סֵפֶר הַפְטָרוֹת

THE BOOK OF HAFTAROT

FOR SHABBAT, FESTIVALS, AND FAST DAYS

AN EASY-TO-READ TRANSLATION
WITH COMMENTARY

סֵפֶר הַהַפְטָרוֹת

THE BOOK OF HAFTAROT

FOR SHABBAT, FESTIVALS, AND FAST DAYS

AN EASY-TO-READ TRANSLATION
WITH COMMENTARY

by
SOL SCHARFSTEIN

KTAV PUBLISHING HOUSE INC.

Copyright © 2006 KTAV Publishing House, Inc.

Library of Congress Cataloging-in-Publication Data

Haftarot. English

The book of Haftarot for shabbat, festivals and fast days: an easy-to-read translation with commentary / by Sol Scharfstein.

     p. cm.

  Includes index.

  ISBN 0-88125-929-2

  1. Haftarot–Commentaries. I. Scharfstein, Sol, 1921– II.Title.

    BM670.H3S327 2007

    224'.05209–dc22

2006037827

Printed in Hong Kong
Published by
KTAV Publishing House, Inc.
930 Newark Avenue
Jersey City, NJ 07306
Email: bernie@ktav.com
www.ktav.com
(201) 963-9524
Fax (201) 963-0102

TABLE OF CONTENTS

סֵפֶר וַיִּקְרָא   *Book of Vayikra*

סֵפֶר בַּמִּדְבָּר   *Book of Bamidbar*

סֵפֶר דְּבָרִים Book of Devarim

Reading and Haftarot for Special Occasions

TO MY WIFE EDYTHE
Whose patience and support never wavered.
For enduring
"Just give me another ten minutes till I finish this paragraph"–
which often stretched into hours.

In Memorium

In 1921, my parents Asher and Feiga came to America where they established a Jewish Bookstore in the lower east side ghetto of New York City. At first we lived in one room in back of the store with a toilet in the hall. Every Friday we went to the public baths where we purchased towels and soap for a penny. Sometimes we brought our own towels and soap to save the pennies.

Asher and Feiga were young, intelligent and not content to just sell books and sundry religious items. So they began to make lead draydels, Simchat Torah Flags and publish wedding certificates. From this small beginning they began to branch out and publish other books such as siddurim, machzorim and chumashim. In 1947, my father Asher had a brainstorm and assembled the first of its kind Torah reading text entitled Tikkun Torah. This was an immediate success. This Tikkun, 60 years later has gone through innumerable editions and has helped train tens of thousands of Torah readers. It is still in print and is selling well to this day.

In 1947, after World War II, my father received the devastating news that his brothers and their families in the little town of Dinivetz in Russia were murdered by the Nazis.

In 1950, with tears in his eyes and a quivering hand he wrote this hebrew memorium for a new version of the Tikkun entitled the Tikkun Encyclopedia. Unfortunately, this edition was not a success.

Asher's Memoriam Reads:

In memory of my brother Yosef son of Dov and his lovely wife Sara and their son Yisrael and his wife and their two children who never even tasted life. They with all the Jews in the village of Dinivetz were thrown alive into a mine in the forest by the Nazis and the Polish Villagers on the 8th day of the month of Mar Hesvon. May the memory of these murderers be wiped off the face of the earth.

To my nephew Aaron son of Yosef, the engineer, who was killed in the Russian army during the battle for the city of Varenzhev.

To my brother Shmuel and his wife Chava and their two children who in 1942 were burnt alive during a pogrom near the city of Warsaw.

I will never forget them.

Asher son of Dov Scharfstein

DEDICATION

There are times during a restless night, when I see their shadows and hear their cries echo through my dreams. I know that they are reminding me never to forget.

This book is dedicated to my nephews, cousins, aunts and uncles whose joys I will never share and laughter that I will never hear.

P.S. I was born in the murderous town of Dinivetz.

INTRODUCTION

The historical factors which led to Haftarah readings have been lost in the clouds of antiquity, but Jews from the earliest times gathered in groups, sometimes in market places, sometimes in homes to pray and to listen as Levites, Priests, Prophets and later Rabbis explained and taught the message of the Torah to our ancestors.

The Pirket Avot, or Sayings of the Elders tells us that Moses received the Torah from Mount Sinai and passed it on to Joshua. Joshua passed it down to the Elders, they then passed it down to the Prophets and they handed it down to the members of the "Great Assembly". They handed it down to the Rabbis and now the Rabbis are handing it down to you.

All Jews have looked to the prophetic vision as a means of sustaining their faith and have adopted the prophetic writings as a source of comfort in times of stress. The prophetic message calls for justice and peace.

The optimistic prophetic message insures our faith in God and humanity.

Life long Jewish study is the key to Jewish survival. Judaism imposes upon us a multiplicity of obligations, to pray, to observe mitzvoth and "tikun olam": To improve our world based upon our ethical mandate.

Come take my hand, open your Book of Haftarot and join me in a voyage of discovery. I promise you an amazing journey, which will make you proud of your heritage. You will touch and feel the courage, goodness and decency of your ancestors, the prophets. Their ideals are your legacy: justice, mercy, brotherhood, peace and tikun olam (repair of the world).

Who were the brave and fearless prophets who dared to attack the rich and powerful? The prophets were a diverse group; some were farmers and shepherds and some were affiliated with the ruling class. They were all spokesmen for Adonai. No single group in the history of mankind has had such a profound ethical effect on the history of mankind.

The prophets had the power of inner sight and vision. Sight to see things as they were. Vision to see them, as they ought to be. Isaiah gave the Hebrews, meaning you, immortality with an eternal purpose:

"To be a light to the nations."

Now it is your turn to keep the prophetic light burning.

Study, learn and keep the torch alight.

May you go from strength to strength and may the optimistic vision of the prophets shape your lives.

Shlomo ben Asher (Shenash)
Sol Scharfstein

ABOUT THE HAFTARAH

The Hebrew word Haftarah means "conclusion" or "take leave of" and is a section from the Neviim (Prophets), which is read after the reading of the Torah on Shabbat, festivals and fast days. The Haftarah is a portion from a book of the Former or Latter Prophets.

The criteria for selecting a prophetic reading was some reference to an incident mentioned in the Torah reading. Special Haftarot, are determined by the calendar, historical events, festivals and fast days on which appropriate portions are read.

Haftarah Customs

With the completion of the Torah reading, the Sefer Torah is raised and rolled up and then the Haftarah is read. The reader precedes the reading by reciting two blessings and concludes the reading with three blessings. The formula changes on special occasions.

History

The origin of the custom of reading a section from the Prophets after the Torah reading is unknown. Rabbi David Abudarham, who resided in fourteenth century Spain, traced the custom to the persecutions of Antiochus, which preceded the Hasmonain revolt. Antiochus forbade the Torah reading so the Haftarah readings were introduced as a substitute.

THE BOOK OF HAFTAROT

The easy-to-read Book of Haftarot is a sequel to the easy-to-read Torah. The Book of Haftarot contains translations for all the Shabbats as well as the festival readings. The translations are written in clear and simple language, and are geared to students and laymen. The format is designed to be helpful for a basic understanding of the Haftarah and is designed for both personal and classroom study.

Each of the Haftarah lessons is made up of six parts.

1 BOOK: Each of the Haftarot is preceded by a description of the text and biographical material relating to the prophet or the historical figure.

2 HISTORY: To properly understand the prophets, the reader must be familiar with the theological and historical milieu of the period.

3 TEXT: This is a short-guided tour through each of the Haftarah with comments highlighting the thoughts and observations of the prophet.

4 CONNECTION: This section explains why this particular Haftarah was chosen and its connection to the Torah reading.

5 HALACHAH: Each of the special Shabbat and holiday Haftarah contains a Halachah section, which explains some of the special customs and ceremonies associated with the reading of the Haftarah.

6 HAFTARAH: The simplified easy-to-read text is easy-to-understand and captures the essence of the text that is translated into idiomatic English. When necessary, the text is set up in a poetic format.

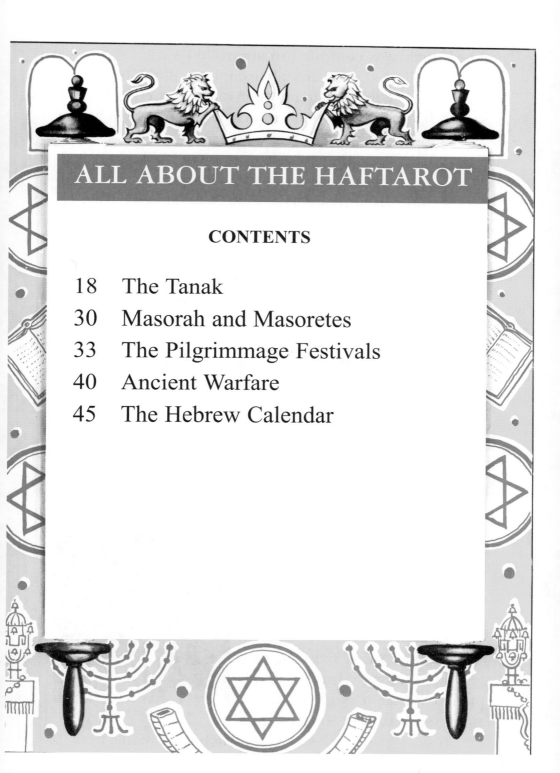

ALL ABOUT THE HAFTAROT

CONTENTS

THE TANAK

The Tanak was compiled in about 200 B.C.E.

Scribes collected and carefully examined all the holy writings. These were put together in the great collection of sacred literature that eventually came to be known as the Tanak—the Hebrew Bible.

TORAH

GENESIS
EXODUS
LEVITICUS
NUMBERS
DEUTERONOMY

PROPHETS

JOSHUA
JUDGES
1 SAMUEL
2 SAMUEL
1 KINGS
2 KINGS
ISAIAH
JEREMIAH
EZEKIEL
HOSEA
JOEL
AMOS
OBADIAH
JONAH
MICAH
NAHUM
HABAKKUK
ZEPHANIAH
HAGGAI
ZECHARIAH
MALACHI

12 minor prophets

WRITINGS

PSALMS
PROVERBS
JOB
SONG OF SOLOMON
RUTH
LAMENTATIONS
ECCLESIASTES
ESTHER
DANIEL
EZRA
NEHEMIAH
1 CHRONICLES
2 CHRONICLES

The complete Hebrew Bible is called TaNaK. It is divided into three divisions: Torah (the Five Books of Moses), Nevi'im (Prophets), and Ketuvim (Writings).

The name *Tanak* comes from the first letters of each of the three divisions. *T* is for Torah, *N* is for Nevi'im and *K* is for Ketuvim.

There are a total thirty-nine separate books in the Tanak. The Torah consists of five books, the Prophets twenty-one books, and the Writings thirteen books. The chapter divisions and the numbering of the verses were introduced into the Tanak to make quoting from it easier. The language of the Tanak is Hebrew except for portions of the books of Daniel and Ezra, which are in Aramaic.

The Torah

The Five Books of Moses are the first five books of the Tanak. The Torah that is read in the synagogue is an exact duplicate of the Torah that Moses gave to the children of Israel.

A Torah scroll must be written by someone who is specially trained. That person is called a *sofer*; (scribe). The Torah is written in a very special script on parchment made from a kosher animal skin.

A sofer at work

An ancient writing instrument, a feather pen, is used to write the Torah.

Each week a different section of the Torah is read in the synagogue. Each section is called a *sidrah*. There are fifty-four *sidrot* in the Torah, just enough for one complete year. At the end of the year, after the Torah has been completely read, there is a special holiday of celebration called *Simchat Torah*. As soon as the reading of all the *sidrot* is completed, the cycle is begun all over again.

A Torah is handwritten in a special script without periods, commas, and punctuation marks. The words have no vowels. The Torah reading is chanted in special musical notes called *trope*.

All Jews, even those who do not know how to read the Torah, are called to participate in the Torah ceremony. This is made possible by calling people to the pulpit to recite special blessings before and after each Torah reading.

The person who recites the blessing is said to have an *aliyah*. The word *aliyah* means "going up" to honor the Torah.

The Torah is also called the Five Books of Moses. The five books are Bereshit, Shemot, Vayikra, Bamidbar, and Devarim.

THE FIVE BOOKS OF MOSES

BOOK OF BERESHIT

בְּרֵאשִׁית
Bereshit

The Hebrew name for Genesis, the first Book of Moses, is Bereshit, from the first word of the book which means "in the beginning." Bereshit describes the creation of the world, its growing and living things, and the first human beings.

It also tells about the origins of the Hebrew people, beginning with the patriarchs, Abraham, Isaac, and Jacob. Bereshit also tells about the Israelites in Egypt, beginning with Joseph.

BOOK OF SHEMOT

Exodus, the second Book of Moses, receives its name from the departure, or exodus, of the Israelites from Egypt. Its Hebrew name is Shemot (names), because it begins with a list of the names of Israel's sons in Egypt. Exodus tells us about the Israelites in Egypt and their escape from slavery under the guidance of Moses. Exodus describes how the Jewish people received the Ten Commandments on Mount Sinai. It pictures the very first Passover celebration. It also details the building of the Sanctuary.

BOOK OF VAYIKRA

The third book of Moses, Leviticus, is called Vayikra in Hebrew, the word with which it begins, meaning "and He called (to Moses)."

Vayikra takes up many important matters dealing with Jewish nationhood. What kind of judges and courts were to be established? What provisions were to be made against the possibility of war? Also discussed in Vayikra are the proper attitude of a Jew toward his parents; his duties toward charity, the poor, the widow, and the orphan; festivals and fasts; and dietary laws.

BOOK OF BAMIDBAR

The fourth Book of Moses is named in Hebrew Bamidbar, from its first important word, meaning "in the wilderness." In English we call it "Numbers," because it begins with the numbering, or census. Bamidbar tells what happened to the Israelites from the time they left Mount Sinai until they reached the borders of Canaan. After forty years of wandering, the Jewish people were prepared to enter the Promised Land.

BOOK OF DEVARIM

Deuteronomy, Devarim in Hebrew, reviews the history and the laws contained in the books of Exodus, Leviticus, and Numbers. It closes with the great song and blessing of Moses just before this great teacher and leader died. The word Devarim means "word" and comes from its first verse, "And these are the words which Moses spoke."

20

The Prophets

Prophets were great men who had visions, special dreams in which Adonai appeared to them and told them what He wanted the Children of Israel to do. The prophets brought Adonai's message to the people. Often the message was a reminder to live by the laws of the Torah, to be kind and fair with one another.

The books of the Prophets are divided into Former Prophets and Latter Prophets. Former prophets tell the history from after the death of Moses to the destruction of the Temple and the exile to Babylonia. The Latter Prophets are the books of classical prophets who lived and prophesied during the time of the kings.

Books of the Former Prophets are Joshua, Judges, Samuel 1 and 2, and Kings 1 and 2. The Latter Prophets are Isaiah, Jeremiah, Ezekiel, and the Terei Asar (Twelve Minor Prophets).

BOOK OF JOSHUA

This first book of the Former Prophets records Israel's history from after the death of Moses to the conquest and settling of Canaan under Joshua's leadership.

BOOK OF JUDGES

The second book of the Former Prophets records the period of the twelve judges, Israel's history from the time of the death of Joshua to that of the birth of Samuel.

BOOKS OF SAMUEL 1 AND 2

Samuel 1 records Israel's history from the time of the birth of Samuel to the death of Saul. Samuel 2 records the reign of King David, under whom the tribes united and grew into one nation.

BOOKs OF KINGS 1 AND 2

The two sections of the books of Kings recount four centuries of Jewish history. They begin with the last days of King David (about 977 B.C.E.) and conclude with the destruction of the First Temple, the Babylonian Exile, and the release of King Jehoiachin from Babylonian prison.

Latter Prophets

BOOK OF ISAIAH

Isaiah was a great preacher who lived in times of tremendous national crisis. He had seen the destruction of Israel, the northern kingdom, by Assyria and feared that the same fate might befall Judah and his beloved Jerusalem. His counsel to Judah for some forty years (740–700 B.C.E.) was chiefly to steer clear of alliances with foreign powers, such as Assyria and Egypt. So strong was Isaiah's belief in Adonai that he dared dream of a golden age, when men would "beat their swords into plowshares."

BOOK OF JEREMIAH

Torn between the desire to save his people and the duty to tell them of the doom that lay in store for them at the hands of Babylonia, Jeremiah was hated. He advised submitting to Babylon, for he believed that only by doing so would Judah find peace. This was an unpopular policy. He also attacked the emptiness of Temple worship without sincere belief in God.

BOOK OF EZEKIEL

Ezekiel was active in Babylon during the Exile. His great task was to teach the people that they could worship Adonai even outside the land of Israel. Because of his message and the place in which he found himself, he became the builder of the first religious Jewish community in the Exile. He helped his people face the uncertain future.

Minor Prophets–Terei-Asar

The books of the Twelve Minor Prophets are short and are included in the Aramaic term Terei-Asar meaning "twelve".

BOOK OF HOSEA

The prophet Hosea wrote and preached in the eighth century B.C.E. in Israel at the time of Jeroboam II and the disorder that followed the king's death. He preached against the immorality of his day, reminding the people that Adonai wants people to be just and compassionate.

BOOK OF JOEL

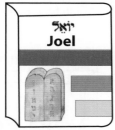

We know next to nothing about Joel, whose book consists of only three chapters. He tells us in very descriptive language of a plague of locusts sweeping over Judah and destroying its fields and vineyards. He calls upon the people to fast in repentance, and he promises that one day Judah will be glorious again, blessed with abundance by the Almighty.

BOOK OF AMOS

Amos, a shepherd from Tekoa, lived during the reign of Jeroboam II. He criticized the northern kingdom of Israel for its frivolity and the great differences between its rich and poor. All men, Amos insisted, were children of the one Adonai. He warned the kingdom against the Assyrians and foretold its doom.

BOOK OF OBADIAH

Fourth Book of the Twelve Minor Prophets of the Bible. Obadiah prophesied the destruction of Edom and the restoration of Israel. This is the shortest book of the Bible.

BOOK OF JONAH

Jonah is a short story about a prophet and was written, according to tradition, by one of the "Men of the Great Assembly." Jonah did not want to bring Adonai's promise of forgiveness to the city of Nineveh. He did not think its evil citizens could learn to be good. So Jonah had to be taught the lesson of Adonai's love for all humankind.

Jonah's being swallowed by the great fish has been interpreted as Israel's captivity.

His being brought forth to safety represents Israel's deliverance by Adonai. The book of Jonah is read in all synagogues on the afternoon of the Day of Atonement, for it preaches Adonai's mercy and goodness to all who atone.

BOOK OF MICAH

Micah, a humble peasant from Gath, prophesied in Judah at the time of Isaiah. He cried out against injustice and dishonesty. "What does the Lord require of you,?" said Micah, "save to do justice, and to love mercy, and to walk humbly with your God." Micah, like Isaiah, envisioned a future when war would cease and all people would be at peace.

BOOK OF NAHUM

In three superb chapters, which comprise the entire book of Nahum, the prophet describes the downfall of the Assyrian empire. The account of the destruction of Nineveh (capital of Assyria, in 612 B.C.E.) is one of the most dramatic recitals in ancient writings. Nahum's book is so sharp in its details that it must have been written during or shortly after this historic event.

BOOK OF HABBAKKUK

Eighth Book of the Minor Prophets of the Bible. Little is known about the prophet himself. In addition to recording his prophecies, he explored the problem of why a wicked man may succeed and a righteous man may suffer. He concluded that man must be just and have faith in Adonai, for He will make the final judgment.

BOOK OF ZEPHANIAH

The prophet Zephaniah preached in the early years of the reign of King Josiah of Judah. He spoke bitterly against the corrupt conditions before Josiah's great reform.

BOOK OF HAGGAI

Tenth of the books of the Twelve Minor Prophets. The prophet Haggai, after returning to Jerusalem from the Babylonian Exile, inspired Zerubbabel and the high priest Joshua to build the Second Temple.

Eleventh of the Twelve Minor Prophets of the Bible. The prophet Zechariah was a contemporary of Zerubbabel, Haggai, and the high priest Joshua. He helped in the building of the Second Temple.

His writings contain visions and prophecies.

BOOK OF ZECHARIAH

BOOK OF MALACHI

Malachi (his real name is uncertain), a prophet of the fourth century B.C.E., talked against the evils of his time and proclaimed that all men are brothers, children of Adonai, and that men should deal justly with one another.

THE HOLY WRITINGS

The Ketuvim or Holy Writings are eleven sacred books on different subjects.

Wisdom and Poetry Books

BOOK OF PSALMS

Psalms, or Tehillim, is a collection of 150 beautiful poems. The book is also called the Psalms of David.

BOOK OF PROVERBS

Proverbs (Mishlei) consists of a collection of wise sayings ascribed to King Solomon.

BOOK OF JOB

Job, a righteous man, was tested by Adonai and was made to suffer great misfortunes. He withstood all the tests and maintained his faith.

FIVE SCROLLS

Ketuvim also contains five scrolls called *megillot*: Song of Songs, Ruth, Lamentations, Ecclesiastes, and Esther. Ruth and Esther tell the stories of great Jewish heroines. Ruth teaches us to be loyal to each other and our religion. Esther tells us how a brave woman saved all the Jews of Persia. The Song of Songs is a book of poetry written by King Solomon. Lamentations is a book of sad and mournful poetry about the destruction of Jerusalem. Ecclesiastes is a book of the teachings of King Solomon.

SONG OF SONGS

Shir Hashirim in Hebrew, this beautiful poem is considered to represent the love between Adonai and Israel. It is ascribed to King Solomon. The poem is read in the synagogue on Passover.

BOOK OF RUTH

A story of friendship and devotion, this book takes its name from Ruth, who refuses to leave her mother-in-law, Naomi, though her husband is dead, Ruth's words have echoed through history: "Beg me not to leave you; for wherever you go, I will go, and wherever you lodge, there will I lodge. Your people shall be my people, and your God my God." At the end of this book, Naomi finds a suitable husband for Ruth in the person of Boaz, and we are told that from this union will descend David, king of Israel. The book of Ruth is read in the synagogue on Shavuot, the harvest festival commemorating the giving of the Torah.

BOOK OF LAMENTATIONS

The book of Lamentations consists of five sad poems describing the sorrows suffered by the Jewish people when the mighty Babylonian armies swooped down upon Jerusalem in 586 B.C.E., destroyed the Temple, and sent the mourning citizens into the Babylonian Exile. Thus was Solomon's Temple laid waste, having been in existence for 410 years. The book of Lamentations is read in the synagogue on Tisha B'av, the day on which both the First and Second Temples were destroyed.

BOOK OF ECCLESIASTES

Ecclesiastes, Kohelet in Hebrew, is a book of wise sayings that begins with the famous "Vanity of vanities, all is vanity." This is considered to be one of the three biblical books written by King Solomon. It is read in the synagogue on Sukkot.

BOOK OF ESTHER

The book of Esther, often called simply "The Megillah" describes how Esther saved the Jews of Persia. It is read on Purim. Many beautiful medieval *megillot* (scrolls) with illustrations and ornaments, mounted on rollers, have been preserved.

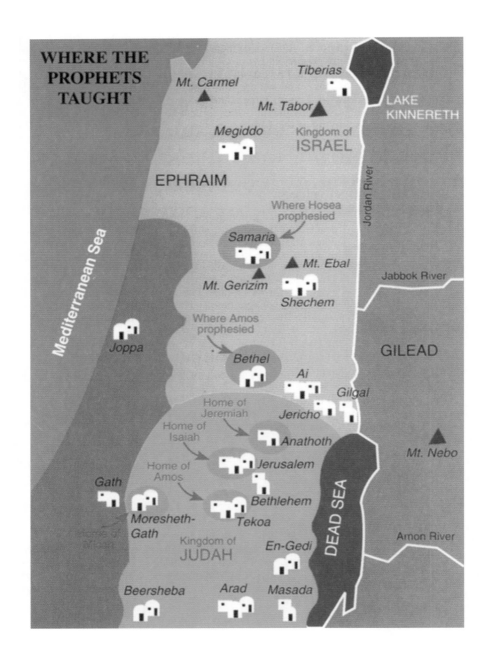

WHERE THE
PROPHETS
TAUGHT

Mt. Carmel

Tiberias

Mt. Tabor

LAKE
KINNERETH

Megiddo

Kingdom of
ISRAEL

EPHRAIM

Jordan River

Where Hosea
prophesied

Samaria

Mt. Ebal

Jabbok River

Mt. Gerizim

Shechem

Mediterranean Sea

Where Amos
prophesied

Joppa

Bethel

Ai

Gilgal

GILEAD

Home of
Jeremiah

Jericho

Home of
Isaiah

Anathoth

Home of
Amos

Jerusalem

Mt. Nebo

Gath

Bethlehem

DEAD SEA

Moresheth-
Gath

Tekoa

Kingdom of
JUDAH

En-Gedi

Amon River

Beersheba

Arad

Masada

HISTORICAL BOOKS

There are five historical books in Ketuvim: Daniel, Ezra, Nehemiah, and Chronicles 1 and 2. Daniel is the story of Daniel's triumph in the court of ancient Babylon. Chronicles 1 and 2, Ezra, and Nehemiah give us a history of the ancient land of Israel. Chronicles ends with the exile of the Jews to Babylonia. Ezra and Nehemiah were the men who led Israel when the Jews returned from Babylonia to Jerusalem. These books tells about the rebuilding of Jerusalem.

BOOK OF DANIEL

Daniel, who was living in the court of Nebuchadnezzar, king of Babylonia, was the only one able to explain the king's strange dreams. He said that soon Adonai would take away the ruling power of proud Babylonia. Daniel and his three friends refused to worship the king's golden image, so they were thrown into a fiery furnace, only to emerge unharmed.

Daniel explained the strange handwriting the king saw on the wall in his dream: the king would go the way of all tyrants. As a final test, Daniel was thrown into a den of hungry lions, but the beasts did not harm a hair of Daniel's head.

BOOKS OF EZRA AND NEHEMIAH

The books of Ezra and Nehemiah are often counted as a single book because they deal with one period. Ezra was the scribe, who replaced the prophets, in about 450 B.C.E., after the Israelites' return to Judea from the Babylonian exile. The scribes carefully copied the Torah and taught it to the people. Nehemiah, who was a cup bearer of the king of Persia, returned to Jerusalem as its governor and led the people to rebuild the walls of the Temple.

BOOK OF CHRONICLES

In two books, Chronicles retells the history of the Jewish people from the creation of the world to the end of the Babylonian exile. Chronicles emphasizes that God rules the world and that history is created by Providence and does not happen by accident.

With Chronicles we have come to the end of the Writings, the third and final division of the books of the Bible.

MASORAH AND MASORETES

The term masorah is derived from the root *masar*, "to hand down," and means the work of preserving the traditional Bible text. The men who performed this function were known as Masorites or Masoretes, and the present Hebrew text of the Torah is known as the Masoretic text.

The necessity for instituting a special watch over the text was felt at an early time. In the period of the Second Temple, the Torah was the source of all Jewish law, and great attention was paid to the exact wording of the text. There were numerous disputes that turned on the question of whether a certain passage was actually a part of the Hebrew text, or how it was to be read. The Masoretes dealt with these questions by carefully comparing and annotating the texts that were in existence at that time.

The task that lay before the Masoretes was twofold, because of the particular nature of the Hebrew language and the way in which it was written. In all the early manuscripts only the consonants appear, the vowels being omitted. Hebrew reading consists of fitting a set of vowels to a group of letters; the same set of letters may be used for a number of words, just by changing the vowels. The Masoretes worked to preserve not only the correct consonantal text, but also the correct readings.

One of the first tasks of the Masoretes was to indicate the irregularities, deviations, and unique places found in the text. They then had to decide which words had to be read (*kere*) differently from the way they were written (*ketiv*), and those places where words were written but not read aloud (*ketiv velo kere*).

They made note of and counted points that are occasion-
ally to be found over words, even in the oldest Bible manuscripts (as in Genesis 16:5 or Numbers 3:39), and which
seem to have been used to indicate variant readings. In this
same way, they noted anything that was unusual in Bible
manuscripts.

These irregularities are recognized as serving a definite purpose. For example, large letters are used at the beginning of
important passages and to prevent the possibility of error.
Thus the letter *dalet* is large in Deuteronomy 6:4 to show
that the last word is read as *echad* ("one"), instead of *acher*
("other").

שְׁמַע יִשְׂרָאֵל יְהוָה אֱלֹהֵינוּ יְהוָה אֶחָד

The large *vav* in the word gachon (Leviticus 11:42) marks
the middle of the Torah.

לְכֹל הוֹלֵךְ עַל גָּחוֹן וּלְכֹל הוֹלֵךְ עַל אַרְבַּע עַד כָּל מַרְבֵּה

The Masoretes also divided the text into larger or smaller
paragraphs and verses and stated the number of these
verses and paragraphs. The division into larger sections
(*sidrot*) and smaller sections (*parashiyot*) as well as into
verses was already known in ancient times; on the other
hand, there was no designation of numbered verses and
chapters until the thirteenth century. When Torahs are
printed in book form, at the end of each of the five books
the total number of verses as well as the number of *sidrot*
and *parashiyot* and the middle verse of each book are
given; this information is followed by a mnemontechnical
verse, the letters of one or more words of which amount
to the sum given. This work of registration was intended
to place a permanent check upon the size and the state of
the text, especially to prevent insertions or deletions.

The punctuation, or vocalization of the biblical text was a continuation of the Masorah. It was not until the eighth century C.E. that a complete system of vowels and accent marks, such as is used today, came into existence.

וַתֹּאמֶר שָׂרַי אֶל־אַבְרָם חֲמָסִי עָלֶיךָ אָנֹכִי נָתַתִּי

The oldest dated manuscript of the Bible is the Petersburg code in the year 1008.

Tiberias was the seat of a series of authorities who were engaged in Masoretic studies, and the family of Aaron ben Moses ben Asher was especially active. Ben Asher, a contemporary of Saadia, was regarded as

Colophon of the Masoretic Codex of Ben Asher (897 C.E.).

the supreme authority in the field of Masorah, and with him the work of the Masorah may be regarded as concluded. His codex of the Bible, provided with Masoretic notes, was hailed as the only authority.

After the eleventh century, the Masoretes who occupied themselves with the biblical text were called punctuators (*nakdanim*). They were primarily biblical scribes who placed vowels and accents in the texts. Sometimes two of them participated in this work, one writing the text and the other adding the points and accents.

Page from the Rules of Accents by Jacob ben Asher in the 10th century. This momentous work established the rules of punctuation and spelling in the Bible

THE PILGRIMAGE FESTIVALS

At the *bikkurim* festival of the first fruits, all the age groups of the kibbutz participate.

The Torah mandates: "Three times each year, every man in Israel must appear before Adonai." The three times referred to were the holidays of Sukkot, Pesach, and Shavuot, known in Hebrew as the *Shalosh Regalim*, or "Three Pilgrimage Festivals."

According to the sages, everyone was required to appear before Adonai except women, minors, the infirm, and the aged. Even those who were not required to attend often participated in the pilgrimage. In practice, whole families made the pilgrimage together. The pilgrims were called *olei regel*, meaning "those who go up by foot." They were so called because Jerusalem is located high in the hills of Judea and the pilgrims had to climb by foot to reach the Temple. Ancient sources state that hundreds of thousands made their way to the Temple during each of the *Shalosh Regalim*. The Talmud notes that Jews from as far as Babylon, Persia, Egypt, Ethiopia, Asia Minor, and Rome came to worship in the Temple on the Three Pilgrimage Festivals.

The Romans conquered Jerusalem in 70 C.E. and burned the Temple to the ground. All that remained was the Western Wall, which became a sacred place where Jews prayed. All through the centuries of exile Jews have worshiped at the Western Wall. Today Jews write prayers and requests and place them in the cracks between the stones of the Wall.

33

The pilgrims traveled in large groups or caravans, with flying banners announcing the names of their clan, town, or village. Many of the caravans were accompanied by musicians who played marching songs. Psalms 120-134 are designated as Psalms of Ascent and were sung as the pilgrims ascended to Jerusalem.

Bikkurim

The object of the pilgrimage was to bring *bikkurim* (first fruits) to offer as a sacrifice at the Temple. The Torah also commands, "You must not appear before Adonai with empty hands. Everyone shall bring an offering in proportion to the blessings that Adonai has given him." (Deut. 26: 26-17).

The sages decided that the minimum offering was three pieces of silver. The proceeds were to be used for the upkeep of the Temple and to care for the sick, aged, and infirm.

As the marching groups approached Jerusalem, they were met by the priests and Levites, who welcomed them to the city and led the pilgrims to their designated tent grounds.

The Necessity for Pilgrimages

Pilgrimages were a cultural, political, and religious weapon in the battle for the survival of the Jewish state. The pilgrimage reunions helped mold the separate tribes into a single cultural, political, and military entity.

Israel was surrounded by idol-worshipping nations whose religious rituals during the harvest seasons were enticing to isolated Israelite farmers and shepherds. The pilgrimages to Jerusalem helped combat the pagan rites of the idol worshippers and kept the ancient Jewish traditions alive. They reinforced the faith and reaffirmed the covenant with Adonai that was made at Mount Sinai. In the city squares, priests and Levites lectured the pilgrims on Jewish law and on the teachings of the Torah.

Israelite farmers and shepherds lived dull, hard, lonely lives. They worked from early light to

Tilling the soil the old-fashioned way with a hand-held plow and a donkey. The ancient Israelites tended their farms in the same way.

total darkness, raising their crops and tending their animals. The pilgrimages were also social occasions: a time for them to celebrate, a relief from the arduous daily regimen.

Ripe Fruits

Just about the time the wheat was harvested, the first fruits began to ripen on trees and vines in Israel. The Torah commanded the farmers to bring their first fruits as an offering of thanks to God. At the Temple in Jerusalem our ancestors expressed their gratitude to Adonai for a bountiful harvest.

The Bible says, in Deuteronomy 8:7-8

Adonai is bringing you to a fertile land with flowing streams and with springs gushing from valleys and mountains. It is a land overflowing with wheat, barley, grapes, figs, and pomegranates—a land of olive and honey-date trees.

Of these "seven kinds" listed, every farmer was to bring his first fruits as a thank-you offering to Adonai. That is why one name for Shavuot is *Chag Habikkurim*, the Festival of First Fruits.

The rabbis in the Mishnah tell how the first ripe fruits were selected. Upon visiting his field and seeing a ripe fig, or cluster of grapes, or pomegranates, the owner would tie a thread around the fruit, saying, "Behold, these are the *bikkurim.*"

35

THE SEVEN KINDS

Each of the seven kinds of fruits mentioned in the Bible played an important part in the Torah and in Jewish history.

Chitah is the Hebrew word for wheat, one of the seven kinds. The quotation in this illustration reads, "He brought them to high mountaintops,/And they feasted on the crops of the land;/He fed them honey from the rocks/And olive oil from stony soil./He fed them yogurt from the flocks/And milk from the herds./He fed them fat lambs and male goats,/And rams pastured in Bashan/With the best of grain" (Deuteronomy 32:13-14)

Wheat and Barley

Israel's rainfall is heaviest during the winter months, so the best harvests come from the winter crops of wheat and barley. Barley ripens about Pesach time and was brought to the Temple during the holiday of Shavuot in the spring. Wheat needs more rainfall and ripens later. So important was the harvest that it was used to record events and dates. The arrival of Ruth and Naomi in Bethlehem, for instance, is dated not by the name of a month but by the fact that they came at the beginning of the barley harvest.

Grapes

Grapes need plenty of rainfall for growth and lots of sunshine to allow the leaves and fruit clusters to develop. Israel has both. The first grapes ripen early in the month of Sivan, in time for Shavuot. The spies sent by Moses to Canaan brought back a cluster of grapes so heavy that "It needed two men to carry it

The grape harvest at a kibbutz vineyard. The Hebrew word for grapes is *gefen*. Israeli wines, because of the quality of the grapes, have won many worldwide competitions.

on a pole" (Numbers 13:23). The Bible says, "And Judah and Israel dwelled safely, every man under his vine and under his fig tree" (1 Kings 5:5).

Figs

The Torah has been likened to a fig. All fruits have some waste material: seeds, pits, or rind; the entire fig, however, can be eaten, and so it is with every word in the Torah. The Talmud says: "When you see a fig tree, say: 'How pleasant is this fig tree; blessed is the Omnipresent, who created it!'"

Pomegranates

The pomegranate had many uses in ancient Israel. It was used as a dye and for writing ink. In addition, ancient doctors used the juice of the pomegranate for medicinal purposes. Its juice is also an excellent thirst quencher.

The spies sent by Moses to Canaan brought back pomegranates. Because they ripen in late summer, the blossoms were used to adorn the sheaves of grain brought to the Temple on Shavuot, and the fruit was brought after it had ripened. Farmers quenched their thirst with pomegranate juice, and the rind was used to make dyes and ink. The clothes of the *kohanim* (priests) in the Temple were decorated with artistically carved pomegranates, and the silver ornaments used to crown the Torah scroll are called *rimmonim* (pomegranates).

Olives

The olive tree is very common in the Mediterranean.

Its small leaves are covered with a thick, shiny coat and can well stand the scorching summer sun. The branch of the olive tree has become a symbol of peace. Noah's dove, sent from the ark to

An oil press from talmudic times. Ripe olives were crushed and olive oil was extracted.

find out whether the flood had abated, brought back an olive branch. Olives, and olive oil, was a basic food in ancient Israel. It was also used to light the Temple menorah, and was one of the most important exports of ancient Israel.

Dates

During the picking season dates are moist and juicy; later they are dried. The best area for dates in Israel is the Jordan Valley. The date palm is sown not with seeds but with shoots, which sprout from its roots. The Midrash says:

"A righteous person will flourish like a date palm" (Psalm 92:13). Why a date palm?

None of it is useless: Its dates are eaten; its branches are used to thatch roofs; its fibers are made into ropes; its leaves to fabricate sieves; its trunks are used for building the house. So, too, none of Israel is worthless: Some study Torah, some the Mishnah, some the Talmud, some the Aggadah. (Bereshit Rabbah 41:1, Lech Lecha)

After they left Egypt, the Israelites wandered through the desert for forty years. They traveled from one oasis to another for cool, fresh water and shade from the hot desert sun.

Then and Now

In ancient Israel, a long procession would wind its way through the streets of Jerusalem, made up of men, women, and children carrying baskets filled with the produce of the soil, the first fruits, to the Temple.

Today in modern Israel this custom has been revived. Long lines of children march with their baskets and guide beautifully decorated floats. The fruits are sold for the benefit of the Jewish National Fund.

Three times a year—on Sukkot, Passover, and Shavuot—the Jews of ancient Israel would march on foot to the Holy Temple in Jerusalem. Today in modern Israel the age-old pilgrimage ceremony is reenacted. Here pilgrims ascend Mount Zion to the blowing of shofars.

THE GEZER CALENDAR

Ancient Israelites depended primarily on agriculture for their livelihood. A tenth-century agricultural calendar engraved in an ancient Hebrew script on a stone tablet, which was found in the excavation in Gezer, provided a seasonal list of the farmers' tasks. The sequence of activities described the planting and harvesting of the biblical seven kinds.

1. Two months for the olives
2. Two months for planting grain
3. One month for planting flax
4. One month for the barley harvest
5. One month for harvest and feasting
6. One month for vine tending (grapes)
7. One month for summer fruit

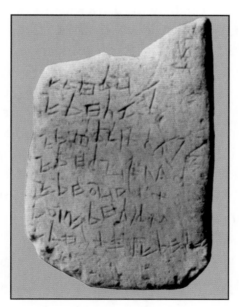

The Gezer Calendar

Notice that some of the seasons last for two months and some for only one month. The month of feasting most likely includes a pilgrimage to Jerusalem.

ANCIENT WEAPONS OF WAR

The land of Israel "was a land flowing with milk and honey." Unfortunately, Canaan was in a geographically dangerous position. It was the bridge between Europe and Asia, and it continually reverberated with the march of armies fighting each other. In addition, the tribes living around Israel did not appreciate Israel's presence in their midst.

Israel was almost constantly in a state of military preparedness, and its army, though weak and often poorly armed, was ready to repel raiders and invaders.

The bow (*keshet*) and arrow (*chetz*) are frequently mentioned in the Tanak. These were long-range weapons and were used in hunting and in combat.

Another long-range weapon was the sling. David killed the giant Goliath with a rock from his sling (*Kela*).

The sling was made of leather straps with a wide pocket, in which was placed a round stone. The sling was whirled until it hummed like a bee. The stone was then released with nearly the speed of a bullet. It hurtled to its target and could cause death or serious injury.

The sword and the knife were designed to stab, hit, and slice in infantry attacks. The sword (*cherev*), which was designed to stab as well as cut, was introduced by the Philistine forces from Crete. Swords were also the favorite weapons of the soldiers in chariots.

The preferred weapon in the ancient Near East was the bow. This Egyptian painting shows instructors teaching their pupils the art of marksmanship with the bow.

David killed the giant Goliath with a stone from a sling. Soldiers with slings fought side by side with the archers. A sling consisted of two leather straps and a stone-holder. This orthostat from the time of David and Solomon shows how the sling was used in battle.

The axe was a heavy hammer with a sharp pointed end. The development of leather and metal body armor made the battle axe (*mapetz*) a necessity. The axe could cut through armor and wound or kill an opponent.

The idol Baal was the warrior god of the Canaanites. Notice the sword and shield. This bronze figurine of Baal was found at Megiddo.

The spear (*romach*) was a medium-range weapon and was developed to keep the enemy at a distance. Spears were long heavy poles with a sharp, pointed metal top. Some spears (*chanit*) were designed to be thrown.

This picture of Pharaoh Tutankhamen in his chariot was found in his tomb. The chariot reins are tied around his waist, freeing his arms and enabling him to shoot the arrows.

Numerous types of horse-drawn chariots were in use in the Middle East. In the Exodus from Egypt, the Israelites were pursued by Egyptian chariots; the riders were drowned in the Sea of Reeds. 1 Kings 10:26 mentions that King Solomon had 1,400 chariots (*rechev*) and 12,000 horses.

Soldiers defended themselves with shields (*maginnim*), which consisted of layers of leather attached to a wooden frame. They also wore heavy leather garments reinforced by metal plates (*shiryon*). A bronze helmet called a *kova* protected their heads.

Initially the Israelite army was composed of farmers and shepherds who enlisted for a special campaign. After the battle the civilian soldiers returned to their farms. These civilian soldiers were called to arms by people who, like Paul Revere, rode through the territories calling the troops to arms. Sometimes shofar blowers stationed on the hilltops signaled the troops to assemble to repel

A group of wooden Nubian soldiers excavated from the tomb of an Egyptian prince. Such models were placed in tombs in the belief that they would serve the owner in the afterworld.

an invasion. King David was the first to assemble a professional regular army.

Most Israelite soldiers were poorly armed and untrained. What they lacked in training they made up in spirit, bravery, and surprise attack, ambushes, and tactical superiority.

Large cities, such as Jericho, were fortified by thick stone and stucco comprised of boulders and stones plastered together. There were holes in the walls through which archers could shoot fire arrows at the enemy. The walls were thick enough for soldiers to stand on to repel attackers who tried to climb the walls using scaling ladders.

Sometimes the enemy would build a mound against the wall so attackers could climb it and enter the city.

Another tactic was excavating a tunnel under the wall and weakening it until it fell apart. Attackers would also shoot flaming arrows into the wooden city gates, allowing them to enter the fortified city.

Battering rams and siege engines were armaments. Some battering rams were attached to armored towers from which archers could shoot into the besieged city.

A Greek soldier under attack. He wears a metal helmet and breastplate. This painting was found on an ancient stone coffin.

Another sophisticated war machine was the catapult. These throwing engines could hurl a heavy stone through the air, crushing anything it hit. The catapults were used against small fortifications. Sometimes barrels of burning oil were sent flying through the air, causing fires and spreading fear among the defenders. Life was not easy for a small country like Israel.

The Greeks also used elephants to carry soldiers into battle and to demoralize their enemies. Elephants were used against the Maccabees. Many Maccabees were killed attacking the Syrian Greeks. Eliezer the Maccabee was killed attacking an elephant.

The Israelite infantry was divided into four groups: archers, slingers, spearmen, and auxiliaries. The spearmen, who were the assault troops of the army, defended themselves with shields, but the archers and slingers were without shields. Infantry battles took place in open fields, and attacks were made on fortified cities with no change of equipment. The cavalry (*parashim*) took part in battles as raiders or as the mobile defense for the chariots.

The main development in offensive weapons was the battering ram (*kar*). Jews served as mercenaries for the Persian king at Elephantine in Egypt. They were organized into companies called a *degelim* and had their own temple.

The rebels under Judah Maccabee gradually acquired military skill and captured Seleucid arms. Judah's strategic and tactical skills helped him achieve victories over the superior Seleucid forces.

Jewish battles were always the few against the many, the citizen soldiers against the heavily armed and trained professionals.

A Syrian war elephant. These huge beasts with sharp-shooting bowmen were the armored tanks of the ancient world.

THE HEBREW CALENDAR

In the earliest days of our history, in the days of the patriarchs, Abraham, Isaac, and Jacob, the Jewish people were shepherds who wandered in search of green pastures for their flocks. They often went to bed at sunset and got up at sunrise. Men, women, and children thought of the sun as a wonderful friend.

Then someone said, "While you have been sleeping at night, I have been watching the moon and the stars. Sometimes the moon is full and round, sometimes it is only half its size, and sometimes I can't find it at all."

Report to the Sanhedrin

Special observers were placed at stations to wait for the appearance of the new moon. As soon as the slightest crescent showed in the sky, the observers rushed to Jerusalem to the Sanhedrin, the High Court of the Jewish people. "We testify that we have seen the new moon," they swore. They stated the moment it had made its appearance.

It was a moment of high excitement. Once the Sanhedrin had proclaimed the new month, runners were dispatched to light fires on the highest hills ringing the capital city. As soon as these signals were seen by the inhabitants of the next town, they in turn lit a fire on their highest hill. At last the signals reached the farthest communities. The new month had officially begun.

Jews of far-off countries like Persia and Italy and Egypt could not rely on messages that sometimes arrived very late. "We will observe the thirtieth day and the day after it as the new month," they decided. "In that way, we will be certain not to go astray." That is why, according to tradition, our forefathers added an extra day to the Pesach, Shavuot, Sukkot, and Rosh Hashanah holidays.

A Written Calendar

In the year 359 C.E., Hillel the Second—so called to set him apart from the famed Hillel who lived in the days of the Second Temple—set the rules for making a calendar.

Taking quill in hand, he wrote that the length of the Jewish month is the time it takes the moon to go around the earth. This month is 29 days, 12 hours, and 44 minutes. "We must be practical," said Hillel. "We will reckon the months by full days." So the law was laid down that some months should have thirty days and others twenty-nine. From that day Jews everywhere could determine the calendar for themselves and observe the festivals on the same day.

Jews, however, number the years from the time of the creation of the world as accounted for in the Bible. In place of B.C. and A.D., which mean "Before Christ" and "Anno Domini" (in the year of our Lord), we use B.C.E. and C.E., which mean "Before the Common Era" and "Common Era." The latter abbreviations are used in this book.

Where did the months get their names?

Originally, the Israelites used numerals to distinguish one month from another. The month in which the spring season began was the first month; the other months were called accordingly the second, third, and so on.

The Hebrew names of the months, as we know them, were adopted when our people lived in the Babylonian Exile after the destruction of the First Temple in 586 B.C.E. The names were derived from the Babylonian calendar.

Now we know about the way our calendar began, but that does not explain how we number our years. Why is the Jewish year called 5718 instead of 1958, or 5719 rather than 1959? The answer to this question lies, as is very often the case, in the lap of Jewish tradition.

From the beginning of recorded time, calendar makers have used events great and small as starting points for their date guides. The Romans, for example, counted time from the founding of their capital city. Early Christians dated events from the birth of Jesus, which they called "the year 1." Our everyday calendar follows that rule. It is called the Gregorian calendar, because it was revised by Pope Gregory XIII in 1582, and was adopted by England for herself and her American colonies in 1752.

The Hebrew Days

The Jewish week begins on Sunday. It ends on Saturday, or Shabbat. The names of the days are really numbers. They tell what day of the week it is. This is how the days are named in Hebrew:

Sunday—Yom Rishon (The First Day)
Monday—Yom Sheni (The Second Day)
Tuesday—Yom Shelishi (The Third Day)
Wednesday—Yom Revi'i (The Fourth Day)
Thursday—Yom Chamishi (The Fifth Day)
Friday—Yom Shishi (The Sixth Day)
Saturday—Shabbat (The Sabbath)

Observe that the day, in Jewish reckoning, begins at sunset. Saturday, which is the seventh day of the week, begins on Friday evening. That is because the Torah tells us, in the story of the Creation, that "there was evening and there was morning, one day." The very first day, the day of Creation, began not with daybreak but with sunset. All our holidays follow this order and begin at sunset of the day before.

A detailed Jewish calendar tells us when the sun sets on the eve of a Sabbath or holiday; it informs us to light candles about 18 minutes before the sunset.

Look again at the calendar. It will tell you which portion of the Torah and Prophets will be read in the synagogue next Saturday.

47

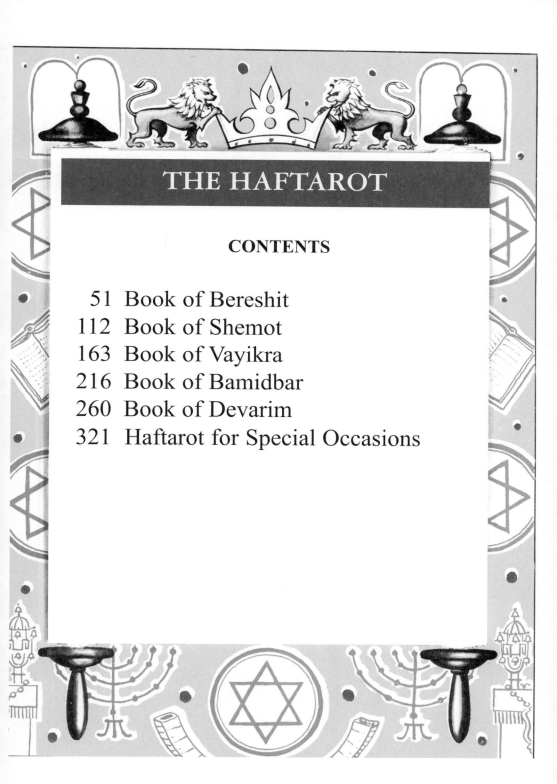

THE HAFTAROT

CONTENTS

INTRODUCTION TO
HAFTARAH for BERESHIT
Isaiah 42:5–43:10

Book of Isaiah The Book of Isaiah belongs to the division called *Nevi'im Rishonim*, meaning Early Prophets. The Book of Isaiah contains 66 chapters. Some scholars believe that the book should be divided into two major segments. Chapters 1–39 are credited to Isaiah ben Amoz. Chapters 40–66 are believed to have been written by an unknown Second Isaiah during the end of the Babylonian exile ca. 550 B.C.E.

History King Cyrus of Persia is mentioned in the prophecy of Second Isaiah (45:1): *Adonai said to his chosen one Cyrus, whose right hand I held to conquer nations.*

Cyrus was an efficient administrator and a monarch of great tolerance. He granted religious freedom to all, believing that a nation flourished best under such conditions. Many of the peoples of Babylonia regarded Cyrus as their liberator. Under his rule, Persia became a great nation.

The Persian conquest of Babylonia in 539 B.C.E. was a great boon for the Jewish exiles. Cyrus was sympathetic to them and soon issued a decree permitting them to return to Jerusalem and restore their Temple. Great was the rejoicing in the Jewish communities. Scores of exiles prepared to make the long-dreamed-of journey back to their homeland.

From the biblical Book of Ezra we learn that about 42,000 Jews from all over Babylonia joined in the exodus to Judah. Their long, difficult journey took them through the lands of the Fertile Crescent, retracing Abraham's trek of ancient days.

Text This prophecy of Restoration is addressed to the thousands of Judeans who had been deported in 586 B.C.E. after the destruction of Jerusalem.

Second Isaiah consoles the homesick Jews and assures them that Adonai will restore them to their homeland.

Do not be afraid,
for I am with you.
I will return your children from the east
and gather them from the west. **43:5**

He also reminds them of the covenant between Israel and
Adonai, that they will open the eyes of the spiritually blind.

I, Adonai, have chosen you to live right.
I took you by the hand and I will treasure you;
I made a covenant with you
to be a light to the nations. **42:6**

Connection   The theme between the sidrah and the haftarah is found in the opening words, which speak of Adonai
as the creator of the cosmos and planet Earth.

Adonai, the creator of cosmos
who stretched out the skies;
who formed the planet
and everything in it,
He gave life to the people upon it,
and intelligence to those who live on it. **42.5**

The sidrah also describes the creation of the cosmos and
planet Earth.

42

5 This is what Adonai says:
Adonai, the creator of cosmos
who stretched out the skies;
who formed the planet
and everything in it;
He gave life to the people upon it,
and intelligence to those who live on it.
6 I, Adonai, have chosen you to live right.
I took you by the hand and I will treasure you;
I made a covenant with you
to be a light to the nations,
7 to open the eyes of the blind,
to release the captives out of prison,
and those who sit in darkness
in the dungeons.
8 I am Adonai.
Adonai is My name.
I will not share my glory with another
and neither will I praise idols.
9 Behold, events
have occurred as I predicted and
now I am predicting new events.
I am revealing them to you
before they happen.
10 Sing a new song to Adonai;
sing His praises to the ends of the earth;
sing all you who sail the seas and beyond,
to the islands and their inhabitants.
11 Tell the inhabitants of the desert and its cities
to join the chorus;
tell the villages that Kedar inhabits
to let the inhabitants of Sela sing.
Let them shout praise from the tops of mountains.

12 Let them honor Adonai
and proclaim His praise in the islands!
13 Adonai shall go forth as a champion.
As a warrior,
He is filled with anger;
He challenges and shouts aloud;
He shall be victorious against His enemies.
14 For a long time I was quiet;
I kept still and controlled Myself.
Now I will cry out,
screaming and groaning
like a woman in childbirth.
15 I will destroy mountains and hills
and remove all their vegetation.
I will dry up rivers into islands
and dry up the watery places.
16 I will lead the blind in unknown ways.
I will guide them on roads
they have never traveled.
For them,
I will make the darkness into light
and pave the road ahead of them.
I will perform these miracles,
and I will not forsake them.
17 Those who pray to idols
and say to manmade idols,
"You are our gods,"
shall be greatly ashamed.
18 Listen, You who are deaf,
listen and pay attention.
Look, you who are blind, open your eyes!
19 Why is My servant blind?
Why is My messenger
whom I send deaf?
Why is My devoted one as blind as Adonai's people?
20 You have seen many things,
but they do not heed.

His ears are open,
but he does not pay attention.
21 Adonai was happy
to make the Torah great and glorious.
22 But Israel is now a robbed and plundered nation.
All of them are trapped in holes
and hidden in prisons.
They are victims
with no one to rescue them,
robbed with no one willing to say:
Send them back.
23 When will you ever listen?
When will you will pay attention
and listen to what is coming?
24 Who allowed Israel to be plundered by robbers?
Was it not Adonai himself
against whom you have sinned?
They would not follow His commandments,
nor did they obey His teachings.
25 He was angry and
then punished them with wars.
They were engulfed in fire
and they still did not care;
they were burning, but He did not take it to heart.

43 But now, says Adonai,
I who created you, Jacob,
and I formed the nation of Israel:
Do not be afraid,
for I have saved you;
I have chosen you,
and now you belong to Me.
2 When you pass through the deep waters,
I will be with you;
and when you cross swift rivers,
they will not drown you.
When you walk through the fire,

you will not be burned.
3 For I am Adonai,
the Holy One of Israel,
who saved you.
I gave Egypt as your ransom,
Ethiopia and Seba in exchange for you.
4 In my eyes, you are precious,
and honored,
and I love you;
I traded the lives of people and nations
To save you.
5 Do not be afraid,
for I am with you.
I will return your children from the east
and gather them from the west.
6 I will say to the north,
"Let them go!"
and to the south,
"Do not hold them back.
Return My children from afar,
and My daughters from the corners of the earth.
7 Return everyone who believed in Me,
all whom I created for My glory,
all whom I formed
and whom I have made."
8 Gather the blind people
who have eyes,
and gather the deaf who have ears.
9 Gather the nations together.
Assemble the inhabitants.
Who among them declared this
and predicted past events?
Let them bring witnesses to convince us
they were right
so that others can hear and say,
"Yes it is true."

10 Adonai says:
Israel, you are My witnesses,
and you are My servant whom I specially chose,
so that you will know
and trust Me
and understand that I am He.
Before Me there was no god.
After Me there will still be nothing.

HAFTARAH for NOAH
Isaiah 54:1–55:5

Book of Isaiah   See haftarah Bereshit, page 51.

History   Ezekiel (ca. 590 B.C.E.) had never faltered in his conviction of deliverance, even during the worst hours of the Exile, but he did not live to see his faith vindicated. Only a few decades after the end of Ezekiel's career, however, the Babylonian empire was on the brink of dissolution. The Persians and Medes had begun to take their place as major powers in the Mesopotamian region late in the seventh century. Eventually the new power was to include territories extending all the way from the Indus to the Mediterranean, and from the Caucasus to the Indian Ocean.

During this turbulent period, a great prophet arose to proclaim to his fellow Jews in Babylon that they were entering a new epoch. He is now called the "Second" Isaiah, to distinguish him from Isaiah ben Amoz, who prophesied in Jerusalem some 200 years earlier. The writings of this exilic prophet are found in chapters 40–66 of the Book of Isaiah. They are easily differentiated from those of the First Isaiah by literary style, historical perspective, and theological emphasis. Some believe that chapters 55–56 were written by a Third Isaiah.

Text   Isaiah sends a message of hope to the Babylonian exiles:

Widen the space of your tent, and extend the tent curtains;
continue lengthening the cords of your tents;
tighten the pegs of your tent. **54:2**

Soon Jerusalem will be rebuilt and Israel will reemerge victorious. The gates of the restored and powerful Jerusalem will be opened wide to welcome those who are thirsty for the spirit of Adonai.

If you are penniless, just come and eat.
Come; it is all free.
Come, drink wine and milk;
it is all on the house—free. **55:1**

Adonai continues to console the exiles; He promises:

Look, you will command nations
that you do not know,
and a nation that did not know you
will run to obey you
because Adonai, your Savior, . . . has honored you. **55:5**

Connection The Torah reading contains the story of Noah and the flood which destroyed the evildoers and paved the way for a new and moral humanity. Adonai also promises Noah:

I have set My rainbow in the clouds,
It shall be a sign of a covenant
between Me and planet earth. **Gen. 9:13**

The haftarah also talks about the water of Noah. Isaiah compares the destruction of the flood and the emergence of rejuvenated and more moral Israelites:

This to me is like the waters of Noah.
As I swore that the waters of Noah
would never again flood the earth,
I swear that I will not
be angry with you or rebuke you. **54:9**

Isaiah also recalls the covenant:

My love will never leave you
and My covenant of peace with you
will never be broken. **54:10**

Haftarah for Noah נֹחַ
(Isaiah 54:1-55:5)

54 Adonai says,
"Childless one,
you, who never had children,
break into a joyful song,
and sing aloud,
you women who were abandoned
will now give birth to more children
than those who have a husband.
2 Widen the space of your tent,
and extend the tent curtains;
continue lengthening the cords of your tents;
tighten the pegs of your tent.
3 Your families
will continue to grow
to the right and to the left,
until they conquer the land
of other nations
and repopulate the abandoned cities.
4 Do not fear,
do not be ashamed.
Do not be discouraged,
for you will not be disappointed;
you will forget the disgrace of your youth,
the shame of your widowhood.
5 Remember your Creator will support you;
Adonai Tzvaot is His name.
The Holy one of Israel is your Redeemer;
He is known as the Creator of the whole cosmos.
6 Yes, Adonai will call you back
as if you were an abandoned and brokenhearted wife.
"A wife of your youth only to be abandoned?"
Adonai, your redeemer says.
7 For a moment I rejected you,

but now, with great love,
I will take you back.
8 In a moment of anger I left you;
and now, with great tenderness,
I will take you back.
9 For me, your exile is like the time of Noah:
I promised that never again
would the waters of Noah drown the earth;
I also swore that I would not be angry with you,
and I would never punish you.
10 Mountains may disappear,
and the hills may be flattened;
but My love will never leave you,
and My covenant of peace with you
will never be broken,
says Adonai, who has mercy on you.
11 Unhappy, storm-tossed city;
I will rebuild you
with precious jewels in fair colors,
and strengthen your foundations with sapphires.
12 I will construct your towers with rubies,
and your gates with diamonds,
and all your walls of precious gems.
13 And all your children
will be taught Adonai's commandments;
great will be the peace,
and your children will live in peace and happiness.
14 Your rulers will be honest and fair.
Terrorists will not attack you;
you will not be afraid,
and you will be far from terror;
and you will live in peace.
15 Nations may gather to attack you,
but it will not be
because I sent them to punish you;
you will defeat any nation
that comes to attack you.

16 Remember,
it is I who created the blacksmith
who fires the coals beneath the forge
and who produces weapons of destruction.
I also created the armies who destroy.
17 Adonai promises.
No weapons that attack you shall succeed;
and those who condemn with lies will be proven false,
promises Adonai.
These will be the rewards
enjoyed by Adonai's servants,
and their victory will come from Me.

55 Anyone who is thirsty, come and drink.
If you are penniless,
just come and eat.
Come; it is all free.
Come, drink wine and milk;
it is all on the house—free.
2 Why waste your money on that junk food?
Why spend money stupidly?
Listen to Me carefully
and eat nutritious food.
Let your body grow
with lots of healthy food.
3 Pay attention and come to Me.
Listen, so that your soul will live;
because of the promises I made to King David,
I will make an everlasting covenant with you.
4 I made him a leader
and commander to the nation.
5 Look, you will command nations
that you do not know,
and a nation that did not know you
will run to obey you because Adonai, your Savior,
the Holy One of Israel,
has honored you.

INTRODUCTION TO
HAFTARAH for LECH LECHA
Isaiah 40:27–41:16

Book of Isaiah   See haftarah Bereshit, page 51.

History   In 539 B.C.E., Cyrus, king of Persia, defeated Babylon and became the new power in the Meso-East. Second Isaiah hails him as Adonai's liberator of the Jewish people. In Isaiah 44:28 Cyrus is referred to in this way: *He is my shepherd and he will fulfill my wishes. He will say of Jerusalem, "It shall be built and the Temple shall be founded."*

Adonai tells Second Isaiah to comfort the Jews in Babylon and assure them that he has not abandoned them. He also assures them that they will return to their homeland and Adonai will liberate the Israelites "from the ends of the earth."

Text   Isaiah reveals that Babylon in the near future will be overthrown by Cyrus the Persian, and he will allow the exiles to return to their homeland.

> *Who aroused the ruler [King Cyrus] from the east?*
> *Who is victorious in every battle?*
> *He conquers nations*
> *And forces kings to surrender to Him.*
> *With His sword,*
> *He turns them into dust;*
> *He scatters them like straw with his bow.* **41:2**

In ca. 539 B.C.E. the Babylonian army was defeated by the Persians. Isaiah prophesies that Israel will become like a powerful force.

> *I will remake you into a threshing machine*
> *with sharp teeth;*
> *you will grind the mountains,*
> *crush them,*
> *and reduce the hills to dust.* **41:15**

The Persian conquest was a great boon to the Jewish exiles. Cyrus soon issued decrees allowing them to return to Jerusalem and restore the Temple. In 520 B.C.E. the exiles led by Zerubbabel, a prince of the House of David, led the pioneers back to their devastated land.

Connection   The connection between the sidrah and the haftarah is the covenant (*brit*) that Adonai made with Abraham and renewed with Isaac and Jacob. In the covenant Adonai assures Abraham:

> *I will bless you*
> *and make your descendants*
> *into a great nation.* **Gen. 12:2**

In the haftarah, Isaiah comforts the Israelites and reminds them:

> *But you, Israel,*
> *My servant, Jacob,*
> *whom I have chosen,*
> *the descendant of My friend Abraham,*
> *I gathered you from the ends of the earth*
> *and said,*
> *"You are My servant,*
> *I have chosen you."* **41:8–9**

Haftarah for Lech Lecha לֶךְ לְךָ
(Isaiah 40:27–41:16)

40
27 Jacob, why do you complain,
and Israel, why do you grumble?
How dare you complain
that Adonai does not care for you?
28 Don't you know?
Haven't you heard?
Adonai, the Everlasting,
the Almighty and Creator of the universe,
can never get tired.
No one can measure the depths of His wisdom.
29 He gives power to the faint,
and to the feeble.
30 Even young people grow faint and tired,
and strong men will stumble and fall.
31 But those who trust in Adonai
will renew their strength.
They will spread their wings like eagles;
they will run
and never tire;
they will walk and not faint.

41
Islands, in the sea, be quiet and listen to me.
Feel your power, and come close, and speak;
let us decide on a verdict.
2 Who aroused the ruler [King Cyrus] from the east?
Who is victorious in every battle?
He conquers nations
and forces kings to surrender to Him.
With His sword,
He turns them into dust;
He scatters them like straw with His bow.
3 He chases them
and advances safely,

hardly touching the road with His feet.
4 Who has performed such mighty deeds?
He who created mankind:
I, Adonai, am the first
and I am the last; I am He.
5 The islands and foreign nations saw, and panicked;
the ends of the earth trembled;
nations came together.
6 Everyone encouraged his neighbor
and comforted each other,
"Be brave."
7 The carpenter encouraged the goldsmith,
and he who flattens with his hammer
encouraged the smithy,
who strikes the anvil,
complimenting the soldering,
saying, "It is excellent";
and they fastened the idol with nails
so that it would not topple and fall over.
8 But you, Israel,
My servant, Jacob,
whom I have chosen,
the descendant of My friend Abraham,
9 I gathered you from the ends of the earth
and said,
"You are My servant,
I have chosen you."
10 Do not be afraid, for I am with you.
Do not be frightened,
for I am Adonai. I will give you strength;
I will help you; I will defend you
with My strong right hand.
11 Be sure,
all your enemies who are angry at you
will be disgraced and shattered;
those who battle against you
will be destroyed

and will disappear.

12 You will hunt
for those who quarreled with you,
but they will be gone.
The enemies who made war against you
shall be as nothing.

13 For I, Adonai the Almighty,
will grasp your right hand
and promise you,
"Do not be afraid, I will help you."

14 Jacob, nation of Israel,
do not feel weak like a worm.
Adonai says,
I am your help, your Redeemer,
I am the Holy One of Israel.

15 I will remake you into a threshing machine
with sharp teeth;
you will grind the mountains,
crush them,
and reduce the hills to dust.

16 You will throw them into the air,
and the wind will blow the dust away,
and the whirlwind will scatter them.
Then you will celebrate with Adonai.
And you will praise the Holy One of Israel.

HAFTARAH for VAYERA
2 Kings 4:1–37

Books of Kings I and II The Books of Kings I and II belong to the part of the *Tanak* called *Nevi'im Rishonim*, meaning Early Prophets. These two books tell the beginning history of the kingdoms of Israel and Judah from the time of King Solomon and the building of the First Temple until the destruction of the Temple and Jerusalem by the Babylonians. These two books cover the period from about 960 to 560 B.C.E.

History Elisha the prophet lived in the Northern Kingdom of Israel during the reigns of four kings: Jehoram, Jehu, Jehoahaz, and Jehoash. Elisha was the son of wealthy landowner Gilead.

Elisha was a member of the "Sons of the Prophets." These were bands of zealous religious patriots who wore "garments of haircloth," lived in groups, and were supported by donations. They were completely opposed to the irreligious and idol-worshipping policies of the government. The leader of these bands was Elijah, and Elisha eventually assumed Elijah's mantle of leadership.

Elisha was Elijah's disciple. The Bible tells how Elijah recruited him. While passing through the Jordan Valley, Elijah saw Elisha plowing a field with a team of oxen. From a distance, he sensed the extraordinary power in the sweat-soaked farmer. Without hesitation, Elijah removed his mantle and flung it around the young man's shoulders. This was an ancient symbolic call to prophetic service, which Elisha eagerly accepted.

Elisha performed miracles and was active in the political and military life of Israel. When the Israelite army attacked Moab, he saved the day by finding water for the troops.

Elisha's fame as a miracle worker was so great that legend attributed power to him even after his death. One day, mourners at a funeral were attacked by Moabite bandits. The frightened mourners threw the corpse into the nearby tomb of Elisha and fled. On contacting the prophet's bones, the corpse came to life and walked away.

Text The text shows Elisha's love for ordinary people and his efforts to bring Adonai's blessings to those in need. The haftarah describes three miracles performed by the prophet.

Elisha performs a miracle by saving the children of a widow who will be sold into slavery if she cannot pay her debts. Then Elisha helps a charitable but troubled woman who cannot have a child. Then some years later, Elisha revives that same child, who is dying of a mysterious ailment.

Elisha was a courageous prophet and was devoted to the preservation of the worship of Adonai. His constant concern was seen in the miracles he performed.

Connection The connection between the sidrah and the haftarah are Abraham and Elisha. Both of these towering personalities were concerned about the welfare of humanity. They looked for and found opportunities to practice loving kindness and hospitality.

Abraham was hospitable to the three strangers of Mamre, and Elisha performed many miracles of hospitality. A farmer brought Elisha a gift of bread and grain. Elisha told his servant to feed the hundred "Sons of Prophets." To everyone's astonishment, there was enough for all of them.

Haftarah for Vayera וַיֵּרָא
(2 Kings 4:1-37)

4 One day, the widow of one of the prophets complained to Elisha, "My husband is dead; and you know that he was faithful to Adonai; but now the creditor has come to take my two children to be his servants."

2 So Elisha said to her, "How can I help you? Tell me, what do you have in the house?" She replied, "Your maidservant has nothing in the house, except for a small jar of olive oil."

3 So Elisha said, "Go borrow as many jars as you can from all your neighbors. **4** Then go into your house and shut the door behind yourself and your sons. Then pour oil into all the jars, setting them aside as they are filled."

5 So she left Elisha and shut the door behind herself and her sons. They brought the jars to her and she poured.

6 When the jars were full, she said to her son: "Bring me more jars." He said to her, "There are no more jars." Then the oil stopped flowing.

7 She went and told the messenger of Elohim, who said, "Go, sell the oil, and pay your debts; now you and your sons can live on what is left."

8 One day, Elisha went to Shunam, and a wealthy woman invited him in to eat with her. Later, whenever he passed that way, he stopped there to eat with her.

9 She said to her husband, "I know that his man who always passes our way is a holy messenger of Elohim. **10** Let's make a little room on the roof of our house, and put in a bed, a table, a chair, and a lamp, so that whenever he comes to eat he will have a place to rest."

11 One day he came and went to the room on the roof to rest. **12** He said to Gechazi, his servant, "Call this Shunammite." When he had called her, she appeared before him.

13 And he said to [his servant], "Tell her: 'Look, you have

70

taken all this trouble for us; what can we do for you? Do you want me to speak on your behalf to the king, or to the commander of the army?'" She answered, "No! I have everything I need."

14 Elisha said to his servant, "Is there anything we can do for her?" And Gechazi answered, "Her husband is old and she has no children."

15 Elisha said, "Call her." She came, and stood in the doorway of his room. **16** He said, "Next year, at about this time, you will give birth to a son." And she said, "No, my lord, man of God, do not lie to your maidservant."

17 But the woman soon became pregnant and gave birth to a son, just as Elisha had predicted.

18 One day, when the child had grown, he went to help his father, who was among the harvesters. **19** He complained to his father, "My head, my head hurts!" [The father] said to his servant, "Carry him home to his mother."

20 He sat on his mother's lap until noon, and then he died. **21** She went up to Elisha's room, laid the dead son on the bed of Elohim's messenger, and left. **22** She then said to her husband, "Call one of the servants and a donkey so I can hurry to the messenger of Elohim and return."

23 Then he said, "Why go to him today? It is not the New Moon or the Sabbath." She replied "Everything will be fine."

(Sephardim conclude here)

24 Then she saddled a donkey and said to her servant, "Let's hurry! Don't slow unless I tell you to."

25 She rode, and came to the messenger of Elohim at Mount Carmel. When Elisha saw her approaching, he said to Gechazi, his servant, "Look, there is that Shunammite woman. **26** Run at once to meet her, and ask her, "Are you well? Is your husband well? Is your child well?" She answered, "Everything will be fine."

27 But as soon as she reached the man of God on the mountain, she fell to the ground and took hold of Elisha's feet. Gechazi tried to push her away, but the messenger of Elohim said, "Let her alone for she is sad; and Adonai hid it from me and has not told me why."

28 Then she said, "My master, did I ever ask Adonai for a child? Didn't I say, 'Do not raise my hopes'?"

29 Elisha said to Gechazi, "Get ready to move; take my walking stick and go; if you meet anyone, do not stop to talk to them, and if anyone talks to you, do not answer; and place my walking stick on the child's face."

30 Then the child's mother said, "As Adonai lives, and as you yourself live, I will not leave you." So Elisha stood and followed her.

31 Gechazi hurried on ahead and placed the staff on the child's face; but there was no sign of life. So he went to meet Elisha and told him, "The child is not yet awakened."

32 When Elisha came to the house, he saw that the child was dead, lying on his bed. **33** So he went in and shut the door upon the two of them, and he prayed to Adonai. **34** Then he went and lay upon the child's body and placed his mouth on the child's mouth, his eyes on the child's eyes, and his hands on the child's hands. Then, as he stretched himself upon him, the child's body became warm. **35** Then Elisha returned and walked back and forth in the house, and went up and stretched himself upon the child. Suddenly the child sneezed seven times and opened his eyes.

36 Elisha called Gechazi and said, "Call this Shunammite woman." So he called her, and when she came, he said, "Here is your son! Take him."

37 She came and fell down at his feet in gratitude. She picked up her son and left.

HAFTARAH for CHAYAY SARAH
1 Kings 1:1–31

Books of Kings I and II   See haftarah Vayera, page 68.

History   Few rulers in history led a more adventurous and colorful life than the shepherd boy, David, the "sweet singer of Israel." As a teen he killed the Philistine giant Goliath, and after many death-defying adventures became the deliverer of the Israelites, the unifier of the nation, the founder of Jerusalem as the religious capital of Israel, the author of the Book of Psalms, and the founder of a dynasty.

David influenced all kinds of people by his personal charm, his strength of character, and his passionate loyalty to Adonai.

Text   King David was old and gradually retired from conducting state affairs. He suffered from fits of shivering, so his servant brought Avishag, a beautiful young girl, to care for and nurse the king.

In the midst of his declining health, David's children began competing for the succession to the throne.

David's son Adonijah claimed the throne and enlisted Joab, the commander-in-chief of the army, and Abiather, the high priest, as his allies. Adonijah enforced his claim and invited all the other princes except Solomon to his inaugural party.

In the meantime, David's wife Bathsheba entered David's bedroom and reminded him that he promised to make her son Solomon his successor. Then Nathan the prophet confirmed her story. David from his deathbed said to Bathsheba:

And the king swore and said, "As surely as Adonai lives, who has saved my life from many dangers, I swear to you by Adonai, the Savior of Israel, saying, 'Today, I proclaim that Solomon your son will rule after I die, and he will sit on my throne in my place.'" **1:29–30**

On his deathbed, David instructed Nathan and the priest Zadok to anoint Solomon with holy oil from the Ark. They performed the ceremony and Solomon became the King of Israel.

Connection   The sidrah discusses Abraham's old age and his concern for the continuation and the future of his family.

In the haftarah, a dying David, in spite of his infirmity, summons the strength to settle the succession and appoint Solomon as king.

Haftarah for Chayay Sarah חַיֵּי שָׂרָה
(1 Kings 1:1-31)

1 King David was old and advanced in years; he could not become warm even when they dressed him. **2** So his servants suggested, "Let them find for the king a young virgin; and let her care for the king and be his servant; let her lie close to the king and keep him warm."

3 So they searched for a beautiful maiden throughout all of Israel, and they found Avishag the Shunammite, whom they brought to the king. **4** The maiden was very beautiful, and she waited on the king and cared for him; but the king had no intimate relations with her.

5 Now Adoniyah the son of Chaggith boasted, saying "I will be the next king," so he assembled chariots and horsemen and recruited fifty men to run ahead of him. **6** His father had never questioned him by saying, "Why have you done all of this?" He was a very handsome man and was born after Avshalom. **7** So he consulted Joab the son of Tzuruya, and with Evyathar the priest, and they supported Adoniyah and helped him. **8** But Tzadok the priest, and Benayahu the son of Yehoyada, Nathan the prophet, and Shim'i and Re'i, and David's warriors did not support Adoniyah.

9 Adoniyah sacrificed sheep and oxen and fat calves near the stone of Zocheleth, at En-rogel; and he invited all his relatives, the king's sons, and all the men of Judah, the king's servants. **10** But Nathan the prophet, and Benayahu, the warriors, and Solomon his brother, he did not invite.

11 Then Nathan spoke to Bathsheba, Solomon's mother, saying, "Have you heard that Adoniyah the son of Chaggith has made himself king, and David our lord does not know it? **12** Now, let me give you advice, so that you may save your own life and the life of your son Solomon. **13** Go at once to King David, and say to him:

75

'My lord the king, did you not swear to me, saying, "Your son Solomon will rule after me, and he will inherit my throne"? Now why does Adoniyah reign?' **14** Then while you are still talking with the king, I will come in after you, and confirm everything you said."

15 So Bathsheba went in to the king's bedroom; the king was very old and Avishag the Shunammite was caring for him. **16** Bathsheba bowed before the king, and the king asked, "What can I do for you?"

17 She said to him, "My lord, you swore to me in the name of Adonai the Lord, 'Solomon your son will rule after me, and he will inherit my throne.' **18** And now Adoniyah rules, and my lord the king does not even know about it.

19 "He has sacrificed many oxen, fat calves, and sheep, and he has invited all the king's sons, Evyathar the priest, and Joab the captain of the army; but he has not invited your servant Solomon. **20** And you, my lord the king, the eyes of all Israel are upon you, to tell them who will inherit the throne of my lord the king after him. **21** Otherwise, when my lord the king dies, I and my son Solomon will be counted as enemies."

22 Nathan the prophet entered while she was still talking with the king. **23** The king's advisers announced, "Nathan the prophet." When he came in before the king, he bowed before the king with his face to the ground.

24 And Nathan said, "My lord, the king, did you decide, 'Adoniyah will be king after me, and he will sit on my throne and rule'? **25** Today Adoniyah has sacrificed many oxen, calves, and sheep and has invited all the king's sons, and the commanders of the army, and Evyathar the priest; and now they are partying and drinking with him, and toasting him: 'Long live King Adoniyah.' **26** But me, your servant, Tzadok the priest, or Benayahu the son of Yehoyada, and your servant Solomon were not invited.

27 "My lord the king, have you not informed your servant? Have you decided who will sit on your throne after him?"

28 Then King David said, "Summon Bathsheba." So she entered and stood before the king.

29 And the king swore and said, "As surely as Adonai lives, who has saved my life from many dangers, **30** I swear to you by Adonai, the Savior of Israel, saying, 'Today, I proclaim that Solomon your son will rule after I die, and he will sit on my throne in my place.'"

31 Then Bathsheba bowed humbly down to the king, saying, "May my lord, King David, live forever."

INTRODUCTION TO
HAFTARAH for TOLDOT
Malachi 1:1–2:7

Book of Malachi   Malachi is the last of the Twelve Minor Prophets. The book of Malachi belongs to the Latter Prophets, *Nevi'im Achronim*. It belongs to the subdivision called *Trey Asar*, meaning twelve—The Twelve Minor Prophets.

History   Malachi means "my messenger." From the description of the text, Malachi prophesied during the Persian period, about 450–425 B.C.E. in Jewish history, about 50 years after the completion of the Second Temple—before the missions of Ezra and Nehemiah. Ezra was Judea's spiritual advisor and Nehemiah was its political advisor.

During this time, the Jewish community was completely disillusioned. The crops were very poor, religious observance was at a low point, and Jews were intermarrying with the pagan women.

Text   Malachi loved his people and demanded the revival of the true faith.

> *Adonai says to the priests*
> *who despise Me,*
> *"A child respects his father,*
> *and a servant respects his master.*
> *If I am a father,*
> *where is My respect?*
> *And if I am a master,*
> *who respects Me?*
> *And you ask,*
> *"How have we despised Your name?"* **1:6**

Adonai says, "Stop the pretenses and the posturing. I know who you really are.

> *I wish there were at least one among you*
> *who would just shut the Temple doors*
> *and stop the useless sacrifices.*
> *Adonai Almighty says.* **1:10**

Connection   The connection between the sidrah and the haftarah are in the opening verses.

Jacob and Rebecca were the parents of twin sons and the parents of two nations.

Edom was founded by Esau, and the Israelites were descended from Jacob. Malachi highlights Adonai's attitude toward the two nations.

Adonai hates the Edomites because Esau rejected his birthright from his father Jacob.

Adonai loves Jacob because he eagerly accepted the covenantal relationship. Although they came from the same parents, the two men were totally different. Later the two nations were neighbors and had a long and bloody rivalry, being often at war with each other.

Haftarah for Toldot תּוֹלְדוֹת
(Malachi 1:1–2:7)

1 This is the message that Adonai sent to Israel through Malachi:

2 Adonai says, I have intensely loved you.
Yet you ask,
"How have You loved us?"
Wasn't Esau Jacob's brother?
Yet I loved Jacob,
3 But I detested Esau;
I devastated his hill country,
and his territory
became a desert filled with jackals.
4 Adonai says,
If Edom should say,
"We are devastated,
but we will return
and rebuild our ruined homes,"
they may rebuild,
but I will demolish them again.
They will be known as the land of evil,
and the nation with whom Adonai is continually angry.
5 You, with, your own eyes will see
the destruction, and you will say:
"Adonai is mighty.
His power reaches
far beyond the border of Israel."
6 Adonai says to the priests
who despise Me,
"A child respects his father,
and a servant respects his master.
If I am a father,
where is My respect?
And if I am a master,
who respects Me?"

And you ask,
"How have we despised Your name?"
7 By offering forbidden sacrifices on My altar;
and then you ask,
"How have we insulted You?"
You insult Me when you say,
"Adonai's altar deserves no respect."
8 Adonai the Almighty says,
Is it not disrespectful
when you offer blind,
lame, and sick [animals] for sacrifice?
Just try to present such gifts to your ruler,
and you will see how pleased he is with you.
9 Adonai Almighty says,
And now you beg Adonai
that He be merciful to you!
When you bring Him that kind of gift,
will He show favor to any of you?
10 I wish there were at least one among you
who would just shut the Temple doors
and stop the useless sacrifices.
Adonai Almighty says,
I have no respect for you,
and I will not accept any sacrifice
that you bring.
11 Adonai Almighty says,
My name is great all over the world,
and in every place
pure offerings are presented to My name.
12 But the priests insult Me
when they say,
Adonai's altar is unimportant,
and its sacrifices are useless.
13 You also say,
"This is a complete waste,"
and you turned up your nose at it.
You have presented offerings

that were stolen by violence,
or that are sick and lame.
Adonai asks,
Should I accept this kind of offering from you?
14 Cursed is the liar
who has a healthy animal in his flock
and donates it,
then substitutes a sick animal for sacrifice
to Adonai;
Adonai the Almighty says,
I am a great Ruler,
and My name is respected everywhere.

2 Priests, pay attention!
This is what I want you to do.
2 Adonai Almighty says,
I want you to listen closely,
and if you do not honor My name,
then I will send the curses upon you,
your blessings will became curses.
Yes, I curse the priests,
because they have not taken my warnings seriously.
3 Beware!
I will punish your descendants
and rub their faces in the dirt,
even into the ashes of your sacrifices;
and you will be buried among the ashes.
4 Adonai Tzvaot says,
I gave you this warning,
so that My covenant
with the Levites can remain in force.
5 My covenant with the tribe of Levi
was a covenant of life and peace,
and I kept my agreement with him
because he respected Me
and honored My name.
6 They obeyed the laws of the Torah of truth,

and they did not lie or cheat.
They obeyed me
and lived in peace and righteousness,
and turned many away
from lives of sin and evil.
7 The priests are the messengers of Adonai Almighty;
their mission is to preserve knowledge,
and people should learn the Torah from them.

INTRODUCTION TO
HAFTARAH for VAYETZE
Hosea 12:13–14:10

Book of Hosea The Book of Hosea belongs to the division called *Nevi'im Achronim*: the Latter Prophets. It is part of the subdivision called *Trey Asar*, the Twelve Minor Prophets.

Hosea was the son of Be'eri and lived in the Northern Kingdom of Israel during the reign of Jeroboam II, ca. eighth century B.C.E.

Hosea had a very unhappy marriage. He was told by Adonai to marry a prostitute named Gomer. They had three children, and each of them was given a name that symbolizes the sinful conduct of the Israelites' behavior toward Adonai.

History About fifteen years after Amos (ca. 760 B.C.E.) prophesied, Hosea (746 B.C.E.) began to speak about the evils of the Northern Kingdom.

A time of prosperity began for Israel, and Samaria, the capital, was a flourishing city. Jeroboam II (784–748 B.C.E.) restored Israel's wealth and power but had no understanding of the people's religious and societal needs. He neglected the laws of the Torah and encouraged the people to worship idols. The kingdom of Jeroboam looked strong and powerful but internally it was rotten and unjust.

Like Amos, Hosea possessed spiritual and political wisdom. He predicted Assyria's invasion of Israel and warned the people against the imminent danger. He identified with the poor and attacked the pagan influence which had engulfed Israel. He warned his people that unless they repented, they were doomed. In 722 B.C.E. the Northern Kingdom was defeated and the capital Samaria destroyed. Much of Israel's population was deported to Persia to prevent further uprisings.

Text Hosea reminds the people that Adonai through his prophet Moses brought the nation into being. He condemns in strong terms the idolatry and the fertility cults which had inundated the country.

After the fierce condemnation in chapter 13, the last chapter is filled with love and pleading. Hosea begs the Israelites to repent and return to the worship of Adonai and find forgiveness.

> *Israel, return to Adonai;*
> *you have stumbled because of your sins.*
> *Ask for forgiveness,*
> *and return to Adonai.*
> *Say to Him,*
> *"Forgive our sins, and be kind to us,*
> *so we will offer the repentance instead of sacrifice"* **14:2–3**

The haftarah ends with Hosea completing his prophecy and stating:

> *Wise people understand these things;*
> *whoever is understanding will know.*
> *Adonai's laws are just,*
> *and the righteous follow them,*
> *but sinners fall and stumble in them.* **14:10**

Connection   The connection between the sidrah and the haftarah are the verses

> *Jacob fled to the land of Aram,*
> *and [there] Israel worked as a shepherd*
> *to earn a wife.*
> *There, Moses, Adonai's prophet,*
> *led the Israelites out from Egypt,*
> *and they were saved.* **12:13–14**

Hosea reminds the Israelites of their ancestor the patriarch Jacob and the sojourn and the redemption of the Israelites from Egypt.

Haftarah for Vayetze וַיֵּצֵא
(Hosea 12:13–14:10)

12
13 Jacob fled to the land of Aram,
and [there] Israel worked as a shepherd
to earn a wife.
14 There, Moses, Adonai's prophet,
led the Israelites out from Egypt,
and they were saved.
15 But the tribe of Ephraim
committed a bitter offense;
they brought bloodshed upon themselves,
and they will be punished.

13
When Ephraim spoke,
everyone trembled.
Everyone respected the tribe in Israel,
but when they started worshipping the idol Baal,
they were doomed.
2 Now they continued to sin
more and more,
and have cast idols of silver.
It is said of these people,
"They offer human sacrifices
and kiss animals shaped by human hands.
3 Therefore they will disappear
like the morning clouds,
and like the dew
that vanishes in the morning,
like the straw from the threshing-floor
that is blown away in the wind,
and like smoke escaping from a chimney.
4 I am Adonai
Who rescued you from the land of Egypt;
You have no Savior except Me.
5 I protected you in the wilderness,

in that dry land of great thirst.
6 But when you had eaten
and were filled,
then you became arrogant and forgot Me.
7 So I will behave like a lion,
and like a leopard
I will lie in wait.
8 I will attack them
like a bear whose cubs have been stolen,
and I will rip their hearts open
and devour them there like a hungry lion.
9 Israel, soon I will destroy you,
Do not expect any help from Me.
10 Where is your king now?
Can he save you now?
Where are your judges,
of whom you demanded,
"Give us a king and princes"?
11 In My anger, I gave you a king,
and now in my anger,
I will take him away.
12 The sins of the kingdom of Ephraim
are collected and are stored and recorded.
13 Pains like a woman in childbirth
will torment him.
He is like a senseless baby
who refuses to leave the womb.
14 Shall I save them
from the power of the grave?
Should I save them from death?
No! send your plagues!
Send your destruction!
I refuse to show mercy!
15 Grow like the reeds,
but an east wind from Adonai
will blow from the wilderness;
and his streams

and his wells will dry up.
That wind will scorch all growing things.

14

Samaria, capital of the kingdom (Israel), is guilty,
for she has rebelled against Elohim.
Her people will die by the sword;
their babies will be crushed,
and their pregnant women
will be ripped open.
2 Israel, return to Adonai;
you have stumbled because of your sins.
3 Ask for forgiveness,
and return to Adonai.
Say to him,
"Forgive our sins,
and be kind to us,
so we will offer the repentance instead of sacrifice"
4 Assyria cannot save us,
and armored chariots are useless,
nor will we say again to the manmade idols,
"Idols, you are our gods,"
for only in You
does the orphan find mercy.
5 I will stop their backsliding,
I will love them freely;
for My anger is turned away from him.
6 To Israel, I will be like the dew;
Israel shall blossom like the lily
and grow roots like the cedars of Lebanon.
7 Its branches will spread
and become beautiful
like the olive trees,
and as perfumed
as the forests of Lebanon.
8 Those who live in exile will return;
they will grow like corn
and blossom like the grapevine;

their fragrance will be like the wines of Lebanon.
9 Ephraim will say,
"I will have nothing to do with idols."
I will care for you;
I am like a tree, always giving fruit.
10 Wise people understand these things;
whoever is understanding will know.
Adonai's laws are just,
and the righteous follow them,
but sinners fall and stumble in them.

INTRODUCTION TO
HAFTARAH for VAYISHLACH
Obadiah 1:1–21

Book of Obadiah   This is the shortest book in the *Tanak* and consists of only one chapter.

It belongs in the division called the *Nevi'im Achronim*, the Latter Prophets. The text is part of a subdivision called *Trey Aser*, meaning twelve. This consists of twelve so-called Minor Prophets. There is nothing known of Obadiah's origin and the date of this prophecy.

History   The primary theme is the sister nation of Israel, (Esau) Edom. According to the Torah, Jacob and Esau were the twin children of Isaac and Rebecca. Isaac was one of the patriarchs of the nation of Israel, and Esau was the founder of the nation of Edom.

They were a desert people who occupied an area around the southern end of the Dead Sea.

In 587 B.C.E., after the kingdom of Judah was defeated by the Babylonians, the Edomites, like vultures, moved in and occupied Judean territory near Jerusalem.

Text   In the haftarah, Obadiah severely criticizes the Edomites for collaborating with Babylon. He condemns the Edomites and promises:

> *Shame will cover you;*
> *you will be disgraced*
> *because of your violence*
> *against your brother Israel,*
> *and you will disappear forever.*   **1:10**

Obadiah prophesied that the defeated remnants of Israel will once again rise up and retake the land, and the Edomites will pay the price, and

> *Israel will be like a strong fire,*
> *and the house of Joseph a roaring flame,*
> *but the house of Esau will be consumed like straw.*

They will set Esau on fire,
and it will consume them.
The house of Esau will not survive;
Adonai has passed judgment. **1:18**

Connection The twin brothers Jacob and Esau are the con-nection between the sidrah and the haftarah. The brothers were rivals from the day of their birth and the enmity wors-ened when Jacob, at his mother Rebecca's insistence, used trickery to obtain the birthright.

Haftarah for Vayishlach וַיִּשְׁלַח
(Obadiah 1:1-21)

1 The prophecy of Obadiah.
Adonai the Almighty appeared
to the prophet Obadiah
with a message about Edom:
I, Adonai, have dispatched a messenger
to the nations in the area,
"Rise up and attack Edom!"
2 I, Elohim, will reduce you
to the smallest among the nations;
you are now the most despised.
3 Your arrogant heart has fooled you,
you who live in rocky fortresses.
You who live on the top of that mount,
say to yourself,
"Who can pull me down to the common folk?"
4 Even though
you build your nest high like the eagle,
and build your nest high among the stars,
I, Adonai, will bring you down to Earth.
5 If robbers attack you at night,
would they not steal only enough for themselves?
If grape pickers came to you,
would not they always leave some gleanings?
6 Esau will be completely looted,
and his hidden treasures will be found!
7 Your allies
have pursued you to the border;
your friends
who were with you at peace
have deceived you
and dominated you;
those who eat your bread
have set a trap for you,

and you are not aware of it.
8 Adonai says,
On that day I will
destroy the wise men of Edom,
and intelligent ones from the mount of Esau.
9 Your mighty warriors
from the city of Teman
will be confused,
and all the descendants of Esau from the mount of Esau
will be slaughtered.
10 Shame will cover you;
you will be disgraced
because of your violence
against your brother Israel,
and you will disappear forever.
11 When you stood silently by
and you behaved as one of the enemy,
as strangers carried off the riches of Israel,
and captured the city,
and cast lots for Jerusalem,
You were like one of them.
12 Why did you gloat
on the day of your brother's misfortune?
Why did you rejoice over the people of Judah
on the day of their destruction?
You should not have boasted
on their day of distress.
13 You should not have entered
into the gates of Jerusalem
on the day of their disaster;
you should not
have gazed on their sorrow
on the day of their calamity.
You should not have stolen their property.
14 You should not have stood
on the roads,
to cut down refugees;

you should not have betrayed
the survivors on the day of distress.
15 Adonai's revenge is coming
to all the nations.
Just as you have tormented Israel,
so you will be tormented;
your evil deeds will be heaped
atop your own head.
16 In my anger,
I punished the people of Judah
who inhabit My sacred mountain.
And now the neighboring nations
will also be punished,
but they will forever vanish
without a trace.
17 They will find safety in Jerusalem,
and it will be holy;
and Israel will recapture their own land.
18 Israel will be like a strong fire,
and the house of Joseph a roaring flame,
but the house of Esau will be consumed like straw.
They will set Esau on fire,
and it will consume them.
The house of Esau will not survive;
Adonai has passed judgment.
19 The people of Israel
who live in the (south) Negev
will conquer the mount of Esau,
and those who live on the coastal plain
the land of the Philistines;
they will conquer
the lands of Ephraim and Samaria,
and Benjamin will occupy Gilead.
20 The exiled of the children of Israel
who live among the Canaanites,
as far as Zarepahath,
and the exiles of Jerusalem,

who are in Sepharad,
will occupy the cities of the (south) Negev.
21 Liberators will ascend Mount Zion
to rule over Mount Esau,
and the kingdom will belong to Adonai.

HAFTARAH for VAYESHEV
Amos 2:6–3:8

Book of Amos The Book of Amos belongs to the section of the *Tanak* called the *Nevi'im Achronim*, meaning the Latter Prophets. The book of Amos is the third book in the subdivision called *Trey Asar*, meaning "twelve" and referring to the twelve prophetic books in the group.

Amos was a shepherd in the village of Tekoa in the hills of Hebron about ten miles from Jerusalem. He first appeared in the town of Bethel and preached against the lack of social consciousness and the selfishness of the people.

History A time of prosperity now began for Israel. Samaria, its capital, was a flourishing city. The reign of Jeroboam II, son of Jehoash, saw foreign merchants coming once more to Israel's markets. New trade pacts were signed with the Phoenicians of Tyre.

Unfortunately, Israel's new prosperity was limited to the nobles and the merchants, who failed to remember that the poor were their brothers. Workers and small farmers paid high taxes and lived in huts, while the rich lived in luxury.

Jeroboam II (784–748 B.C.E.), like other rulers before him, restored Israel's material wealth and power but had no understanding of people's inner needs. He encouraged his people to adopt the idol-worshipping ways of Damascus and Tyre.

Now another strong voice arose in the land, crying out against the oppressors who were forcing the greater part of the people to endure poverty and injustice. Amos, a shepherd from Tekoa, spoke openly in the streets of Samaria, declaring that the sacrifices made by the rich on the altar at Bethel were meaningless as long as the donors did not act justly.

Amos possessed great knowledge of the political problems of the day. He warned that all the wealth of Samaria would be useless against the Assyrian threat unless the kingdom of Israel was united and strong. This would come about, he declared, only if the nation kept the laws of the Torah.

Text   Israel's wealthy class forced Amos to leave Samaria, but he continued to speak out fearlessly, telling the rich that Adonai would be more pleased by acts of justice than by costly offerings.

> *So says Adonai:*
> *For three sins of Israel,*
> *yes, for four,*
> *I will not repeal [the punishment;*
> *because they sell the poor for silver,*
> *and the poor for a pair of sandals.*
> *With the dust of the earth,*
> *they cover the heads of the poor*
> *and push aside the helpless.* **2:6–7**

In this selection, the prophet condemns sinners. In sorrow, Amos says, "I must reveal this from Adonai."

> *The lion has roared;*
> *everyone is in a panic.*
> *Adonai Almighty has spoken;*
> *who can tell*
> *what will happen in the future?* **3:6**

Connection   The connection between the sidrah and the haftarah is the sale of an innocent boy, Joseph, into slavery in Egypt. The haftarah also focuses on the sale of the poor into slavery. Amos says:

> *I will not repeal [the punishment];*
> *because they sell the poor for silver,*
> *and the poor for a pair of sandals.* **2:6**

Haftarah for Vayeshev וַיֵּשֶׁב
(Amos 2:6–3:8)

2 **6** So says Adonai:
For three sins of Israel,
yes, for four,
I will not repeal [the punishment];
because they sell the poor for silver,
and the poor for a pair of sandals.
7 With the dust of the earth,
they cover the heads of the poor
and push aside the helpless.
Father and son sleep with the same woman
and my Holy Name is disgraced.
8 They lie down
beside every altar
on pledged garments,
and they drink wine in the Temple of Adonai
bought with priestly fines.
9 I destroyed the Amorites,
who were as tall as cedars,
and as mighty as the oaks;
I destroyed their fruit above the ground
and their roots below the ground.
10 I delivered you from the land of Egypt,
and led you in the desert
through the forty years,
to conquer the land of the Amorite.
11 I raised your sons
to be prophets,
and some of your men
as Nazirites.
Adonai asks,
Children of Israel, isn't it true?
12 Then you forced the Nazirites to drink wine
and ordered the prophets not to prophecy.

13 Now I will crush you
just as a wagon filled with grain presses down.
14 The swift will not escape,
and the strong
will lose their strength;
and the warrior not save his own life.
15 The archer will retreat;
and the swift runner will not escape;
and the trained horseman
will not save his life.
16 Adonai says, On that day,
The bravest and the mighty
will run away.
I Adonai have decreed it.

3 Children of Israel,
listen to the word
that Adonai has
spoken about you,
and against the children of Israel,
which I brought up from the land of Egypt.
2 From all the nations on the earth,
I have chosen only you;
therefore I will punish you
for all your sins.
3 Would two people walk together
without being friends?
4 In the forest,
would a lion roar
when he cannot find prey?
Would a lion roar in his den
if he has caught nothing?
5 Would a bird fall into a cage
where there is no bait for it?
Would a trap spring up from the ground
if it has caught nothing?
6 In the city,

when a shofar sounds a warning,
don't the people tremble with fear?
Can a disaster happen to a city,
unless Adonai has ordered it?
7 Whenever Adonai Almighty
plans to do anything,
He reveals His decision
to His servants,
to the prophets.
8 The lion has roared;
everyone is in a panic.
Adonai Almighty has spoken;
who can tell
what will happen in the future?

HAFTARAH for MIKETZ
1 Kings 3:15–4:1

Books of Kings I and II   See haftarah Vayera, page 68.

History   David and his son Solomon were the two out-standing Hebrew monarchs, each in his own way. David rose from a shepherd boy and, with brute strength and bravery, carved out an empire. Solomon was born with a silver spoon in his mouth and, like a trained executive, consolidated his kingdom and gave it forty years of prosperity and peace. Solomon is remembered for his wisdom, for erecting the Temple, and for his huge harem of token wives.

In addition, Solomon is credited with the Apocryphal book, the Wisdom of Solomon. The king was reputed to have composed three thousand proverbs and more than a thousand songs.

Solomon was a clever ruler and was gifted with great wisdom. Since the Temple had not yet been built, the politically wise king made it a practice to worship and offer sacrifices in different tribal areas, thereby uniting the various factions by not exhibiting any favoritism.

Text   One day Adonai appeared to Solomon in a dream and asked him what he wanted most. In the dream, Solomon answered:

> *"Give me an understanding mind to rule Your people, to distinguish between good and evil, so I can rule the people fairly."* **3:9**

Adonai granted his wish and gave him a wise mind.

Solomon's wisdom is soon tested by two harlots who each claim to be the mother of a child. Solomon orders the living baby cut in half so each woman can have half. One of the women accepts the verdict, but the true mother cries,

"My lord, let her have the living child, but please do not kill it." **3:26**

Then the king answers,

"Give the living child to the first one; do not kill it; for she really is its mother." **3:27**

Word of Solomon's wise judgment quickly spread.

When the Israelites heard of the king's decision, they stood in awe of the king; for they saw that Adonai had given him great wisdom, to judge wisely.
And King Solomon was king over all Israel. **3:28**

Connection   In the sidrah, Joseph interprets the Pharaoh's dreams and credits Adonai for granting him the wisdom to do so.

Solomon also has a dream and does not ask for riches or power. Solomon only asks for the wisdom to rule and judge his subjects fairly and with an understanding heart.

Haftarah for Miketz מִקֵּץ
(1 Kings 3:15–4:1)

3 **15** King Solomon woke up, and realized that Adonai spoke to him in a dream. Then he went to Jerusalem. There he stood before the Holy Ark (of God's covenant) and brought burnt and peace offerings, and invited all of his officials to a feast.

16 Then two prostitutes came to the king and stood before him for judgment. **17** One woman said, "My master, we two live in the same house; and I gave birth to a child while she was in the house. **18** On the third day after I had my child, this woman also gave birth, and we were together; there was no one else with us in the house, only the two of us were in the house.

19 That night, this woman's child died because she rolled over on it. **20** Then she quietly got up at midnight, while I slept, and took my son from beside me, and placed her dead child at my breast. **21** In the morning, when I arose to nurse my child, I saw it was dead; but in the morning, when I looked at it closely, I saw that it was not my son."

22 The other woman said, "No, the living son is mine and the dead one is yours." The first said, "No, the dead son is yours and the living one is mine." Thus they argued before the king.

23 Then the king said, "One woman says, 'My son is the one who is alive; your son is dead'; and the other says, 'No, your son is dead; and my son is the living one.'"

24 Said the king, "Someone bring me a sword." So they brought a sword to the king. **25** The king said, "I am going to divide the living child in half, and in that way I will give half to one, and half to the other."

26 Then the woman whose child really was the living one said, because her heart ached for her son, "My lord, let her have the living child, but please do not kill it." But the other said, "Neither of us will have the child; cut it in half."

27 Then the king answered, "Give the living child to the first one; do not kill it; for she really is its mother."

28 When the Israelites heard of the king's decision, they stood in awe of the king; for they saw that Adonai had given him great wisdom, to judge wisely.

4 And King Solomon was king over all Israel.

INTRODUCTION TO
HAFTARAH for VAYIGASH
Ezekiel 37:15–28

Book of Ezekiel The three major classical prophets are Isaiah, Jeremiah, and Ezekiel. Ezekiel served as a priest in the Temple of Jerusalem, and when the Babylonians in 586 B.C.E. destroyed Jerusalem, he was carried away to captivity in Babylonia. Ezekiel settled in the city Tel-Abib, situated along the Chebar river.

The Book of Ezekiel belongs to a section the *Tanak* called *Nevi'im Achronim*, the Latter Prophets, and consists of 48 chapters, divided into four fantasy-filled visions.

Some of the Jewish leaders in Babylon were poets who sang of the bitterness of the exile and of the longing for home. One of the outstanding leaders of that time was the prophet Ezekiel.

Ezekiel, the son of the priest Buzi, was born in Israel about 622 B.C.E. His call to prophecy came about 539 B.C.E., five years after his exile to Babylonia.

The Book of Ezekiel describes a Jewish community enjoying religious freedom and well integrated into Babylonian society. In fact, some of the Jews did not even consider themselves exiles.

History In 608 B.C.E. Neco, king of Egypt, appointed Jehoiakim as king of Judah. Jehoiakim was an obedient vassal. He installed Egyptian gods in Judah, followed Egyptians laws, and paid heavy tribute. Like a bone between two huge ferocious dogs, Judah found itself a small, weak nation, with Egypt on one side and the advancing armies of Nebuchadnezzar of Babylon on the other.

Egypt sought to undermine the power of Babylonia by encouraging its new vassals to revolt. King Jehoiakim of Judah, encouraged by Egyptian promises of assistance in the case of a Babylonian attack, refused to pay tribute to Nebuchadnezzar. The Babylonian king promptly sent an army. But little Judah stood firm under Jehoiachin, who was only eighteen years old when he succeeded his father, Jehoiakim.

Remembering the ravaged battlefields of Judah, Ezekiel likened them dramatically to a desolate valley of dry bones. Adonai, he declared, would breathe life into these dry bones, and the desolate valley would be transformed into a place of new life. Restored, the people would return to their own land to achieve this restoration.

Text   Necbuchadnezzar himself took command of his troops, destroyed many cities of Judah, and marched up to the gates of Jerusalem. The promised Egyptian assistance never materialized, and in 597 B.C.E. Nebuchadnezzar took the city by storm, carrying young Jehoiachin and many important families into captivity. Among the captives was the young priest Ezekiel.

In this selection, Ezekiel prophecies that the nation of Israel will be reborn and live again. The two warring kingdoms, the states Israel and Judah, will become one nation under one king, a descendant of the House of David.

Ezekiel predicts a future golden age. He says:

> *My dwelling place will be in their midst,*
> *I will be their Adonai,*
> *And they will be My people.*
> *Then nations will realize that*
> *I, Adonai, have made Israel holy when My Temple is forever*
> *in their midst.*   **37:27–28**

Connection   The connection between the sidrah and the haftarah is the theme of reunification.

Joseph is reunited with his parents and his brothers. The prophet Ezekiel predicts that the Israelites will return to their homeland and the kingdoms of Israel and Judah will unify into one single entity.

Haftarah for Vayigash וַיִּגַּשׁ
(Ezekiel 37:15-28)

37

15 And a message from Adonai came to Ezekiel, saying: **16** Ezekiel, son of man, take a stick, and write on it, "The Kingdom of Judah, and the Israelites living there"; then take another stick, and write on it, "This stick represents Joseph, this stick represents Ephraim, and all the House of Israel, and its people." **17** Join them together into one stick, joined together in your hand. **18** When your people ask you, "Will you tell us what these two sticks mean?" **19** say to them, "This is what Adonai Almighty says: Watch, I will join together the stick of Joseph, which is in the hand of Ephraim and the tribes of Israel, and put it together with the stick of Judah, to form one stick, so that they can become one in My hand. **20** Hold the sticks on which you write in your hand so that everyone can see them. **21** Now say to them: "Adonai the Almighty promises, I will gather together the children of Israel from among the nations into which they have been exiled; and I will gather them from every foreign land and return them to their own land. **22** I will make them one nation in the land, and upon the mountains of Israel. Only one king will rule over them all, and they will no longer be two separate nations divided into two kingdoms.

23 Never again will they corrupt themselves by worshipping idols or their detestable things, or by commiting any other transgressions; wherever they live I will save them from their sins and I will cleanse them. Then they will truly be My people, and I will be their Adonai.

24 My servant David will be their king, and they will all have one leader. They will follow My commandments, observe My statutes, and fulfill them. **25** They will live in the land in which your ancestors lived, in the land which I promised to My servant Jacob; they and their children, and their grandchildren will live there forever; and My servant David will be forever their ruler. **26** In addition, I will make an everlasting covenant of peace with them; and I will bless them and multiply them, and I will establish My Temple in their midst for all time. **27** My dwelling place will be in their midst, I will be their Adonai, and they will be My people. **28** Then nations will realize that I, Adonai, have made Israel holy when My Temple is forever in their midst.

INTRODUCTION TO
HAFTARAH for VAYECHI
2 Kings 2:1–12

Books of Kings I and II   See haftarah Vayera, page 68.

History   David found it difficult to decide which of his sons was to succeed him as king. He realized that in order to prevent strife over the succession, he had to announce his choice before he died. Summoning Nathan the prophet, he told him that he had selected the wise Prince Solomon, son of Bathsheba. Solomon was anointed by Zadok, the high priest, and proclaimed king. The rams' horns sounded and the people shouted, "Long live King Solomon!"

King David's work was done. When he died, all Israel mourned the passing of the sweet singer whose many accomplishments had included the composition of the beautiful poems that comprise the biblical Book of Psalms. David died in 965 B.C.E.

Text   When David lies dying, he instructs Solomon as follows:

"I am about to die; I want you to be strong and courageous.
You must keep the charge of Adonai, follow in His teachings, and observe His statutes, commandments, judgments, and testimonies, as it is written in the Torah of Moses, so that you may succeed in all you do and wherever you go. **2:2–3**

David, a fierce warrior to his last dying breath, instructs the young newly crowned boy how to deal with his friends and take revenge against his enemies.

Be aware and wise, and do not let him [Joab] go to his grave peacefully.
Be kind to the sons of Barzillai the Gileadite, and let them eat at your table; for they helped me when I escaped from your brother Absalom. **2:6–7**

Connection   In the sidrah, the dying patriarch Jacob speaks
to his children, giving them guidance and blessing them.
David, the dying king, also blesses his sons before he dies.

Haftarah for Vayechi וַיְחִי
(2 Kings 2:1–12)

2 As David was dying, he said to Solomon:
2 "I am about to die; I want you to be strong and courageous. **3** You must keep the charge of Adonai, follow in His teachings, and observe His statutes, commandments, judgments, and testimonies, as it is written in the Torah of Moses, so that you may succeed in all you do and wherever you go. **4** If you do, then Adonai will keep His promise, which He made me, saying: If your descendants are faithful, and follow Me with all their heart and soul, then one of your descendants will always sit on the throne of Israel.

5 "You are aware of what Joab the son of Tzeruya did to me, and what he did to the two captains of the Israelite army: He murdered Abner the son of Ner and Amasa the son of Yether, spilling the blood of war in time of peace, and staining the blood of war on his belt, about his waist, and on the shoes on his feet as if he were in battle.

6 "Be aware and wise, and do not let him go to his grave peacefully. **7** Be kind to the sons of Barzillai the Gileadite, and let them eat at your table; for they helped me when I escaped from your brother Absalom. **8** Remember Shimi the son of Gera, the Benjamite from Bachurim, who cursed me with a terrible curse when I fled to Machanaim. When he came down to meet me at the Jordan River, I swore to Adonai saying, 'I will not kill you with my sword.'
9 "Do not consider him blameless. You are a wise man; you must find a way to deal with him; you must arrange a bloody death for him."

10 Then David died and was buried in the city of David.
11 David ruled over Israel for forty years; he ruled for seven years in Hebron and thirty-three years in Jerusalem.
12 Then his son Solomon inherited the throne of David his father; and the kingdom was firmly in his control.

INTRODUCTION TO
HAFTARAH for SHEMOT
Isaiah 27:6–28:13, 29:22–23

Book of Isaiah   See haftarah Bereshit, page 51.

History   The people of Judah had become vassals of Assyria. Now Egypt, in an attempt to restore her empire, was trying to unite the small states around Palestine to stage a revolt against Assyria. Though Egypt promised to support a rebellion militarily, she was in no position to supply aid. Isaiah correctly analyzed the situation and warned Judah that they were pawns in the deadly chess game between Egypt and Assyria. A politically influential party in Jerusalem favored joining the conspiracy. Despite Isaiah's warning, Judah revolted in 714 B.C.E., leading to the destruction of the Jewish state and the exile to Babylonia of numerous important Judeans.

Text   Isaiah uses agricultural imagery to comfort the Israelites. He says:

The time is nearing, And Jacob will put down roots, Israel will blossom and flower and carpet the face of the earth with its fruit. **27:6**

Now Isaiah criticizes and predicts the doom of the people who have lost faith and hope. He says:

The fortified cities of Israel will be empty and filled with abandoned and lonely houses.
It will be like the wilderness, where the calves will rest and graze and eat from the branches. **27:10**

Isaiah continues and aims his prophecy at the Northern Kingdom.

The arrogant crown of the drunkards of Samaria will be trampled underfoot. **28:3**

He mocks the people of Samaria:

He feeds us in bits
rule by rule,
line by line,
a little here,
and a little there. **28:10**

Now, Adonai talks to Israel,
tiny rule by rule,
tiny line by line,
a little bit here
and a little bit there.
Yet they do not understand.
They go forward,
then they fall backwards. **28:13**

The haftarah concludes with a message of hope:

Israel will no longer shiver with fear,
nor will their face turn white with panic.
When they see their children,
and My blessings, in their midst,
then they bless My name
and they will bless the Holy One of Jacob
and will praise Adonai the protector of Israel. **29:22–23**

Connection   There are two themes that connect the Torah reading with the haftarah.

Both readings dwell upon suffering. The Israelites suffered in slavery in Egypt, and the Israelites suffered during the time of Isaiah.

Also the Israelites in Egypt were angry at Moses because of his seeming lack of progress in his confrontations with Pharaoh. The Israelites were also unhappy with Isaiah's prophecies, which predicted doom and destruction.

Haftarah for Shemot שְׁמוֹת
(Isaiah 27:6–28:13, 29:22–23)

27

6 The time is nearing,
and Jacob will put down roots,
Israel will blossom and flower
and carpet the face of the earth with fruit.
7 Has Adonai struck (Israel) as strongly
as He struck those who harmed them?
Were they killed
just as the killers themselves were slain?
8 In full measure, by exile you will contend with her.
He has removed her with His rough blast in the day of
the east wind.
9 This is the only way Israel will be cleansed.
When He must crush all the stones
of the altars into pieces,
so that the Asherim
and the pagan altars
will never again rise.
10 The fortified cities of Israel will be empty
and filled with abandoned and lonely houses.
It will be like the wilderness,
where the calves will rest and graze
and eat from the branches.
11 The people are like dried-out branches.
The women will gather them
and burn them as fuel.
Israel is a foolish nation
so I will have no pity on them.
He who freed them from slavery
will not show them any pity.
12 The time will come and Adonai will gather the grain
from the Euphrates River to the Brook of Egypt, and all
of the Israelites will also be gathered one by one.
13 On that day, a great trumpet will be blown and

the people of Israel, who are captives in the land of Assyria, and those who are scattered in the land of Egypt, will come and worship Adonai on His holy mountain at Jerusalem.

28

Destruction will come to the drunkards of Ephraim, and to the fading flower of His glorious city of Samaria, which is located in a rich valley of beauty, because its returned leaders are overcome with wine.
2 Adonai is mighty and strong,
like a powerful hailstorm,
a mighty wind,
like a torrent of raging waters over the face of the earth.
3 The arrogant crown of the drunkards of Samaria
will be trampled, underfoot,
4 and the white flower of his glorious splendor,
overlooking the rich valley,
will be like the first ripe fig before summer comes,
which one eats as soon as it is found.
5 On that day, Adonai Almighty
will become Israel's crown of glory,
for the remnants of His people Israel;
6 He will be a spirit of righteousness,
which sits in judgment, and courage to those who repel their enemy at the city gate.
7 The priests and prophets, who are filled with wine and reel from whiskey,
they who reel from strong drink and are confused with wine,
they cannot see straight and make judgments.
8 All the tables are covered with vomit filth.
9 There is no one to teach
and no one to understand Adonai's message.
Does Adonai think that we are like babies who suck milk from their mother's breast?
10 He feeds us in bits
rule by rule,

line by line,
a little here
and a little there.

11 But with a stammer He will speak to His nation in foreign language and say,

12 His people had a resting place where the tired can be refreshed. But you refused to listen.

13 Now Adonai talks to Israel,
tiny rule by rule,
tiny line by line,
a little bit here
and a little bit there.
Yet they do not understand.
They go forward,
then they fall backwards;
they will be wounded and caught and taken captive.

29

22 Adonai, who redeemed Abraham,
says this about the house of Jacob:
Israel will no longer shiver with fear,
nor will their face turn white with panic.

23 When they see their children,
and My blessings, in their midst,
then they will bless My name
and they will bless the Holy One of Jacob
and will praise Adonai the protector of Israel.

HAFTARAH for VA'ERA
Ezekiel 28:25–29:31

Ezekiel   See haftarah Vayigash, page 105.

History   Prophets were highly intelligent individuals who were blessed with intuitive wisdom and were gifted with visionary powers. They were dedicated to preserving the religious life of the Israelites in the Holy Land and in exile. The prophets were also astute political observers and offered advice on political strategies and military alliances.

In 587 B.C.E. Jerusalem was destroyed by the army of King Nebuchadnezzar of Babylon. Ezekiel was most likely a priest in the Temple of Jerusalem. After the destruction, Ezekiel was one of the tens of thousands of leaders and notables who were carried away into exile to Babylon, where he began to prophesize.

After the kingdom fell, Ezekiel preached fiery messages of hope and future restoration. He assured the exiles that deliverance would come if the Israelites obeyed Adonai, kept away from idol worship, and observed the commandments. Ezekiel also directed a series of scathing attacks against neighboring nations, including Egypt, Sidon, and Tyre, allies who rejoiced and took advantage of Israel's defeat.

Text   The prophet was especially angry at its primary ally Egypt, who made a half-hearted attempt to assist the Israelites during the fatal siege. Ezekiel portrays Pharaoh Hofrah, who was a pompous, prideful monarch who believed that he was a god:

> *The Pharaoh boasts:*
> *The Nile is mine.*
> *I created it myself.*   **29:3**

This boastful bravado exposed the land of Egypt to Adonai's anger. Now the prophet compares Egypt to a huge crocodile, who, despite his size, can easily be caught with tiny hooks.

I will place hooks into your jaws
I will cause fish to stick to your scales
And I will remove you from the river. **29:4**

In 572 to 568 B.C.E. Nebuchadnezzar continued his campaign to subjugate the crocodile Egypt.

The haftarah also mentions the kingdom of Tyre, another ally who abandoned Israel. In 594 B.C.E., after a long siege of thirteen years, Tyre, a rich island fortress just a half-mile off the Phoenician coast, was captured by Nebuchadnezzar.

Connection The connection between the sidrah and the haftarah is Egypt: the land of misery and Israelite slavery in the time of Moses. Once again, in the time of Ezekiel, the villainous Egyptians are responsible for Israelite repression, this time with Babylon.

Even today, the modern state of Israel is once again placing its trust in Egypt by allowing them to patrol the borders between Gaza and Egypt to prevent arms smuggling and the movement of terrorists.

Ezekiel 28:25-29:21

28 **25** This is what Adonai says: When I gather the people of Israel from among the nations where they were scattered, then I will reveal My holiness. And every nation will see My holiness, and the Israelites will once again live in their own land, which I gave My servant Jacob. **26** They will live there in safety and build houses and plant vineyards. They will live safely after I punish all those who have humiliated them and Israel will know that I am Adonai.

29 In the tenth year of the tenth month, on the twelfth day of that month, Adonai appeared to me saying: **2** Son of man, condemn Pharaoh king of Egypt. Prophesy against him and all the people of Egypt. **3** Speak and say: This is what Adonai says:

I am your enemy, Pharaoh king of Egypt.

You are like a huge crocodile

lying in the midst of his rivers,

who boasts, "The Nile is mine and I created it."

4 I will place My hooks in your jaws.

I will cause the fish to stick to your scales

and remove you from the river

with all the fish of your rivers sticking to your scales.

5 I will drag you into the wilderness,

you and all the fish of your rivers, into the desert.

You will not be buried.

Your body will be given as food for the beasts of the earth and birds of the sky.

6 Then all the inhabitants of Egypt will realize that I am Adonai, because they acted like a bunch of reeds when Israel needed your help. **7** When they leaned on you, you broke and caused them to stagger. **8** Therefore Adonai says: Behold, I will send an enemy against you and they will destroy your people and your animals. **9** The land of Egypt will become a desolate wasteland and then you will know that I am Adonai—because you boasted, "The Nile is mine and I created it."

10 Know this, I am your enemy and the enemy of your rivers and I will make the land of Egypt into a desolate wasteland, from Migdol to Syene as far as the borders of Ethiopia. **11** For forty years no human or animal will pass through your land.

12 I will make the land of Egypt the most barren among the depressed countries. Every city in Egypt will be in ruin for forty years. I will scatter the Egyptians among the nations and spread them through many countries.

13 Adonai says: At the end of forty years I will bring back the Egyptians from the places I have scattered them. **14** I will bring them back from their captivity and return them to the land of Pothros, the land of their ancestors. They will be a weak kingdom. **15** It will be the weakest of kingdoms and will never again be a power. I will weaken them and they will never again rule other nations.

16 The House of Israel will never again trust Egypt. They will remember their sin when they turned to Egypt for help. They will finally realize that I am Adonai.

17 Adonai spoke to me in the twenty-seventh year, in the first month on the first day of that month.

18 Son of man, King Nebuchadnezzar of Babylon and his army attacked the city of Tyre. Every head became bald and every shoulder was blistered, but he and his army did not succeed in their battle to capture Tyre. **19** Therefore, this is what Adonai says: I will hand over the land of Egypt to King Nebuchadnezzar of Babylon and he will plunder her and carry off her treasure. He will give her wealth to his troops as spoils of conquest.

20 Adonai says: As a reward for his efforts, I have given him the land of Egypt because he followed my plan.

21 On that day, I will give the nation of Israel strength and I will give you (Ezekiel) the power to speak to them. Then they will realize that Adonai has caused these events to happen.

HAFTARAH for BO
Jeremiah 46:13–28

Book of Jeremiah   Jeremiah was born in the village of Anathoth, near Jerusalem. He came from a wealthy and prestigious family of priests. As a young man, Jeremiah received the call to prophecy. He went to the Temple and preached that Judea was too weak and must accept the Babylonian yoke of vassaldom or be destroyed. The leaders were shocked and Jeremiah was arrested and thrown into jail. After he was released, he continued to suggest advice to King Jehoiakim but his messages were disregarded.

After ten years of isolation, Jeremiah once again pleaded with King Zedekiah to reject revolt against Babylonia. Once again the patriot's advice was ignored and he was imprisoned.

In 586 B.C.E. the Babylonians captured Jeremiah but King Nebuchadnezzar allowed him to travel to Egypt, where he died.

History   In 597 B.C.E. King Nebuchadnezzar of Babylonia captured the city of Jerusalem, and Judah became a vassal of Babylon. For ten years King Zedekiah (598–587 B.C.E.) of Judah had been wavering between revolt against Babylon and the peaceful acceptance of vassaldom. Meanwhile, Judah's neighbor Egypt supported all efforts against her archenemy Babylonia. Egypt begged Zedekiah to join the alliance against Babylon. He began preparing Judah for a long war by raising an army and fortifying the invasion routes.

Text   The prophet Jeremiah, now an old man, warned that Judah was too small and weak to challenge the mighty Babylonian Empire. He also denounced the Egyptians as unreliable allies. In 665 B.C.E. the Babylonians defeated the Egyptians in the battle of Charchemish.

Jeremiah warns the Judeans:

> *Pharaoh, king of Egypt, is a braggart,*
> *who boasts and does nothing.* **46:17**

Jeremiah predicted:

> *Egypt will be put to shame;*
> *she will be delivered*
> *and captured by the enemy*
> *from the north.* **46:24**

The haftarah concludes on a hopeful note:

> *But you, Israel, my servant,*
> *do not be afraid, do not be dismayed.*
> *O Israel, be assured,*
> *I will save you and your offspring*
> *from the land of their captivity,*
> *and Jacob will return again in peace.* **46:27**

Connection   The connection is the perfidious land of Egypt. Egypt was the land of slavery in the times of Moses. Egypt again wishes to harm Israel by involving it militarily in a hopeless war.

Haftarah for Bo בֹּא
(Jeremiah 46:13-28)

46 **13** Adonai told Jeremiah the prophet, that Nebuchadnezzar, king of Babylon, was coming to attack the
land of Egypt:
14 Shout in Egypt, and tell it in Migdol;
trumpet it in Noph
and in Tahpanhes.
Say: "Stand and be ready,
for the sword has destroyed
everything around you.
15 Why is your champion flattened?
He did not survive
because Adonai leveled him.
16 Many stumbled;
they fell upon each other.
They said:
"We will rise up and return to our own people,
to our homeland,
far from the deadly sword."
17 They cried there,
"Pharaoh king of Egypt is a braggart
who boasts and does nothing.
18 Surely as I live, says the King,
who is Adonai the Almighty,
Surely one shall come like Tabor
among the mountains,
and like Carmel by the sea.
19 Citizens of Egypt,
prepare to go into exile,
for Noph will become a desolated ruin
without life.
20 Egypt is a beautiful cow,
but the enemy from the north is coming.
21 Her soldiers are strong,

but they also retreated
and fled together.
They did not stand;
their day has overtaken them,
this is the time of their punishment.
22 They shall slink away
like a doomed serpent,
for they invade with an army,
and attack her with axes,
like those who cut down trees.
23 They will cut down her trees,
says Adonai, although the forest is thick,
because they are more numerous
than the grasshoppers.
24 Egypt will be put to shame;
she will be delivered
and captured by the enemy
from the north.
25 Adonai Tzvaot,
the Adonai of Israel, says,
I intend to punish Amon the god of Thebes,
and Pharaoh, and Egypt, and her gods,
and her kings;
Pharaoh, and those who rely on him.
26 Adonai promises that He will place them
into the hand of those who seek to kill them,
into the hand of Nebuchadnezzar,
king of Babylon,
and his warriors.
Afterwards, it will again be inhabited,
as in days gone by,
Adonai says.
27 But you, Israel, My servant,
do not be afraid, do not be dismayed.
O, Israel, be assured,
I will save you
and your offspring

from the land of their captivity,
and Jacob will return again in peace,
and no one will harm him.
28 Adonai says,
Jacob my servant, do not fear
for I am protecting you.
I will destroy all the nations
to which I have driven you.
But you I will punish.
I will discipline you,
but I will not destroy you.

HAFTARAH for BESHALLACH
Judges 4:4–5:31

Book of Judges   The seventh book of the *Tanak* is named after the Judges (*shoftim*) who ruled Israel from the death of Joshua to the time of the Prophet Samuel. After the initial invasion of Canaan by Joshua, the Israelites deteriorated into a loose coalition of tribes with no single unifying political or military authority.

Though these leaders were called "judges," their principal function was to act as military commanders in time of trouble. The Hebrews in most cases were forced to share the land with their Canaanite neighbors. All around them, their enemies were poised to invade them at the slightest indication of weakness.

The text describes the career of each of the thirteen judges. Each biography starts with a military disaster brought on by a religious relapse into idolatry. The Hebrews lived as neighbors with their pagan enemies and this situation became for them a moral and spiritual degradation. Then a judge was chosen, who became the military deliverer. The thirteen *shoftim* are Othniel, Ehud, Shamgar, Deborah, Gideon, Abimelech, Tola, Jair, Yiphthach, Ibzan, Elon, Abdon, and Samson.

History   During the centuries after Joshua there were twelve judges. No longer half-starved desert nomads, the Israelites had now become farmers, shepherds, artisans, and city dwellers.

Their new way of life, however, was beset with dangers from all sides.

Canaanite soldiers often raided Israelite farms and storehouses. Though the Israelites bravely fought off the attackers, their efforts were futile against the armed might of Jabin, the most powerful Canaanite king. Jabin's army, commanded by his general, Sisera, was well trained and equipped with heavy iron chariots and weapons.

Text In the hill country of Ephraim lived a female judge named Deborah. People came from far and near to consult her. Deborah held court near her home at a place between Ramah and Bethel. Here she would sit beneath a palm tree and the people would come and tell her their problems.

Deborah resolved that Jabin must be defeated. When the time was ripe, she summoned Barak, an able warrior from the tribe of Naphtali, and she ordered him to muster every available Israelite soldier and prepare to attack.

Together, Deborah and Barak led the warriors of Israel up the sides of Mount Tabor, a mountain that rises over the great plain of Jezreel near the Kishon River.

> *Deborah, a prophetess, the wife of Lappidoth, was a judge and the leader of Israel at that time. She used to sit under the palm tree of Deborah, which was between Raman and Bethel in the hill country of Ephraim; and the Israelites would come up to her to settle their disputes.* **4:4**

Confident of an easy victory over this small army equipped with inferior weapons, the mighty King Jabin and his general, Sisera, assembled their troops and their iron chariots and waited at the base of Mount Tabor for the Israelites to strike.

Shouting their battle cry, the Israelite warriors charged down the mountain and attacked the Canaanites. In the midst of the battle, the skies opened and rain poured down.

> *Deborah said to Barak, "Get ready! Today, Adonai will help you defeat Sisera. Adonai has prepared his defeat." So Barak led his ten thousand men and charged down from Mount Tabor.* **4:14**

The Kishon, normally a quiet stream, became a raging torrent, rolling and rushing across the plain. The heavy iron wheels of Sisera's chariots were mired in thick, slippery mud. Weighed down by their heavy armor, the Canaanite soldiers were no match for the Israelites.

The Canaanites fled in utter confusion. Sisera sought refuge in the tent of Jael, begging for water to quench his thirst. Jael gave the great warrior a dry cloak and some milk to drink, then stood guard at the door of the tent.

Unaware that Jael and her husband, Cheber, were friendly with the Israelites, Sisera thought himself safe and fell into a deep sleep. And while he slept, Jael slew him. According to the Book of Judges, Jael took a sharp tent peg, quietly crept close to the sleeping Sisera, then hammered it through his temple.

> *Then, while he was in a deep sleep, Jael, Cheber's wife, took a tent peg and a hammer in her hand, and crept to him softly, and drove the peg through his temple until it hit the ground. So he breathed his last and died.* **4:21**

Great was the rejoicing of the Israelites when they learned that Sisera was dead and that the fierce Canaanite warriors had fled in confusion. Deborah, the prophetess who had so fearlessly led her people, sang a song of praise to Adonai.

With the Israelite victory at Mount Tabor, the power of the Canaanites came to an end. The successful conquest of this troublesome enemy gave the Israelites a much firmer hold on their new land.

Connection Both the sidrah and the haftarah contain songs of thanksgiving, one by Moses and the other by Deborah. In celebration of their victory, Moses and the children of Israel sang a song to Adonai.

In the haftarah, Deborah and Barak also sing a song of victory, after their defeat of Jabin, the king of Canaan, and the Canaanites.

Haftarah for Beshallach בְּשַׁלַּח
(Judges 4:4–5:31)

(*Ashkenazim begin here*)

4 **4** Deborah, a prophetess, the wife of Lappidoth, was a judge and the leader of Israel at that time. **5** She used to sit under the palm tree of Deborah, which was between Ramah and Bethel in the hill country of Ephraim; and the Israelites would come up to her to settle their disputes.

6 One day, she sent for Barak the son of Abinoam from Kedesh-naphtali, and said to him, "Adonai has commanded: Assemble ten thousand men of the tribe of Naphtali and the tribe of Zebulun, and march to Mount Tabor.

7 I will trick Sisera, the captain of Jabin's army, with his chariots and warriors, to meet you by the brook of Kishon; and I will make you victorious over him."

8 Barak said to her, "I will go if you will go with me; but if you will not go with me, I will refuse."

9 Deborah said, "Yes, I will definitely go with you; but no one will credit you with the victory; for Adonai will deliver Sisera into the hand of a woman." Then Deborah rose and accompanied Barak to Kedesh.

10 At Kedesh, Barak assembled the tribes of Zebulun and Naphtali to Kedesh, and ten thousand warriors followed him; and Deborah also went up with him.

11 At that time, Cheber the Kenite had moved away from the Kenites and from the descendants of Chobab the father-in-law of Moses, and had pitched his tent by the oak in Zaanannim, which is near Kedesh. **12** They told Sisera that Barak the son of Abinoam had gone up to Mount Tabot. **13** So Sisera assembled nine hundred chariots of iron, and all his warriors, and they marched, from Harosheth-goyim, to the brook of Kishon.

14 Deborah said to Barak, "Get ready! Today, Adonai will help you defeat Sisera. Adonai has prepared his defeat."

So Barak led his ten thousand men and charged down from Mount Tabor. **15** Adonai panicked Sisera and his chariots, and all his warriors as Barak attacked; Sisera jumped from his chariot and escaped on foot.

16 But Barak pursued the chariots and the army as far as Harosheth-goyim. All the army of Sisera was wiped out. Not a warrior was left. **17** But Sisera escaped on foot to the tent of Jael, the wife of Cheber the Kenite, because there was a treaty of peace between Jabin the king of Hazor and the house of Cheber the Kenite.

18 Jael came out to meet Sisera and said to him, "Lord, come in; do not be afraid." So he went into the tent, and she covered him with a rug.

19 He said to her, "I am very thirsty, please give me a drink of water." So she opened a jar of milk and gave him a drink, then covered him again.

20 He said to her, "Stand at the door of the tent. If anyone comes and asks you, 'Is anyone hiding here?' say 'No.'"

21 Then, while he was in a deep sleep, Jael, Cheber's wife, took a tent peg and a hammer in her hand, and crept to him softly, and drove the peg through his temple until it hit the ground. So he breathed his last and died.

22 As Barak chased after Sisera, Jael came out to meet him and said to him, "Come, and I will show you the man you are looking for." He entered the tent, and there lay Sisera with the tent peg in his temple, dead.

23 On that day, the Israelites, with Adonai's help, defeated Jabin, the king of Canaan.

24 The Israelites' power against Jabin the king of Canaan grew stronger and stronger until they completely destroyed Jabin, king of Canaan.

(Sephardim and some Ashkenazim begin here)

5 On that day, Deborah and Barak the son of Abinoam sang:
2 Blessed is Adonai,
When the leaders of Israel are in command,

when the people willingly follow them.
3 Kings, listen, give ear;
Mighty rulers, pay attention.
For I will sing to Adonai.
I will sing praises to Adonai,
the Savior of Israel.
4 Adonai, when you left Seir,
when you marched out from the land of Edom,
the earth shook,
and the heavens opened;
the skies poured rain.
5 The mountains shook
at the presence of Adonai;
even you, Mount Sinai,
shook at the presence of Adonai,
the Savior of Israel.
6 During the rule of Shamgar
son of Anath,
and in the days of Jael,
the highways were empty,
and travelers sneaked through hidden paths.
7 The rulers were powerless in Israel;
no one listened
until you, Deborah,
a mother in Israel,
came to power.
8 Israel worshipped new gods;
and war came to the city gates.
There were no shields or spears
among the forty thousand warriors in Israel.
9 My heart is with the leaders of Israel,
who volunteered
to lead the people.
Bless Adonai,
10 Tell about it,
you who ride on white donkeys,
you who sit on rich carpets,

you who walk on the road,
you can now travel in safety.
11 Listen to the voice of musicians
at the wells;
they shall describe
the righteous deeds of Adonai,
and the righteous deeds
of rulers in Israel;
then Adonai's people
went down in safety
to the city, to the gates.
12 Deborah, awake, awake!
Awake, awake, sing a song!
Arise, Barak, son of Abinoam,
and lead your captives.
13 Then He set a remnant
to rule over the nobles
and the people.
Adonai gave me dominion
over the mighty.
14 Some came from Ephraim,
a land that once belonged to Amalek;
Benjamin was with your kinsmen.
Out of Machir
came leaders,
and out of Zebulun
came military officers.
15 The leaders of Issachar
were with Deborah
and Barak.
They followed Barak into the valley,
but the troops of Reuben
did not join the struggle.
16 Why did you remain among the sheep,
just to listen to the bleating of the animals?
Among the soldiers of Reuben,
there was no resolve to fight.

17 Gilead remained on the east bank of the Jordan,
and Dan stayed on the ships.
Asher remained at the seashore,
safe in its harbors.
18 Zebulun is a tribe
who fought bravely;
also Naphtali
joined the battle of Canaan.
19 The kings came
and battled at Taanach
by the waters of Megiddo;
but they gained no spoils.
20 In heaven, the stars fought.
Their orbit influenced the battle against Sisera.
21 The Kishon River swept them away;
that ancient river,
the river of Kishon.
O, My soul,
continue to march with courage.
22 Then came the cavalry,
rapidly charging,
the galloping of the mighty warhorses.
23 The angel of Adonai said,
"Cursed be the people of Meroz!
Cursed are its inhabitants
because they did not come to help Adonai,
to help Adonai against the enemy.
24 Jael, the wife of Cheber the Kenite,
shall be the most blessed
of the women who live in the tents.
25 He asked for water,
and Jael gave him milk.
She brought him yogurt
in a bowl fit for kings.
26 With her hand,
she grasped the tent pegs,
and with her right hand,

she swung a heavy hammer;
she pounded Sisera.
The peg pierced his temples
and crushed his head.
27 He sank at her feet;
he fell,
he lay;
he sank,
he died.
28 The mother of Sisera looked out
and peered through her window.
"Why is his chariot not coming?
Why don't I hear the wheels of his chariots?"
29 Her wisest ladies answer her;
in fact, she answers herself:
30 "They must be finding
and dividing the captured spoils;
a pretty girl or two for every man;
for Sisera, colorful garments,
spoils of dyed embroidered garments,
two embroidered garments
for the neck of every soldier."
31 Adonai,
may all Your enemies perish like Sisera.
But they who love You
shall be as strong
as the sun rising.
And Israel lived at peace for forty years.

HAFTARAH for YITRO
Isaiah 6:1–7:6, 9:5–6

Book of Isaiah   See haftarah Bereshit, page 51.

History   Divinely inspired dreams are a feature of the *Tanak* from the period of the patriarchs onward. Dreams and visions were closely associated with prophecy as revelations of Adonai. All the three major prophets (Isaiah, Jeremiah, and Ezekiel) tell how Adonai first came to them in a dream or vision.

Text   In the year 740 B.C.E., when King Uzziah died, five-year-old Isaiah had a vision of Adonai sitting upon his throne in his Temple. He was surrounded by angels (*seraphim*), and the thunder of their voices shook the foundations of the Temple. In panic, Isaiah cried out, "Woe is me! I am lost!"

One of the angels touched Isaiah's lips with a burning coal from his altar. Then Isaiah heard the voice of Adonai saying, "Whom shall I send?" Then Isaiah said:

> *"I am here! Send me!*
> *I will be Your messenger."* **6:8**

This was Isaiah's call to prophecy.

Connection   The sidrah describes the revelation at Mount Sinai which turned Israel into a Holy Nation. It was at this juncture that Adonai revealed the Torah to the Israelites and they accepted the obligations of the commandments.

The haftarah records the revelation that came to Isaiah, who accepted his mission of prophecy. The seraphim were singing:

> *"Holy, holy, holy is Adonai, Almighty;*
> *The whole cosmos is filled with His glory."* **6:3**

Haftarah for Yitro יִתְרוֹ
(Isaiah 6:1–7:6, 9:5–6)

6 In the year when King Uzziah died, I saw Adonai sitting upon a high and regal throne, and His heavenly robe filled the Temple. **2** The angels stood up above Him. Each angel had six wings; two covered his face, two covered his feet, and with two they flew. **3** And one sang to another,
"Holy, holy, holy is Adonai the Almighty;
the whole cosmos is filled with His glory.
4 The foundations of the Temple shook, and the entire Temple was filled with smoke.
5 Then I cried,
"I am dead!
For I am lost;
because I am a sinner, and I am living in a nation of sinners;
yet my eyes have seen
the Ruler, Adonai Almighty."
6 Then one of the angels, with a glowing coal in his hand which he had taken with tongs from the altar, flew over to me. **7** He touched my lips with the burning coal, and said,
"This burning coal has touched your lips;
your sins are forgiven and cleansed."
8 I heard Adonai's voice saying,
Whom shall I send,
and who will be our messenger?
Then I answered,
"I am here! Send me!
I will be Your messenger."
9 And He said:
Go, and carry this message to this people:
You hear,
but do not understand;
you see,
but do not comprehend.

10 Make the minds of the people stubborn,
deafen their ears,
and blind their eyes;
then they will not see with their eyes,
not hear with their ears,
and not understand with their heart,
and then they will not repent and be healed.
11 Then I asked,
"Adonai, how long must I do this?"
And He answered,
Until the cities are destroyed
and deserted without people,
and houses without people,
and the fields are completely desolated.
12 Until Adonai has exiled the people
to faraway lands,
and the land is in total ruins.
13 If even one tenth of them remain in it,
then even they will be destroyed;
but like a pine or an oak tree,
whose stump remains when it is felled,
the holy ones will be like the tree stump.

(*Sephardim conclude here*)

7 When Ahaz the son of Yotham, the son of Uzziah, was king of Judah, Retzin the king of Aram, and Pekach the son of Remaliah, king of Israel, attacked Jerusalem, but could not conquer it. **2** When the kingdom of David was told, "Aram is allied with Ephraim (Israel)," his heart and the heart of his people trembled like trees of the forest shaken in strong wind.
3 Then Adonai said to Isaiah: I want you and your son Shear-yashuv to go to confront Ahaz near the aqueduct of the upper pool, on the road of the washerman's field. **4** Assure him and say to him, "Stay calm and collected; do not be afraid, and do not panic over them; they are just

two burned-out coals, the anger of Retzin and Aram, and the son of Remaliah. **5** Because Aram with Ephraim (Israel) and the son of Remaliah have plotted to destroy you, saying,

6 "Let us attack Judah, besiege it, and crown the son of Tabeel as its puppet king."

9 **5** A child has been born; we have been blessed with a son who will rule over us; and his name is called "Pele-yoez El-Gibbor Avi-Av-Sar-Shalom" (wonderful counsel is God the mighty, eternal Father, peaceful Ruler). **6** For the increase of the realm and for peace without end, He will rule forever from the throne of David, and upon his kingdom, to strengthen it and to govern it with justice and with righteousness. The devotion to Adonai Almighty will do this.

HAFTARAH for MISHPATIM
Jeremiah 34:8–22, 33:25–26

Book of Jeremiah   See haftarah Bo, page 122.

History   Zedekiah was installed by Nebuchadnezzar as a puppet ruler. He was Judah's last king and ruled from 598 to 597 B.C.E. For ten years Judah had been wavering between revolt against Babylonia and peaceful acceptance of vassaldom. Zedekiah and his allies were about to decide in favor of revolt. Again the courageous Jeremiah raised his voice against this plan.

He carried a wooden yoke on his shoulder and preached Adonai's message of submission as the price of survival.

The people listened to the aged prophet when he appeared among them. He warned that Judah was far too small and weak to challenge the mighty Babylonian empire. He begged them to preserve what freedom remained and comforted them by predicting that someday the captives would return from Babylon and Judah would be rebuilt.

Meanwhile, Egypt continued to support all efforts at revolt against Babylonia and sought allies for a last stand against the new empire.

When Judah's neighbors approached Zedekiah to form an alliance against Babylonia, he veered back to the side of the war party and began preparing his country for a long siege. Fortifications were strengthened, food and arms were stored, and all able-bodied men were trained for defense.

Text   In despair over these preparations for another war, the prophet Jeremiah renewed his warnings. He was denounced and again cast into prison.

An alliance was formed between Judah, Edom, Moab, Ammon, and the Phoenician cities of Tyre and Sidon. Pharaoh Apries of Egypt assured the allies of his support.

In the ninth year of his reign, after a long perod of indecision, Zedekiah, the last king of Judah, revolted against Nebuchadnezzar of Babylon. The year was 586 B.C.E.

Nebuchadnezzar dealt swiftly with the rebellion. His army of charioteers, infantry, and cavalry far outnumbered the combined forces of the allies.

Zedekiah realized that he needed manpower to defend the country against the Babylonians, so he ordered the release of the Hebrew slaves and thereby enlarged his army.

At first the Israelite owners released their slaves, but as Nebuchadnezzar left in 586 B.C.E., they broke their promise and forced their bondsmen back into slavery.

Now Jeremiah expresses Adonai's anger:

But you have broken the agreement and shamed My name, when each of you forced your male and female slaves, whom you had set free, back into slavery again. **34:16**

The final siege of Jerusalem began in 588 B.C.E.

Jeremiah prophesied that because the slaves were forced to return to bondage, Adonai would punish Judah and the Babylonians would return.

The haftarah ends with a message of hope, predicting the return from Babylonian captivity.

I will never desert the descendants of Jacob, and of My servant David, and not choose one of David's descendants as ruler of the descendants of Abraham, Isaac, and Jacob.
I will return them to their land and have mercy on them. **33:26**

Connection The sidrah starts with the ordinance that secures the rights of the bondsmen. From the time he was sold, a Hebrew slave was to be freed after six years of service.

The haftarah also deals with the freeing of the slaves by Zedekiah:

That every one should free his male and female Hebrew slaves; so that no one should enslave a fellow Jew. **34:9**

34

8 This is the message that came to Jeremiah from Adonai, after King Zedekiah made a covenant with all the people in Jerusalem, to liberate all the Hebrew slaves. **9** That every one should free his male and female Hebrew slaves; so that no one should enslave a fellow Jew. **10** And everyone obeyed, all the officials and all the people who had entered into the covenant obeyed, that everyone would set free his male and female Hebrew slave; they obeyed and released them. **11** But later, they changed their minds and forced their former servants and the handmaids whom they had set free to return. **12** Adonai spoke to Jeremiah.

13 This is what Adonai the Savior of Israel says: I made a covenant with your ancestors when I rescued them out of the Egyptian land of slavery. **14** I told them that at the end of seven years, each of you must release his fellow Hebrew who has been sold to you and has served you six years. You must let him go free. However, your ancestors did not obey Me. **15** And now you repented and did what was right in My eyes, by freeing all your Hebrew slaves; you even made a covenant before Me in My Temple. **16** But you have broken the agreement and shamed My name, when each of you forced your male and female slaves, whom you had set free, back into slavery again.

17 Therefore, this is what Adonai has decided: Because you have not obeyed Me by freeing your fellow slaves, I now proclaim freedom for you, freedom to die by the sword, to be destroyed by the plague, and by the famine; you will be a disgrace to all the nations of the earth. **18** Because you have broken the terms of the covenant which were made with Me, I will treat you like the calf that is cut in two and passed between its parts; **19** the rulers of Judah and the rulers of Jerusalem, the officers, the priests, and all the people of the land, who walked between the parts of the calf. **20** I will hand them over to their enemies, to those who wish to kill them. Their dead bodies will be for food to the birds and wild animals, and to the beasts of the earth. **21** And I will hand over Zedekiah king of Judah and his officers to their enemies, to those who wish to kill them, to the army of the king of Babylon, which has withdrawn from Jerusalem; **22** and they will attack, and capture it, and burn it down; the cities of Judah will become a wasteland, without inhabitants.

33

25 This is what Adonai says: I would no more reject My people than I would change the sequence of day and night. **26** I will never desert the descendants of Jacob, and of My servant David, and not choose one of David's descendants as ruler of the descendants of Abraham, Isaac, and Jacob. I will return them to their land and have mercy on them.

HAFTARAH for TERUMAH
1 Kings 5:26–6:13

Books of Kings I and II   See haftarah Vayera, page 68.

History   David and his son Solomon grew up in totally different circumstances. David arose from humble beginnings and, after numerous dangerous adventures, established an empire. His son Solomon, born to a king, consolidated David's empire and gave it 40 years (965–926 B.C.E.) of peace and prosperity.

Solomon carefully calculated Israel's assets and its possibilities. He completed the fortifications that his father David had begun and signed a series of political and military alliances with the surrounding nations.

Solomon acquired a reputation for great wisdom. Three biblical books, Proverbs, Ecclesiastes (Kohelet), and Song of Songs (Shir HaShirim), are attributed to him.

Text   Now Solomon turned to the project that would demand his greatest effort, the one most dear to his heart and the hearts of his people—the building of the Holy Temple (*Bet Hamikdash*) on Mount Zion.

> *He began to build the temple 480 years after the Israelites left the land of Egypt, in the fourth year of Solomon's rule over Israel, in the month of Iyar, which is the second month.* **6:1**

Until then, Israel had worshipped Adonai in the simple sanctuary in Shiloh, that housed the Holy Ark. Solomon wanted a magnificent Temple that would be the grandest structure in all Jerusalem and in all the land of Israel.

From his close friend and ally King Hiram of Tyre, Solomon obtained cedar wood of Lebanon for the Temple. He paid for this precious wood with the produce of Israel—grain and oil, olives and figs—and with copper from the mines of Ezion-Geber.

The Temple was built of stone and precious wood, with great pillars and spacious inner courts, with special places appointed for the rites of the services. The interior was paneled with cedar wood. Gold, newly brought to the land of Israel from other countries in exchange for copper and olive oil, was lavishly used to make Solomon's Temple a dazzling sight to behold.

Moreover, not one iron tool was used in the construction of the Temple, because of iron's association with violence and war.

The Temple was built of stone finished at the quarry, and no hammer or axe or any tool of iron was heard at the Temple, while it was being built. **6:7**

When the Temple was completed, Jerusalem was thronged with jubilant people. Many had come to marvel, and many others came to rejoice and rededicate themselves to their faith.

The Israelites presented their problems and disputes to the judges in the king's court, and they left their sacrifices and offerings in the newly built Temple.

They also brought wares to trade in the busy markets.

Connection   The sidrah and the haftarah are both about building projects.

Moses was instrumental in building a Tabernacle in the desert. King Solomon used all of Israel's material and human resources to build a magnificent and opulent Temple in Jerusalem that was the crown jewel of the Middle Eastern world.

5 **26** And God gave Solomon wisdom, as he promised him; and there was peace between Hiram and Solomon; and they made a treaty together. **27** Then King Solomon drafted 30,000 laborers from out of all Israel. **28** And he sent them to Lebanon in groups of 10,000 a month. They worked one month in Lebanon and two months at home; Adoniram was in charge of the workers. **29** Solomon also had 70,000 carriers, and 80,000 stone-cutters in the mountains; **30** besides Solomon's chief officers who supervised the work, there were 3,300 foremen who supervised the workers. **31** At the king's orders, they quarried great, solid stones, to provide the foundation of the Temple. **32** So Solomon's builders and Hiram's builders and the Gebalites did the cutting and prepared the timber and the stone to build the Temple.

6 He began to build the Temple 480 years after the Israelites left the land of Egypt, in the fourth year of Solomon's rule over Israel, in the month of Iyar, which is the second month. **2** The Temple which King Solomon built for Adonai was 90 feet long, 30 feet wide, and 45 feet high. **3** The walkway in front of the Temple of the house was 30 feet wide, the same as the width of the Temple; and it was 15 feet deep in front of the house. **4** And he made the windows of the Temple wide on the inside, and narrow at the outside. **5** Against the walls and around the Temple of the sanctuary, he built a building with many rooms all around. **6** The lowest floor of the building was $17\frac{1}{2}$ feet wide; the middle floor was 9 feet wide, and the third was $10\frac{1}{2}$ feet wide; on the outside he made ledges in the wall of the Temple, so that the beams could be inserted into the walls of the Temple.

7 The Temple was built of stone finished at the quarry, and no hammer or axe or any tool of iron was heard at the Temple, while it was being built.

8 The entrance to the lowest floor of chambers was on the south side of the Temple. There were winding stairs going up to the second floor, and another set of stairs from the second to the third floor. **9** Solomon built the Temple, and finished it; and then he lined the inside of the Temple with cedar boards. **10** He built the floors of the side structure against the whole house, each $7\frac{1}{2}$ feet high; and they were fastened to the Temple with beams of cedar.

11 Adonai spoke to Solomon, saying, **12** About this Temple which you are building, if you follow My statutes, carry out My judgments, and obey all My commandments, then I will keep My promise with you, which I made to your father David. **13** And I will dwell among the Israelites and will not abandon My people Israel.

HAFTARAH for TETZAVEH
Ezekiel 43: 10–27

Book of Ezekiel   See haftarah Vayigash, page 105.

History   The first vision of Ezekiel relates to the period before the destruction of Jerusalem by the Babylonians. His second vision takes place after the destruction of the kingdom of Judah. Here he preaches a message of hope for a future return.

In his third vision Ezekiel directs his message against the neighboring countries who had taken advantage and gloated at the defeat of Judah.

Text   This haftarah is part of Ezekiel's fourth vision. Here he describes the plan for the rebuilt Temple when the exile is over.

> *If they are truly ashamed of all that they have done, then explain to them the design for the Temple, the specifications, its exits, its entrances, and all its plans, and all its laws, and write them down in their sight; so that they will observe all its ordinances and obey them.*
> **43:11**

He predicts Adonai's return and describes the instructions for the altar for the burnt offerings.

Ezekiel also details some of the rituals for the restored altar and designates the descendants of Zadok for the high priesthood. The office of the high priesthood remained in the Zadokite family until the times of the Maccabees.

> *The priests of Levi from the family of Zadok will be the only ones to serve Me, says Adonai.* **43:19**

Connection   The Torah portion provides a description for the various offerings. The haftarah describes the restored Temple and the ritual for the burnt offering.

Haftarah for Tetzaveh תְּצַוֶּה
(Ezekiel 43:10-27)

43 **10** Son of man, describe the Temple to Israel, so that they may be ashamed of their sins; let them think about it. **11** If they are truly ashamed of all that they have done, then explain to them the design for the Temple, the specifications, its exits, its entrances, and all its plans, and all its laws, and write them down in their sight; so that they will observe all its ordinances and obey them. **12** This is the law for the Temple; the entire area on top of the mountain shall be most holy. This is the law of the Temple.

13 These are the dimensions for the altar. The base of the altar shall be 20 inches high and 20 inches broad, and a 10-inch ledge on the outer rim, and this shall be the base of the altar. **14** From the base on the ground to the lower edge, 20 inches, and the width of 10 inches. **15** And from the smaller ledge to the greater ledge, 40 inches; and from the top of the altar there will be a horn at each of the corners. **16** The top of the altar shall measure 21 feet by 21 feet, square on its four sides. **17** And the upper ledge shall be 24 feet long and 24 feet wide on its sides; with a 20-inch rim about it; with a base 10 inches all around it. The steps leading up shall be on the east side.

18 And He said to me: Ezekiel, Son of man, this is what Adonai says: These are the regulations for offering burnt offerings and for dashing blood against it when the altar is completed. **19** The priests of Levi from the family of Zadok will be the only ones to serve Me, says Adonai. Give them a young bull as a sin offering. **20** You shall take some of its blood and smear it on the four horns of the altar, and on the four corners of the ledge, and all around the rim; in this way, you will cleanse it and make it fit for sacrifice.

21 Then you shall take the bull of the sin offering and burn it in the appointed place, outside the Temple area.

22 Then on the second day you shall sacrifice a healthy he-goat as a sin offering; then you shall cleanse the altar, just as you cleansed it with the bull. **23** When you have finished purifying it, you shall sacrifice another healthy young bull, and a healthy ram. **24** You shall present them to Adonai at the Temple, and the priests shall sprinkle salt on them and offer them up as a burnt offering to Adonai.

25 Each day, for seven days, you shall present a healthy goat as a sin offering; a young, healthy bull, and a healthy ram. **26** For seven days you shall make atonement upon the altar and cleanse it; this is how you shall make it acceptable to Me. **27** And Adonai said: On the eighth day, and from the eighth day on, the priests are allowed to offer burnt offerings upon the altar; and I will be pleased to accept them.

INTRODUCTION TO
HAFTARAH for KI TISSA
1 Kings 18:1–39

Books of Kings I and II   See haftarah Vayera, page 68.

History   After King Solomon's son Rehoboam succeeded his father on the throne, the flourishing kingdom of David and Solomon was divided into two smaller states, the northern kingdom of Israel, under Jeroboam, and the southern kingdom of Judah under Rehoboam.

Throughout the reign of Rehoboam and Jeroboam, there was war between Israel and Judah.

The people of the northern kingdom of Israel still looked to Jerusalem as their sacred city. On festival days, they journeyed there to join the people of Judah in prayers, sacrifices and holiday processions. Jeroboam had altars and shrines erected in the northern cities of Bethel and Dan to entice his people to offer prayers and sacrifices in their own land rather than in Jerusalem.

Because the northern kingdom of Israel never developed a stable succession, it was ruled by nine separate dynasties. It had five kings within a few years of the death of Jeroboam.

Omri, an able general, established order in Israel. He defeated the Moabites and made them Israel's vassals. Omri was not sensitive to the people's spiritual needs and ideals, and as the *Tanak* says, he "did evil in the eyes of God."

When Omri died, Ahab (871–852 B.C.E.) became king. Intent on cementing a pact with Phoenicia, Ahab married a Phoenician princess, Jezebel. She brought her idols and priests to her new home in Samaria. Jezebel, with the priests of Baal, set about teaching the Phoenician way of life to the people of Israel, persecuting anyone who defied her. Many of the prophets were killed at her command.

Text   Not many people had the courage to criticize Ahab and Jezebel openly. There was one, however, who would not be silenced. This was the prophet Elijah. Boldly and passionately Elijah spoke out for the poor, who according to the laws of Israel were to be afforded protection from oppression and unjust taxes.

> *When Ahab saw Elijah, Ahab said to him, "Is it really you, Israel's troublemaker?"*
> *Elijah answered, 'I have not harmed Israel; you and your family are the troublemakers because you have abandoned Adonai's commandments and worshipped the idols of Baal.* **18:17–18**

Elijah also spoke out fearlessly against the priests of Baal. He fought their influence, upholding and defending the ancient traditions and faith of the people of Israel.

Elijah's most famous feat took place on the slopes of Mount Carmel. In order to prove that Baal was a false god, he challenged the Phoenician priests to a contest. While the assembled people watched, Elijah and the priests prepared to offer sacrifices on wood saturated with water. Then the priests urged Baal to set the wood afire, but nothing happened. When Elijah asked Adonai to do the same, the thoroughly soaked wood burst into flames.

At the end of the contest, the Israelites unanimously declared:

> *"Adonai is Elohim*
> *Adonai is Elohim."* **18:39**

Wherever he journeyed, Elijah comforted the poor, healed the sick, and encouraged people to serve Adonai. In many places, he destroyed the shrines of Baal.

Connection   Both the sidrah and the haftarah are concerned with the worship of idols.

In the sidrah, the Israelites in the absence of Moses, who was atop Mount Sinai receiving the Ten Commandments, built and worshipped a golden calf.

In the haftarah, the Israelites, influenced by King Ahab's Phoenician wife, Jezebel, promote the worship of the idol Baal.

Haftarah for Ki Tissa כִּי תִשָּׂא
(1 Kings 18:1-39)

18 After three years of drought, Adonai said to Elijah, Go, and present yourself to Ahab, and tell him that I will send rain upon the land.

2 So Elijah went to meet Ahab. The famine was merciless in Samaria.

3 Ahab called Obadiah, who was in charge of the palace—Obadiah faithfully worshipped Adonai.

4 When queen Jezebel was killing the prophets of Adonai, Obadiah saved a hundred prophets and hid them by fifties in a cave, and fed them with bread and water.

5 And Ahab said to Obadiah, "Check all the springs of water, and all the brooks in the land; perhaps we may find grass to keep the horses and mules alive, and not lose all our animals.

6 So they divided the search area between them; Ahab went alone one way, and Obadiah himself one way.

7 Elijah met Obadiah as Obadiah was searching his area, and he recognized him, and bowed down and said, "My master Elijah, is it really you?"

8 He answered him, "Yes! It is I; go, tell your master that Elijah is here."

9 Then Obadiah said, "How have I sinned, that you would send your servant to Ahab, so he can kill me?

10 "As I swear to Adonai, my master has hunted you in every nation and kingdom; and when they said, 'He is not here,' he made that kingdom and nation swear that they had not found you.

11 "But now you say, 'Go, tell your master, "Elijah is here."' **12** I know that as soon as I leave you, the spirit of Adonai will carry you to a secret place unknown to me, so that if I tell Ahab, and he cannot find you, he will kill me; yet I, your servant, have worshipped Adonai from my youth. **13** Haven't you heard what I did when Jezebel killed the prophets of Adonai, how I hid a hundred men of God's prophets in a cave by fifties, and fed them with bread and water? **14** And now you say, 'Go, tell your master, "Behold, Elijah is here,"' and he will kill me."

15 And Elijah said, "As the Adonai Almighty lives, whom I serve, I will appear before him today."

16 So Obadiah went to meet Ahab and told him where to find Elijah.

17 When Ahab saw Elijah, Ahab said to him, "Is it really you, Israel's troublemaker?"

18 Elijah answered, "I have not harmed Israel; you and your family are the troublemakers, because you have abandoned Adonai's commandments and worshipped the idols of Baal. **19** Now call together and assemble everyone in Israel to meet me at Mount Carmel. Make sure to bring the four hundred and fifty prophets of the idol Baal, and the four hundred prophets of the idol Asherah, who are supported by Jezebel."

(Sephardim begin here)

20 So Ahab assembled all the Israelites, and gathered the prophets together at Mount Carmel.

21 Elijah addressed the people and said, "How long will you sit on the fence? If you choose Adonai, worship Him; but if you choose Baal, then follow him." The people remained silent. **22** Then Elijah said to the people, "I alone am God's prophet; but Baal has four hundred and fifty prophets. **23** Bring us two bulls; and let them choose one bull, and cut it into pieces and place it on the wood of your altar without lighting it. I will prepare the other bull, and place it on the wood of my altar, and I will not light it. **24** Now you call on your god, and I will call on Adonai. The one who answers by fire, he is the true Elohim." All the people answered, "It will be as you say."

25 Then Elijah said to the prophets of Baal, "Choose one bull for yourselves; prepare it first, and then call on the name of your god, but set no fire to the wood." **26** They chose a bull, and they prepared it, and prayed to Baal from morning until noon, saying, "O Baal, answer us." But there was no response, and no one answered. And they danced around the altar which was made. **27** At noon Elijah teased them, saying, "Cry louder, for he is a god; either he is thinking or sleeping, or on a trip, or perhaps he is sleeping and must be awakened."

28 So they shouted louder, and cut themselves with knives and swords until the blood poured out. **29** They raved all afternoon until the time for the evening offering, but there was neither sound nor answer, and no reply.

30 Then Elijah said to the people, "Gather around me"; and all the people came close to him. And he repaired the altar of Adonai that had been thrown down.

31 Elijah took twelve stones, one for each of the tribes of Jacob's sons, to whom Adonai had said, Israel shall be your new name. **32** With the stones he built an altar in honor of Adonai, and he dug a trench in honor of Adonai around the altar, large enough to hold three gallons of seed. **33** He arranged the wood, cut the bull in pieces, and placed the pieces on the wood. **34** Then he said, "Fill four jars with water, and pour it over the burnt offering, and on the wood." And he said, "Now pour water a second time"; and they poured a second time. And he said, "Pour it a third time"; and they poured it a third time. **35** Now the water flowed around the altar, and also filled the ditch with water.

36 At the time of the evening offering, Elijah the prophet came near, and said, "Adonai of Abraham, of Isaac, and of Israel, let it be known this day that You are the Elohim of Israel, and that I am Your servant, and that I have done all these things at Your word. **37** Adonai, hear me. Adonai, answer me; let the people know that You are Adonai, for You did turn their heart backward."

38 Then a fire from Adonai flashed, and consumed the burnt offering, the wood, the stones, and the dust, and dried up the water that was in the trench.

39 When all the people saw it, they bowed down, and they said, "Adonai is Elohim! Adonai is Elohim!"

HAFTARAH for VAYAKHEL
1 Kings 7:40–50, 13–26

Books of Kings I and II   See haftarah Vayera, page 68.

History   The Temple was a seven-year project and King Solomon spared no expense to make it the most beautiful building in the whole area.

By today's standards it was a small building, 165 feet long, 80 feet wide, and 50 feet high. The inside was divided into three sections: The *Ulam*, the vestibule; *Hechol*, the main hall; and the *Devir*, the Holy of Holies, where the Ark was kept.

The Temple was the home for the Ark and for the *Shechinah*, the Divine Presence which inhabited the *Davir*, the Holy of Holies.

Text   King Solomon hired the master craftsman Hiram of Tyre to cast the bronze decorations.

> *Hiram also made the pots, the shovels, and the basins. Hiram finished everything that King Solomon asked him to make for Adonai's Temple.* **7:40**

For the courtyard he cast two huge bronze decorative pillars, one for each side of the entrance, 40 feet tall and 6 feet in diameter.

For the courtyard he cast a huge bronze bowl called "molten sea." It is estimated that the bowl weighed 60,000 pounds and could hold 10,000 gallons of water.

The beauty of the Temple spread Solomon's fame and added luster to his name.

Connection   The Torah portion and the haftarah describe the craftsmanship and skills of the builder of the desert Tabernacle and the Temple in Jerusalem, respectively.

Haftarah for Vayakhel וַיַּקְהֵל
(1 Kings 7:40–50)

For Ashkenazim

7 **40** Hiram also made the pots, the shovels and the basins. Hiram finished everything that King Solomon asked him to make for Adonai's Temple:

41 two columns, two round decorations on the top of the columns, and two sets of chains to cover the round decorations on the top of the columns, **42** 400 pomegranates hanging from chains, two rows of pomegranates for each set of chains, to cover the two round decorations on the top of the columns; **43** the ten bases, and the ten lavers on the bases; **44** and the one sea, and the twelve oxen under the sea; **45** the pots, the shovels, and the basins, and all these vessels which Hiram made for King Solomon, in the house of God, were made of polished brass. **46** In the plain of Jordan, King Solomon cast them, in the clay ground between Succoth and Zerethan. **47** Solomon did not weigh the utensils, because there were so many of them.

48 Solomon made all the furnishings for Adonai's Temple: the golden altar, the golden table for the showbread; **49** the candlesticks of pure gold, five on the right side, and five on the left, in front of the Sanctuary; the flowers, the lamps, and the tongs, of gold; **50** the cups, the snuffers, basins, spoons, firepans, of pure gold; and two sets of gold hinges, one of them for the doors of the inner house, the most holy place, and one set of hinges for the doors of Adonai's Temple.

For Sephardim

7 **13** King Solomon sent to Tyre for Hiram. **14** He was the son of a widow belonging to the family of Naphtali. His father had been a metal craftsman from Tyre. Hiram was skillful and artistic in the design of bronze objects. King Solomon hired him to work on the Temple. **15** He cast two bronze columns for the entrance hall of the Temple. Each was 27 feet high, eighteen feet round. **16** He cast two capitals for the tops of the columns. Each capital was $7\frac{1}{2}$ feet high. **17** Hiram cast two decorated chairs for the capitals on top of the columns with a woven chain for each of them. **18** He cast the pomegranates: two rows of pomegranates in bronze for each of the chains. **19** The capitals on the columns in the hall had shapes like lilies and were 7 feet high. **20** There were 200 pomegranates for each of the capitals. **21** He erected the columns in the entrance hall of the Temple: the column on the south side was called Joachim and the column on the north side was called Boaz. **22** The capitals on top of the pillars were shaped like lilies. Hiram finished the work on the pillars. **23** Now Hiram cast a large tank called the sea. The sea was 15 feet in diameter, $7\frac{1}{2}$ feet tall, and 45 feet round. **24** The sea was circled below the rim by two rows of gourds, cast in one piece, which was 3 inches thick, curling like lily petals. **25** The sea rested on the backs of twelve bulls, 3 facing north, three facing west, three facing south, and three facing east. All the bulls were facing outwards. **26** The walls of the bronze sea were three inches thick and the rim projected out like a lily blossom. The seas held 11,000 gallons of water.

INTRODUCTION TO
HAFTARAH for PEKUDAY
1 Kings 7:51–8:21

Books of Kings I and II   See haftarah Vayera, page 68.

History   The blocks of stone for the Temple were quarried from the nearby hills of Jerusalem. The cedar wood was supplied by Hiram of Tyre. The logs from Lebanon were floated on rafts to the port of Jaffa and from there hauled up the mountain to Jerusalem. The king also provided masons and carpenters, and Hiram, the metal expert, cast the Temple utensils.

It is estimated that 80,000 men, forced (corvee) labor in shifts of 10,000 a month, were involved in the stone quarries and in cutting trees and transporting them to the building area.

The actual building of the Temple was started in the fourth year of Solomon's reign and was completed in the eleventh year.

Text   A large group of notables from all over the country attended the Temple Consecration Service. The priests carried the Ark of the Covenant into the newly built sanctuary and deposited it in the Holy of Holies. Then a dark cloud, the visible sign of Adonai's presence and approval, filled the Temple.

Now Adonai has kept the promise that He made; as Adonai promised, I have built the Temple for Adonai, the Savior of Israel. And I have made there a place in the Temple for the Holy Ark containing the covenant, which He made with our ancestors, when He brought them out of the land of Egypt. **8:20–21**

Connection   The connection between the Torah reading and the haftarah are twofold.

The Tabernacle, the mobile home of Adonai, was built in the wilderness by Moses. The stately, opulent home of Adonai was built by Solomon in Jerusalem.

The second connection is the presence of Adonai both in the movable Tabernacle and in the Holy Temple in Jerusalem.

Haftarah for Pekuday פְּקוּדֵי
(1 Kings 7:51–8:21)

7 **51** King Solomon finished building Adonai's Temple. Now Solomon brought in all the gifts which David his father had donated, the silver, the gold, and the vessels, and placed them into the treasuries of Adonai's Temple.

8 Then King Solomon gathered the leaders of Israel, and the heads of all the tribes of Israel, to Jerusalem, to bring up the ark of Adonai's covenant out of Zion, the city of David. **2** In the month of Tishri, which is the seventh month, King Solomon assembled all the people to feast. **3** All the leaders of Israel came, and the priests carried the ark.

4 And they brought the ark of Adonai, and the Levites brought all of them up. **5** King Solomon and all the Israelites, who had assembled before him in front of the ark, were sacrificing so many sheep and oxen that they could not be counted.

6 The priests brought the ark of Adonai into its place, the Sanctuary of the Temple, in the Holy of Holies, under the wings of the cherubim. **7** The cherubim spread out their wings over the ark and formed a covering over the ark and its poles. **8** The poles were so long that the ends of the polls were seen from the Holy of Holies in front of the Sanctuary; but they could not be seen outside. They are there to this day. **9** There was nothing in the Holy ark except the two tablets of stone (Ten Commandments) which Moses placed there at Horeb (Mount Sinai), when Adonai made a covenant with the Israelites when they left the land of Egypt.

10 When the priests came out of the Holy of Holies, a cloud filled the Temple of Adonai. **11** The priests could not stay to continue to pray because of the cloud; for Adonai's glory filled the Temple.

12 Then Solomon said, "Adonai has said that He would dwell in the thick darkness. **13** I have built for You a beautiful Temple, a place for You to dwell in forever."

14 Then the king turned around, and all the congregation of Israel stood, and he blessed the whole congregation of Israel.

15 He said, "Blessed be the Adonai of Israel, who has with His hand fulfilled His promise to my father David, saying, **16** Since the day that I brought My people Israel out of Egypt, I had not chosen any city in all the tribes of Israel to build a Temple for My name, my presence there; but I chose David to rule over My people Israel. **17** Now it was in the heart of my father David to build a Temple for the name of Adonai, the Savior of Israel. **18** But Adonai said to David, my father, you always intended to build a Temple for My name. **19** But you will not be the one to build the Temple, but your son, who is your own flesh and blood, will build the Temple for My name. **20** Now Adonai has kept the promise that He made; as God promised, I have succeeded my father. I have built the Temple for Adonai, the Savior of Israel. **21** And I have made there a place in the Temple for the Holy Ark containing the covenant, which He made with our ancestors, when He brought them out of the land of Egypt."

HAFTARAH for VAYIKRA
Isaiah 43:21–44:23

Book of Isaiah   See haftarah Bereshit, page 51.

History   This haftarah is thought to be the prophecy of Second Isaiah. It was written against the background of the closing years of the Babylonian exile, beginning about 550 B.C.E.

This prophecy is delivered to a people living in exile in Babylon after the destruction of the First Temple. The prophet criticizes the exiles for their failure in the past to worship Adonai properly and earnestly. He says:

> *You have not honored Me*
> *with offerings,*
> *nor have you honored Me*
> *with your sacrifices.* **43:23**

But despite your neglect, there is hope, for Adonai loves his people and forgives them:

> *For My own sake,*
> *I will forgive your sins*
> *and I will never remember them.* **43:25**

Isaiah reminds the exiles of the contrast between the Adonai and the idols.

He reminds them that Babylonian gods are no more than the work of a human's hand.

> *Part of the tree he burns in the fire;*
> *with this half, he cooks food.*
> *He roasts his meat and is satisfied.*
> *He also warms himself and says:*
> *"Aha, I am warm; I feel the heat."*
> *The rest of the wood*
> *he carves into an idol.*

He kneels and worships.
He prays to it, saying
"You are my god, save me." **44:16–17**

In the end, you must admit your stupidity to return:

People of Israel,
remember you are My servants.
I created you.
Israel, you are My servant;
you must not forget Me. **44:21**

Connection   The Torah reading details the true worship of Adonai during the years of wandering in the desert. The haftarah, on the other hand, contrasts the abandonment of faith in Adonai and the laws of the Torah.

Haftarah for Vayikra וַיִּקְרָא
(Isaiah 43:21–44:23)

43

21 I created Israel
so that they would honor Me
with praises.
22 But, O Jacob, you
have not called upon Me for help;
neither, O Israel,
because you have also grown tired of Me.
23 You have not honored Me
with offerings,
nor have you honored Me
with your sacrifices.
I have not asked you
for cereal offerings,
or demanded sweet incense.
24 You have not purchased spices,
nor given Me the best of your sacrifices;
but you have insulted Me
with your sins and offenses.
25 For My own sake
I will forget your sins,
and I will never remember them.
26 Let us consult together;
present your case
so that you may be judged innocent.
27 Your first ancestor sinned,
and your leaders sinned against Me.
28 That is why
I will not allow priests of the Sanctuary
to serve me,
and have allowed Israel
to be destroyed and disgraced.

44

Jacob and Israel.
I have chosen you to serve Me;
2 I am your creator,
who made you;
I formed you in the womb,
and I will help you:
Israel, do not be afraid,
for I have chosen you
to serve Me.
3 I will pour water on the thirsty land
and streams on the dry land.
My spirit and My blessings
will surround your descendants.
4 They will bloom
in the midst of the grass,
like willow trees near flowing streams.
5 They will worship and say,
"I believe in Adonai,"
and another will say,
"I am a descendant of Jacob";
another will write, "I belong to Adonai"
on his hand, and give himself the name Israel.
6 Adonai, the King of Israel, and Redeemer,
the Adonai Tzvaot says,
I am the first and I am the last;
except for Me there is no other Elohim.
7 Who else can tell you the future—
let him tell you
and prove it to Me—
since I appointed the ancient people?
I dare them to predict the future
and what shall come to pass.
8 Do not be afraid;
didn't I tell you a long time ago?
You are My witnesses.
Is there any other Elohim besides Me?

There is no other Rock;
not one single one.
9 Those who make idols are foolish,
and the images they value are worthless.
They are their own witnesses;
their idols neither see nor think;
is it any wonder
they are put to shame?
10 Who but a fool
would manufacture a useless idol?
11 All the skilled craftsmen
shall be put to shame.
Let them all come together,
and let them stand.
Together they will stand
in fear and shame.
12 The smith makes an axe,
and heats it in the coals,
and shapes it with hammers,
and forges it with his powerful arm.
But he becomes hungry
and loses his strength;
he becomes thirsty and weak.
13 The carpenter measures
and marks out a piece of wood.
He shapes the wood with planes,
marks it out with the compasses,
and carves it into the figure of a man,
a beautiful statue,
to stay in his house.
14 Men cut down cedars;
they plant the cypress, and the oak,
and lets them grow strong
among the trees of the forest.
He plants a cedar tree,
and the rainwater nourishes it.

15 Then a human uses its wood for fuel;
he burns branches and warms himself;
he lights a wood fire and bakes bread.
Then he carves a wooden idol
and worships it
and kneels before it;
16 Part of the tree he burns in the fire;
with this half, he cooks food.
He roasts his meat and is satisfied.
He also warms himself and says:
"Aha, I am warm; I feel the heat."
17 The rest of the wood
he carves into an idol.
He kneels and worships.
He prays to it, saying,
"You are my god, save me."
18 Such stupidity and such ignorance;
their eyes are shut
so they cannot see;
their minds are shut
so that they cannot understand.
19 No one has the common sense to say,
"Half of the wood
I burned in the fire;
I also baked bread on its coals.
I also roasted meat and ate it.
Shall I stupidly make a tree into an idol?
Shall I dumbly kneel to a stick of wood?
20 He pursues after emptiness.
A deluded heart has led him astray,
and he prays to a wooden puppet
that cannot save his soul, or ask,
"Is the doll in my right hand stupidity?"
21 People of Israel,
remember you are My servants.
I created you.
Israel, you are My servant;

you must not forget Me.
22 I have swept away your sins
as though they were clouds and mist.
Return to Me,
for I have forgiven you.
23 O heavens, sing for joy,
for Adonai has done it.
Shout and start singing,
O depths of the earth,
O mountains,
O forest and every tree in it.
For Adonai has rescued Israel
and now displays His glory in Israel.

HAFTARAH for TZAV
Jeremiah 7:21–8:3, 9:22–23

Book of Jeremiah See haftarah Bo, page 122.

History This prophecy was spoken by Jeremiah in 608 B.C.E. to a gathering of officials in the Temple area. It infuriated the priests and placed him in danger. This was a time when it was not safe for him even to enter the Temple itself. The priests and the rival group of prophets disliked him because he denounced the profitable but hollow futility of sacrifice.

Text In those days, when sacrifices and ritual were the mainstay of religion, Jeremiah's words were revolutionary ideas. The new doctrine began to undermine the influence of the priests. The prophetic message attempted to change the mission of the priests from that of a performer of rituals to that of a teacher of Jewish ethics and morality. Jeremiah preached that Adonai wanted higher moral standards.

With these ideas supplied by the prophets, the Jews in Babylonian captivity set about giving Judaism a "new look." This Temple was the place where sacrifices were offered. By making morality superior to sacrifice, the prophets converted Judaism from time and place. Now Jews wherever they lived could build synaguges for religious assembly.

Jeremiah says that the people are substituting sacrifice instead of obedience. He says:

> *This is what Adonai, the Savior of Israel, says: Do away with your burnt offerings to your sacrifices, and eat flesh.* **7:21**

Then Jeremiah continues:

> *When I brought your ancestors out from the land of Egypt, I did not ask them or command them to bring burnt offerings or sacrifices. I commanded them:*

"Obey Me, and I will be your Savior, and you shall be My people. Do as I command you, and all will be well with you." **7:22**

Jeremiah denounces the rites and practices of idolatry, which include the cults of child sacrifice. He says that they have corrupted the Temple.

They have built altars in Topheth, which is in the Valley of Ben Himmon, to sacrifice their sons and daughters in the fire. **7:31**

The haftarah ends with a note of encouragement. Adonai declares:

But one should glory only in the knowledge that he understands and knows Me. I am Adonai who acts with mercy, justice, and righteousness to everyone on earth; for in these gifts I delight, declares Adonai. **9:23**

Connection The connection between the sidrah and the haftarah are the sacrifices which the Israelites brought to Adonai while they wandered through the desert. Now Jeremiah talks about the sacrifices and also denounces the cult of child sacrifice. Instead, Jeremiah emphasizes prayer and obedience as a symbol of devotion to Adonai.

Haftarah for Tzav צַו
(Jeremiah 7:21-8:3, 9:22-23)

7 **21** This is what Adonai, Tzvaot of Israel says: Add your burnt offerings to your sacrifices, and eat flesh. **22** When I brought your ancestors out from the land of Egypt, I did not ask them or command them to bring burnt offerings or sacrifices. **23** I commanded them: "Obey Me, and I will be your savior, and you shall be My people. Do as I command you, and all will be well with you."

24 But they did not listen and did not obey; they followed their own ideas and their stubbornness. They went backward instead of forward. **25** From the time that your ancestors came out from the land of Egypt to this day, from morning until night, I continued to send you My prophets.

26 Yet they wouldn't try to hear or listen to Me; they continued their stubbornness. They were worse than their parents.

27 No matter what you say, they will not listen to you. You can warn them, but they will not respond. **28** Say, "This is the nation that refused to obey the voice of Adonai, and did not accept My teaching. Faithfulness has disappeared; she continues to live a lie.

29 Shave your hair, and throw it away. Mourn upon the high hills; for Adonai, in anger, has rejected and abandoned the generation."

30 Adonai says, The people of Judah have sinned openly. They have placed their idols in My Temple and corrupted it. **31** They have built altars in Topheth, which is in the Valley of Ben Himmon, to sacrifice their sons and daughters in the fire, which I never, ever, commanded them; and the thought never crossed My mind. **32** Adonai says, The time is approaching when the valley will no longer be called Topheth, nor the Valley of Ben Himmon, but the Valley of Slaughter; for they shall dump so many in Topheth till there is no room. **33** And the carcasses of the people will be food for the birds and animals; and there will be no one to scare them away. **34** I will end the sounds of laughter and happy voices, the joyous voices of the bridegrooms and of the brides, for the land shall lie in ruins from the cities of Judah, and from the streets of Jerusalem.

8 Adonai says, At that time, the enemy will scatter the bones of the kings of Judah, the bones of the princes, the bones of the priests, the bones of the prophets, and the bones of the inhabitants of Jerusalem will be removed from their graves. **2** They shall spread them on the ground, open to the sun, the moon, and all the heavenly bodies, which they have loved, which they obeyed, and which they have worshipped. Their bones shall not be gathered or buried; they shall be like garbage on the surface of the earth. **3** Those of this evil family who remain alive shall prefer death rather than life, in the places into which I have driven them.

9 **22** Adonai says, Let not the wise man glory in his knowledge, nor the mighty man in his strength, nor the wealthy man in his riches. **23** But one should glory only in the knowledge that he understands and knows Me. I am Adonai who acts with mercy, justice, and righteousness to everyone on earth; for in these gifts I delight, declares Adonai.

HAFTARAH for SHEMINI
2 Samuel 6:1–7:17

Books of Samuel I and II   The Books of Samuel I and II belong to the section of the *Tanak* called the Early Prophets. It includes the history of the first two kings of Israel, Saul and David, from 1040 to 965 B.C.E.

Samuel was both a judge and a prophet. The Philistine invaders from Crete pressured the Israelites so they asked Samuel to appoint a king who would lead and defend them.

Samuel appointed Saul as the first king of Israel. Saul succeeded in defeating the Philistines, but he was a moody and quarrelsome king who alienated the prophet Samuel.

Saul took David, "the sweet singer of Israel," into his court. David was very popular, and stories of his brave deeds made Saul jealous. Samuel was disappointed in Saul, so he secretly anointed David as the next king of Israel. The king then plotted to kill David, but Jonathan, Saul's oldest son and David's friend, warned him to escape.

The Philistines, sensing the weakness of the kingdom, attacked. Both Saul and his sons were killed in battle, and David ascended to the throne. He reigned until 971 B.C.E. and succeeded in expanding both his power and territories. He captured Jerusalem and made it the seat of his central government. He is also credited with writing the Book of Psalms. The land of Israel under his reign became a thriving nation, and numerous and powerful rulers paid him homage.

History   Hebron was David's capital as long as he ruled only the territory of Judah. The leaders of the northern and central tribes met at Hebron and appointed him as their king. Now that his rule extended over *all* the Israelite tribes, he needed a centrally located capital. The city of Jerusalem was an ideal location.

The Jebusite city was captured by David's warriors, who gained access by creeping through a tunnel that brought water from the spring of Gihon outside the wall.

With Jerusalem established as the political capital, David decided to make it into a religious center.

The Ark of the Covenant had for twenty years been lying almost hidden in the village Kiryat-jearim near Jerusalem. David, at the head of a great procession of leaders and notables, went to bring the Ark to Israel. It was carried on a wagon drawn by oxen and was preceded by bands, dancers, and singers. The wagon was led by two brothers, Uzzah and Ahi. Along the rocky road the Ark started to fall and Uzzah grabbed it to steady it. Uzzah was immediately struck dead. David, fearful of divine displeasure, stopped the project. He then arranged to place the Ark in the custody of Oved-Edom, who lived nearby.

After three months, David decided that it was safe to bring the Ark to Jerusalem. Once again a group of happy notables, leaders, and worshippers brought it to Jerusalem.

David led the dancing as the Ark made its way to its prepared resting place.

His wife Michal watched as her husband leaped and danced in joy. She told David she was ashamed of him, saying:

> *"Did the king of Israel honor*
> *himself today, by exposing himself*
> *today in front of his servants,*
> *just like a vulgar, dirty old man?"* **6:20**

King David lived in his palace, but he wanted to build a palace worthy for Adonai, to house the Ark. The prophet Nathan said:

> *"Go, and do everything that*
> *is in your heart,*
> *for Adonai is with you."* **7:3**

That night Adonai told Nathan to say to David:

> *"When your time on earth is over,*
> *and you join your ancestors,*
> *I will choose one of your sons*
> *to be king.*
> *He will build a Temple for Me.* **7:12–13**

Connection   The sidrah describes the consecration of the Tabernacle in the wilderness. The haftarah describes the transporting of the Ark of the Covenant to its temporary home in Jerusalem.

There are also tragic incidents in both the sidrah and the haftarah.

6 David again mobilized 30,000 specially chosen Israelite warriors. **2** And David with his troops marched to Baalon of Judah, to bring up the Ark of Elohim, which is called by the name of the Adonai of Hosts who is seated between the cherubim. **3** They placed the Ark of Elohim upon a new cart, and drove it to the house of Abinadav, which was on the hill. Uzzah and Achio, the sons of Abinadav, drove the new cart.

4 They moved the Ark of Elohim from the house of Abinadav, which was on the hill; Achio walked alongside the ark. **5** And David and all the leaders of Israel danced before Adonai, playing all kinds of instruments made of cypress-wood, with lyres, with harps, with tambourines, with sistrums, and with cymbals.

6 And when they came to Nakhon's threshing-floor, Uzzah reached out toward the Ark of Elohim and steadied it, because the oxen had stumbled.

7 Then Adonai was angry with Uzzah; and Elohim struck him down there for his crime, and he died on the spot by the Ark of Elohim. **8** And David was unhappy at Adonai's punishment against Uzzah; and that place was given the name of Peretz-Uzzah to this day.

9 That day, David was afraid of Adonai, and he said, "How can the Ark of Adonai come with me?" **10** So David decided not to take Adonai's Ark into the city of David; but David carried it in the house of Oved-Edom the Gittite. **11** The Ark of Adonai remained in the house of Oved-Edom the Gittite three months, and Adonai blessed Oved-Edom and all his family.

12 King David was informed that "Adonai has blessed the household of Oved-Edom, because of the Ark of Elohim." So David went with joy, went and brought the Ark of Elohim from the house of Oved-Edom into the city of

David. **13** And when the bearers of the Ark of Adonai had moved six paces, he sacrificed an ox and a sheep. **14** And David danced before Adonai with all his strength; and David was dressed with a linen ephod. **15** So David and all the house of Israel brought up Adonai's Ark with the blowing of the shofar.

16 As Adonai's Ark entered the city of David, Michal, Saul's daughter, watched from the window and saw King David leaping and dancing before Adonai, and she was ashamed of him and in her heart despised him.

17 They carried Adonai's Ark, and placed it inside the tent that David had erected for it; and David brought burnt offerings and peace offerings before Adonai.

18 After David finished offering the burnt and the peace offerings, he blessed the people in the name of Adonai the Almighty. **19** Then he gave everyone a gift of a loaf of bread, and a cake made in a pan, and a raisin cake. Then all the people left and returned home.

(Sephardim conclude here)

20 When David returned to bless his household, Michal, Saul's daughter, came out to meet David and said, "Did the king of Israel honor himself today, by exposing himself today in front of his servants, just like a vulgar, dirty old man?"

21 David answered Michal: "I celebrated before Adonai, who chose me instead of your father, or anyone in your family, and appointed me ruler over Adonai's people, Israel. **22** I will be even more undignified than this, and common; but with my servants of whom you talked, with them I will get honor."

23 And Saul's daughter Michal was childless to the day of her death.

7 Now King David lived in his palace, and Adonai had given him peace from all his enemies round about.

2 The king said to Nathan the prophet, "It is not right, I live in a palace of cedar, but the Ark of Elohim sits within tent curtains."

3 Nathan said to the king, "Go, and do everything that is in your heart, for Adonai is with you."

4 That night, Adonai said to Nathan, **5** Tell my servant David: "This is what Adonai asks: Do you want to build a Temple for Me to dwell in? **6** I have not lived in a Temple since the day I liberated the children of Israel from Egypt until now. I have moved from place to place in a tent and in a Tabernacle. **7** Wherever I have traveled with children of Israel, I never asked any of the tribes of Israel, who were under My care: Why haven't you built Me a Temple of cedar?"

8 Now, tell My servant David, this is what Adonai Almighty says: "I took you from the pasture and from tending animals to be a ruler over My people Israel.

9 Wherever you went I accompanied you and I helped you destroy your enemies around you. I made you one of the most famous people in all the world.

10 I have given My people Israel a home of their own so they can live in peace and will not any more tremble in fear. Evil conquerors will not oppress them as before.

11 From the time I appointed judges to rule you, I have kept your enemies from attacking you. Adonai promises that you and your descendants will live like kings.

12 When your time on earth is over, and you join your ancestors, I will choose one of your sons to be king. **13** He will build a Temple for Me, and I will establish his kingdom forever. **14** I will be a father to him, and he shall be as a son to Me. If he does wrong, I will punish him. **15** But I will never remove My approval from him, as I removed it from Saul. **16** Your dynasty and your kingdom shall endure forever; your throne will be established forever."

17 Nathan went to David and told him everything he had heard and seen in this vision.

INTRODUCTION
HAFTARAH for TAZRIA
2 Kings 4:42–5:19

Books of Kings I and II   See haftarah Vayera, page 68.

History   The prophet Elisha was Elijah's disciple. The Bible tells how Elijah recruited him. While passing through the Jordan Valley, Elijah saw Elisha plowing a field with a team of oxen. From a distance, he sensed the extraordinary power in the strong, sweat-soaked farmer. Without hesitation, Elijah removed his mantle and flung it around the young man's shoulders. This was an ancient symbolic call to prophetic service, which Elisha eagerly accepted.

Both prophets devoted themselves to the crusade against idolatry, but there was a definite difference between them. Elijah was stern and solitary, while Elisha was gentle and was often found in the company of his disciples.

Elisha performed miracles and was active in the political and military life of Israel.

Text   This haftarah relates two miraculous incidents in the life of Elisha.

During a famine, a devotee of Elisha brought him a small gift of bread and corn and he said, "Give it to the hungry people."

But the servant said, "How can I give this small amount of food to one hundred people?" Elisha said, "Give the people the food; for Adonai has told me: There will be plenty for everyone and there will be some left." **4:43**

This small gift of food was miraculously multiplied by Elisha and grew so that it fed one hundred hungry people.

In the second miracle, Elisha cured Naaman, a famous Syrian general, of his leprosy. Naaman's wife was told by her Israelite maid that Elisha could cure him of his leprosy.

So Naaman drove his horses and chariots to the door of Elisha's house. Elisha sent his message, saying, "Go and immerse yourself seven times in the Jordan, and your skin will be as healthy and clean as before." **5:9**

Naaman was grateful.

Then he and his officials returned to the messenger of Adonai. He came and gratefully stood before him, saying, "Now I am convinced that there is no Adonai in all the world except in Israel. Please accept a gift from your grateful servant." **5:15**

Connection Both the sidrah and the haftarah deal with leprosy, the scourge of the Middle East.

Haftarah for Tazria תַּזְרִיעַ
(2 Kings 4:42–5:19)

4 **42** A man came from Baal Shalishah and brought Elisha the messenger of Adonai bread from the first fruits, twenty loaves of barley, and fresh ears of corn in his sack. Elisha said, "Give the food to the people, so that they can eat."

43 But the servant said, "How can I give this small amount of food to one hundred people?" Elisha said, "Give the people the food; for Adonai has told me: There will be plenty for everyone and there will be some left."

44 So he gave them the food. And, according to Adonai's promise, everyone ate, and some was left over.

5 The king of Aram admired and respected Naaman, the commander of the army, because through him, Adonai had given many a victory to Aram. He was also a brave man of valor, but he was a leper. **2** On one of their raids, the Arameans had captured a girl from the land of Israel, and she served Naaman's wife as her maid.

3 One day, she said to her mistress, "If my master met with the prophet who is in Samaria, he could heal his leprosy!"

4 So Naaman went in and told the king, "This is what my Israelite maid says."

5 The king of Aram said, "Then go ahead, and I will send a letter of introduction to the king of Israel." So he left and took with him 750 pounds of silver, 150 pounds of gold, and ten new suits of clothing. **6** He delivered the letter to the king of Israel. It said, "This letter will introduce my servant Naaman. I want you to cure him of his leprosy."

7 When the king of Israel read the letter, he tore his clothing in fear and cried, "This king sends me a leper to cure?

He thinks that I have the power of life and death? Perhaps it is just an excuse to start another war against me."

8 However, when Elisha, the messenger of Adonai, heard that the king of Israel had torn his clothing in fear, he sent a message to the king, saying, "Why have you torn your clothing in fear? Let Naaman come to me. Then he will know that there is a true prophet in Israel."

9 So Naaman drove his horses and chariots to the door of Elisha's house. **10** Elisha sent his message, saying, "Go and immerse yourself seven times in the Jordan, and your skin will be as healthy and clean as before."

11 Naaman became angry, and went away, raging in anger: "I expected that he would personally welcome me, and stand before me and pray to Adonai, wave his hands over my body, and heal me. **12** Aren't the Amanah and Pharpar, the rivers of Damascus, superior to any river in Israel? Why can't I just immerse myself in them and be healed?" So he angrily drove away.

13 But his servants ran after him and pleaded, "My lord, if the prophet told you to perform a complicated ceremony, wouldn't you have done it? How much more so then, when he simply said to you: Immerse and be cured." **14** So Naaman went down and immersed himself in the Jordan seven times, just as the messenger of Adonai had instructed him; and his skin became as clean as the flesh of a little child. **15** Then he and his officials returned to the messenger of Adonai. He came and gratefully stood before him, saying, "Now I am convinced that there is no Adonai in all the world except in Israel. Please accept a gift from your grateful servant."

16 Elisha replied, "I swear to Adonai whom I serve that I will not accept your gift." Naaman begged him to take it, but he refused. **17** Then Naaman said, "If not, then please give me enough soil from the land of Israel as two mules can carry, because from now on, I will never again offer sacrifices to other gods but to Adonai. **18** I pray that

Adonai will pardon me: When I worship in the Temple of the idol Rimmon, and I bow down there, may Adonai forgive me."

19 Elisha said to him, "Go in peace." Naaman left for home.

HAFTARAH for METZORA
2 Kings 7:3–20

Books of Kings I and II   See haftarah Vayera, page 68.

History   Elisha, meaning, "Adonai is salvation," was the successor to Elijah. He was the son of a wealthy farmer and became a devoted helper to Elijah. He prophesied for fifty years during the reigns of kings Jehoram (849–842 B.C.E.), Jehu (842–815), Johoahaz (815–801), and Jehoash (801–780), and kings sought his advice.

Text   The Arameans, with a great army, laid siege to Samaria, and Elisha advised resistance to the bitter end. The inhabitants were reduced to eating garbage, and some women became cannibals and ate their own children. The king was incensed at Elisha, who had encouraged resistance, and decided to execute him. When Elisha appeared, he announced that the very next day the famine would end and the Syrians would retreat.

> *Adonai had caused the Aramean camp to hear the roar of a great army of chariots and cavalry. So the soldiers said to one another, "The king of Israel has hired the king of the Hittites and Egyptians to attack us."*
>
> *So they got up and fled in the darkness, and abandoned their tents, horses, donkeys, and the camp, and fled for their lives.* **7:6**

Overnight a miracle occurred, and the Arameans had fled. In the morning, four lepers who were living outside the city walls discovered the empty tents.

Connection   The connection between the sidrah and the haftarah is the discussion of leprosy in the sidrah. The haftarah tells about the four lepers who discover the empty Aramean camp.

Haftarah for Metzora מְצֹרָע
(2 Kings 7:3-20)

7 **3** At about this time, four lepers were at the entrance to the gate of the city of Samaria. They said to one another, "Why should we sit here until we die?"

4 If we say, "Let us go into the city," the famine is in the city, and we will die there. If we sit here, we will also die. Come, let us go and surrender to the Arameans. If they spare our lives, we will live; and if they kill us, we will simply die.

5 They arose at dusk to go over to the Aramean camp. But when they entered the outer edge of the Aramean camp, it was completely empty.

6 Adonai had caused the Aramean camp to hear the roar of a great army of chariots and cavalry. So the soldiers said to one another, "The king of Israel has hired the kings of the Hittites and Egyptians to attack us." **7** So they got up and fled in the darkness, and abandoned their tents, horses, donkeys, and the camp, and fled for their lives.

8 When the four lepers marched into the camp, they entered a tent, ate and drank, and took some silver, gold, and clothing, and went and hid them. Then they returned and entered another tent, took valuables from there, and hid them. **9** Then they said to one another, "We are not doing the right thing. This is a day of good news and we are silent. If we wait till morning, we will be punished. Come, let us go and tell the good news to the king's household."

10 They returned and shouted to the guards at the gates of the city and they said to them, "We went to the camp of the Arameans, and it was completely deserted. The horses and donkeys are tied up, and the tents are empty. **11** Then the guards called and told it to the members of the king's household.

12 The king immediately arose and said to his servants, "I will tell you what the Arameans will do to trick us. They know that we are dying of hunger; so they have left the camp and hidden themselves in the field, thinking, 'When they come out of the city, we will capture them alive and take over the city.'"

13 One of his officials suggested, "Let our soldiers saddle five of the remaining horses in the city. Let us send them to see what has happened."

14 They found two chariots in the area with horses; and the king sent the scouts to find the Aramean army, saying, "Go and scout." **15** They followed the Arameans as far as the Jordan; and the road was littered with garments and equipment, which the Arameans had desperately thrown away. The scouts returned and told the king what they saw. **16** Then the people streamed out of the city and plundered the Aramean camp. There was so much loot that a quart of fine flour was sold for a shekel, and two quarts of barley for a shekel, according to Adonai's word.

17 The king appointed the captain on whom he depended to be in charge of the gate; but the people trampled him, so they rushed out of the city, and he died, just as the prophets had predicted when the king came to his house. **18** Elisha said, "About this time tomorrow, a seah of flour will sell for a shekel and two seahs of barley for a shekel at the gate of Samaria."

19 The officer had said to Elisha, "Look, even if Adonai should open the floodgates of the heavens, this could never happen." Then Elisha replied, "You will see it with your own eyes, but you will not eat any of it!" **20** And that is exactly what happened to him, for the people trampled him in the gateway, and he died.

HAFTARAH for ACHARE MOT
Ezekiel 22:1–19

Book of Ezekiel See haftarah Vayigash, page 105.

History Before the destruction of the Temple by Nebuchadnezzar in 594 B.C.E., Ezekiel denounced Israel for the violations of the religious and moral laws.

At first Ezekiel's prophecies were messages of doom, but after the fall of Jerusalem he spoke messages of hope, comfort, and assurance of restoration. Ezekiel believed that a prophet was a watchman, responsible for warning his people of the consequences of sin. Ezekiel said that each person is born with free will and is the master of his own destiny and responsible for his own deeds.

Text Ezekiel condemns Jerusalem for her sin, and says:

This is what Adonai says:
This is a city that shelters murderers,
and its doom has arrived.
You have made yourself guilty
by making idols. **22:3–4**

Ezekiel continues and lists a variety of sins which includes lack of family purity, mistreatment of the widow and orphan, violating the sanctity of the Sabbath, and charging high interest for loans.

Ezekiel predicts the fall of Jerusalem.
Ezekiel, son of man, the house of Israel
has become worthless to Me; they are
as useless to Me as brass, tin, lead,
and iron that remains in the
furnace after the silver has been removed.
So Adonai says that because you all have
become worthless, I will bring all
of you into Jerusalem. **22:18–19**

Ezekiel says that the destruction of Jerusalem is certain and the population will take refuge behind the walls. Now they will all meet their doom.

Connection   Both the sidrah and haftarah deal with the necessity of sexual purity.

Haftarah for Achare Mot אַחֲרֵי מוֹת
(Ezekiel 22:1-19)

22 Adonai's message came to me: **2** Ezekiel, son of man, are you ready to publicly condemn this bloody city? Remind her of her terrible sins. **3** Then say this: This is what Adonai says: This is a city that shelters murderers, and its doom has arrived. You have made yourself guilty by making idols. **4** You are guilty because of murders and the worship of idols which you have made. You have brought your destruction; and you have reached the end of your existence.

I have made you a disgrace among the nations and made you a laughingstock among all the countries.

5 You will be ridiculed over the world and you will became infamous.

6 Every leader of Israel has used his power and might to commit murder. **7** Parents are humiliated and the stranger among you is abused; you have mistreated the orphan and the widow. **8** You have disrespected My sacred laws and violated My Sabbaths. **9** Among you there are those who tell lies so people are condemned to death; and you eat at the shriner mountains to worship idols, and you commit vulgar acts. **10** Children sleep with their fathers' wives and impure women. **11** In your communities there are men who sleep with their neighbors' wives and their daughters-in-law, and who have raped their sisters. **12** Adonai says, Among you there are professional murderers who are paid to kill; you have taken high interest for loans and extorted money from neighbors, and have forgotten Me.

13 I'm angry at your crimes and at the murders which have occurred among you. **14** Can your heart keep beating and can your hands remain strong, in the days to come when I punish you? I, Adonai, have decided to do it.

15 I will scatter you among the nations and through many countries, and will remove the dirt which covers you.

16 You will be laughed at among the nations; and then you will realize that I am Adonai.

17 Adonai continued speaking to me, saying,

18 Ezekiel, son of man, the house of Israel has become worthless to Me; they are as useless to Me as brass, tin, lead, and iron that remains in the furnace after the silver has been removed. **19** So Adonai says that because you all have become worthless, I will bring all of you into Jerusalem.

INTRODUCTION TO
HAFTARAH for KEDOSHIM
Amos 9:7–15

Book of Amos   See haftarah Vayeshev on page 96.

History   The prophet Amos was a well-to-do owner of orchards and a rancher with flocks of cattle and sheep. He prophesied in the mid-eighth century B.C.E., during one of the most prosperous periods in the history of the Northern Kingdom of Israel. The reign of King Jeroboam II, who ruled for forty years (793–753), was a time of prosperity and political influence.

But beneath the veneer of opulence, Amos saw the disparity between the rich and powerful and the poor and downtrodden. Amos was sent by Adonai to denounce the social inequities and the religious corruption of both Judah and Israel. His powerful denunciations shook the royal court. Amaziah, the priest of Bethel, sent a warning to King Jeroboam saying, "Amos is a traitor and is plotting to kill you." King Jeroboam ordered Amaziah to warn Amos to get out of Israel and prophesize in Judah. Amos went to Judah and bravely continued to preach that Israel was ripe for ruin.

Text   The prophet Amos sharply criticizes the people for their sinful ways. He warns:

> *The eyes of Adonai are upon*
> *your sinful kingdom.*
> *I will destroy it from the*
> *face of the earth.* **9:8**

> *All the sinners of*
> *My people shall die by the sword.* **9:10**

After his prophecy of condemnation, the prophet assures the people of Israel and Judah that Adonai will restore the kingdom:

In that day I will raise up
the fallen tabernacle of David,
and repair its breeches.
I will raise up his ruins
and build it as in the days of old. **9:11**

Not only will the kingdom be restored, however.

And I will return the captivity of my people Israel.
They shall rebuild the desolate cities
and inhabit them. . . . And I will plant
them upon their land, and they shall
never again be plucked up from their land which
I have given them. **9:14–15**

Connection The theme of holiness dominates the sidrah: "You must be holy, because I am Adonai and I am holy."

In the haftarah the prophet Amos first criticizes the Israelites who have rejected their ethical and spiritual heritage. But Amos predicts that the time is approaching when Israel will return to the Torah and its message of spiritual holiness.

Haftarah for Kedoshim קְדוֹשִׁים
(Amos 9:7-15)

9 **7** Adonai says, O children of Israel, you are like Ethiopians to me.
Didn't I free you, Israel, from the land of Egypt,
and from Philistines from Caphtor,
and Aram from Kir?
8 Adonai says, The eyes of Adonai
are upon your sinful kingdom.
I will destroy it from the face of the earth.
But I will not completely erase the house of Jacob.
9 I will command, and I will separate
the children of Israel from among the nations,
just as corn is separated in a sieve.
Not a single grain shall fall upon the earth.
10 All the sinners of My people shall die by the sword,
those who say,
"The evil shall not overtake us or confront us."
11 In that day I will raise up
the fallen tabernacle of David,
and repair its breaches.
I will raise up his ruins
and build it as in the days of old,
12 so that they may possess the remnant of Edom,
and all the nations upon whom My name is called,
says Adonai who does this.
13 Behold, the days are coming, says Adonai,
when the plowman shall overtake the reaper,
and the treader of grapes,
the one who sows seed.
The mountains shall drip sweet wine,
and all the hills shall melt.

14 And I will return the captivity of My people Israel.
They shall rebuild the desolate cities and inhabit them;
they shall plant vineyards
and drink their wine;
and they shall make gardens
and eat their fruit.
15 And I will plant them upon their land,
and they shall never again be plucked up
from their land which I have given them,
says Adonai.

Haftarah for Kedoshim קְדוֹשִׁים
(Ezekiel 20:2–20)

(For Sephardim)

20 **2** Adonai's message came to me, saying,
3 Son of Man, speak to the elders of Israel, and say to them, This is what Adonai the Savior says: How dare you come to Me for help? Adonai says, I refuse to give you an answer. **4** Son of Man, you judge them! Remind them of the sins of their ancestors; **5** say to them, This is what Adonai says: When I chose Israel, I helped the descendants of the house of Jacob, and made Myself known to them in the land of Egypt; I swore to them, saying, I am Adonai, your Savior; **6** on that day I swore that I would rescue them out of the land of Egypt and bring them into a land that I had found for them, the best of all lands, a land flowing with milk and honey.

7 Then I said to them, I am Adonai your Savior; all Israelites must rid themselves of their idols. Do not disgrace yourselves with the idols of Egypt. **8** But they rebelled against Me and would not listen. The people did not rid themselves of their idols, and they continued to worship the idols of Egypt. Then I said I would punish them while they were still in the land of Egypt. **9** But I acted to protect the honor of My name, so that My name would not became a laughingstock in the eyes of the nations, among whom they lived, in whose sight I had saved the Israelites by bringing them out of the land of Egypt. **10** I took them out of the land of Egypt and brought them into the wilderness. **11** I gave them My Torah and taught them My commandments, so people could obey them and live a life of peace. **12** I also gave them My Sabbaths, as a day of rest, as a sign between Me and them, and to remind them I am Adonai who made them holy.

13 But in the wilderness the children of Israel once again rebelled against Me; they did not observe My laws, and they rejected my commandments, even though obeying these laws means living a good and peaceful life. They also disgraced My Sabbaths. Then I said I would pour out My anger on them in the wilderness, to destroy them.

14 But I acted for the sake of My name, that it should not be a laughingstock in the eyes of the nations, who had seen me bring the Israelites out of Egypt.

15 However, I also punished them in the wilderness, in that I would not lead them into the choicest of all lands, the one flowing with milk and honey, **16** because they rejected My laws and didn't obey My commandments and disgraced My Sabbaths—and continued to pray to their idols.

17 Nevertheless, I pitied them and I did not destroy them in the wilderness.

18 Then, in the wilderness, I warned their children: Do not follow in the footsteps of your parents or worship their idols. **19** I am Adonai. Follow My laws, and observe My rules, **20** and observe my Sabbaths. If you do, that will be a sign between Me and you that you respect Me and know that I am Adonai.

INTRODUCTION TO
HAFTARAH for EMOR
Ezekiel 44:15–31

Book of Ezekiel See haftarah Vayigash, page 105.

History Ezekiel was the first prophet to receive the call to prophecy outside the Holy Land. He had a vision and was commanded to preach that Jerusalem had been defeated not by the Babylonians but because of the wickedness of Judah, which had angered Adonai.

Ezekiel preached that Adonai was faultless and that Babylon was the instrument with which he had punished Judah. The prophet stressed that those who avoided idol worship and observed the Sabbath would find salvation and redemption. Ezekiel dramatized for the Israelites in exile that their lost homeland would once again come to life.

Text This haftarah in the last part of the book is a vision of hope for a rebuilt Temple which will rise when the exile is over. Adonai was disappointed by the Levites who permitted violations of the Holiness Codes. Ezekiel details the duties of the family of Tzadok, who will inherit the priesthood when the Temple is rebuilt.

Tzadok was the high priest appointed by King Solomon in the Temple. Ezekiel envisions the duties of the priests from the family of Tzadok.

Adonai says, the Levitical priests, the sons of Tzadok, who were in charge of My sanctuary when the children of Israel strayed from Me, they may still approach Me and serve Me; and they shall stand before Me to offer to Me the fat and the blood, says Adonai.

Only they shall enter My Sanctuary and approach My table to serve Me, and they shall perform My service.
44:15–16

They shall act as judges in lawsuits; and they shall judge it according to My rules. They shall observe My teachings and My laws at all My feasts, and they shall preserve the holiness of My Sabbaths. **44:24**

Connection The sidrah is about the numerous priestly duties in the Tabernacle.

The haftarah is also about the priestly duties in the new Temple as envisioned by Ezekiel.

Ezekiel was a religious mystic as well as an ordained priest who was familiar with the details of the Temple ceremonies.

44 **15** Adonai says, the Levitical priests, the sons of Tzadok, who were in charge of My sanctuary when the children of Israel strayed from Me, they may still approach Me and serve Me; and they shall stand before Me to offer to Me the fat and the blood, says Adonai. **16** Only they shall enter My Sanctuary and approach My table to serve Me, and they shall perform My service.

17 When they enter the gates of the inner court, the priests shall wear their linen vestments; they shall wear no wool while they serve inside the gates of the inner court; **18** They shall have linen turbans on their heads and linen undergarments; they shall not wear anything that causes sweat. **19** When they leave and go into the outer court where the people are, they shall remove the vestments in which they performed the holy service, place them in the sacred chambers, and they shall put on regular clothes. In this way they will not transmit holiness to the people by contact with their clothing.

20 They must not shave their heads or let their hair grow long; they shall carefully trim the hair of their heads. **21** No priest may drink wine when he enters the inner court. **22** They shall not marry a widow or a divorced woman; only a virgin of the family of the house of Israel, or a widow of a priest.

23 And they shall teach My people the difference between what is holy and what is godless, and teach them how to differentiate between what is unclean and what is clean.

24 They shall act as judges in lawsuits; and they shall judge it according to My rules. They shall observe My teachings and My laws at all My feasts, and they shall preserve the holiness of My Sabbaths.

25 They shall not contaminate themselves by going near a dead person, for then they may contaminate themselves, except for a father or mother, a son or daughter, or a brother or an unmarried sister. **26** Seven days must elapse until he is purified. **27** Adonai says, On the day that he goes into the Sanctuary, he shall offer a sin offering.

28 I am their only inheritance the priests have. You shall give them no land in Israel; I am their only possession.

29 They shall eat the grain offerings, the sin offerings, and the guilt offerings; and every donated Temple gift shall belong to them. **30** The best of all the first fruits and all of your contributions shall belong to the priests. You shall also give the priest the first of your grain, so that a blessing may reside in your house. **31** The priests shall not eat any birth or animal that died a natural death or that was killed by another animal.

INTRODUCTION TO
HAFTARAH for BEHAR
Jeremiah 32:6–27

Book of Jeremiah   See haftarah Bo, page 122.

History   During the siege of Jerusalem by Nebuchadnezzar in 587 B.C.E., Jeremiah was imprisoned because of his opposition to the military and political policies of King Zedekiah.

Text   At that time, Jeremiah's hometown of Anathoth was already under Babylonian occupation, and landowners were looking for opportunities to sell land and raise cash.

At one of the lowest points in Jewish history, Jeremiah at Adonai's command made a dramatic gesture and purchased land from his cousin Chanamel. As the next of kin, under Jubilee law, Jeremiah had the right to the first offer to keep the property in the family.

So, just as Adonai promised, Chanamel met me in the court of the guard and said to me, "Please buy my field, that is in Anathoth, in the land of Benjamin; you have the right of inheritance, and the redemption is yours; buy it for yourself." Then I knew that this was Adonai's word.

So I bought the field that was in Anathoth from Chanamel, my uncle's son, and paid him seventeen silver shekels. **32:8–9**

Now Jeremiah turns his act into a symbolic act of prophecy. He gives the bill of sale to his secretary, Baruch, and says:

Adonai Tzvaot commands: Take these deeds of sale, one of which is sealed, and this open deed, and place them in a clay jar that they will last for a long time.

This is what Adonai Tzvaot says: This is the way houses and fields and vineyards shall be once again bought in this land. **32:14–15**

Connection The sidrah and haftarah both deal with the redemption of a family inheritance. At the darkest point of Judah's existence, Jeremiah "redeemed" his family's land.

The Torah (in Vayikrah 25) says that every fiftieth year in Israel was to be announced as a Jubilee year. The Jubilee has three features.

1. Liberty was granted to all Israelites who were in bondage to their countrymen.
2. There was to be return of ancestral possessions to those who, because of poverty, were forced to sell them.
3. The farmers were to inaugurate a year of rest for the land. They got to eat whatever grew without cultivation.

Haftarah for Behar בְּהַר
(Jeremiah 32:6–27)

32 **6** Jeremiah said, Adonai spoke to me:
7 Your cousin Chanamel, the son of Shallum your uncle, will soon approach you, saying, "Buy my field that is in Anathoth, since you are his closest relative and you have the right to buy it." **8** So, just as Adonai promised, Chanamel met me in the court of the guard and said to me, "Please buy my field, that is in Anathoth, in the land of Benjamin; you have the right of inheritance, and the redemption is yours; buy it for yourself." Then I knew that this was Adonai's word.

9 So I bought the field that was in Anathoth from Chanamel, my uncle's son, and paid him seventeen silver shekels. **10** I signed the deed, sealed it, called witnesses, and weighed the silver shekels on a scale. **11** Then I took two copies of the deed which contained the terms and conditions, and the unsealed copy. **12** I delivered the deed of purchase to Baruch, the son of Neriah, the son of Machseiah, in the presence of Chanamel, my uncle's son, and in the presence of the witnesses who had signed and witnessed the deed of purchase, and in the presence of all the Jews who sat in the courtyard. **13** In their presence I said to Baruch,

14 "Adonai Tzvaot commands: Take these deeds of sale, one of which is sealed, and this open deed, and place them in a clay jar that they will last for a long time. **15** This is what Adonai Tzvaot says: This is the way houses and fields and vineyards shall be once again bought in this land."

16 After I had given the deed of sale to Baruch the son of Neriah, I prayed to Adonai, saying,
17 Adonai! With Your great power and outstretched

arms, You have made the heaven and the earth. Nothing is too difficult for You; **18** You show love to thousands, but you also punish children for the sins of their parents. Adonai, You are great and mighty. Adonai, You are the Savior of Israel; **19** You have great wisdom and are mighty in deeds; Your eyes see all the ways of men, rewarding everyone according to his conduct, and his actions. **20** You performed miracles and wonders in the land of Egypt and have continued to perform miracles in Israel, and among all mankind. **21** You freed Your people Israel out of the land of Egypt with wonders and miracles, with a strong hand and an outstretched arm, and with great terror. **22** You gave them this land, which You swore to their ancestors to give them, a land flowing with milk and honey. **23** They settled in and took possession, but they did not listen to Your command or Your teachings. They ignored everything that You commanded them to do. That is why You sent disasters upon them. **24** See how the siege towers have surrounded the city to capture it; now Jerusalem will be conquered by the Babylonians who surround it, because of the sword, and the famine, and disease. What You have predicted has happened; You can just see it for Yourself. **25** Yet You, Adonai, said to me, Buy the field for money, and call witnesses, even though the city will soon be captured by Babylonians.

26 Then Adonai's word came to Jeremiah, saying, **27** Behold, I am Adonai, the Creator of mankind. There is nothing too difficult for Me.

HAFTARAH for BECHUKKOTAI
Jeremiah 16:19–17:14

Book of Jeremiah   See haftarah Bo, page 122.

History   Jeremiah was concerned about the immorality of the Israelites. Prophets were not simply oracles. They were Adonai's mouthpiece, sent to warn the Isaelites that they were responsible for their own fate, and that doing evil would eventually lead to ruin.

Nothing was preordained or set in stone. The creator of the universe did not abolish human liberty. Humanity was capable of improvement and influencing divine decisions.

Text   Jeremiah has an optimistic conception of the fate of Israel. After its destruction, Jeremiah assures the Israelites that the time of Redemption and Return (*teshuvah*) will come and redeem the Israelites from Babylonian captivity, not only for Israel, but for all nations. He says:

> *Blessed is the person who trusts in Adonai.*
> *He shall be like a tree planted near water,*
> *with roots that reach into the rivers.*
> *It does not dry out in hot weather,*
> *and its leaves remain fresh and green,*
> *even in a drought,*
> *and never stops producing luscious fruits.*   **17:7–8**

Jeremiah continues to praise Adonai.

> *O Adonai, heal me,*
> *and let me be healed;*
> *save me, and let me be saved;*
> *for You are the one I praise.*   **17:14**

Connection   Reward and punishment are the connecting themes between the sidrah and the haftarah. The sidrah details the blessings and curses that will occur if the people defy the will of Adonai. Jeremiah continues, and then he says:

> *Blessed is the person*
> *Who trusts in Adonai.*   **17:7**

Haftarah for Bechukkotai בְּחֻקֹּתַי
(Jeremiah 16:19–17:14)

16

19 Adonai, You are my strength;
You are my refuge in the time of trouble,
and my fortress;
nations from the ends of the earth
will come to You and say,
"Our ancestors stupidly worshipped nothing
but useless and false idols."
20 Can people make their own gods?
Of course, but their gods are worthless.
21 I will teach them;
I will show them My power
and My strength;
and they will know that My name is Adonai.

17

Judah's sin is engraved with a chisel of iron
with a diamond point.
It is engraved on their hearts,
and on the horns of your altars.
2 Your children have built altars,
and worshipped asherim
under leafy trees upon mountain tops.
3 O you mountain dweller in the field,
I will give all your wealth
and all your treasures,
as well as your altars
and everything you own,
to your enemies.
4 You will lose the land that I gave you;
and I will make you slaves
to your enemies in foreign countries;
for you have made me angry
like a fire that keeps on burning.
5 Adonai says,

Cursed is the person who trusts in humans
and the strength of his arm,
and turns away from Adonai.
6 He shall be like a bush in the desert,
where nothing good grows.
He will live in waterless places
in the wilderness,
in an uninhabited salt-filled desert.
7 Blessed is the person
who trusts in Adonai.
8 He shall be like a tree
planted near water,
with roots that reach into the rivers.
It does not dry out in hot weather,
and its leaves remain fresh and green,
even in a drought,
and never stops producing luscious fruits.
9 Who can understand why
the human heart cannot be trusted
and is very weak?
10 But I, Adonai, search hearts;
I examine thoughts
and reward you for your deeds.
11 Like a bird that hatches eggs
that she does not lay,
so is the person who becomes rich
by cheating.
When they are at the end of their lives,
their wealth just disappears,
and they end up looking like a fool.
12 Your glorious throne is our Temple.
13 Adonai, You are the hope of Israel.
All who reject You shall be shamed;
all those who desert You
will be like words written in the dust,
because they have forsaken Adonai,
the fountain of living waters.

14 O Adonai, heal me,
and let me be healed;
save me, and let me be saved;
for You are the one I praise.

HAFTARAH for BAMIDBAR
Hosea 2:1–22

Book of Hosea   See haftarah Vayetze, page 84.

History   As the moral conscience of the community, the prophet Hosea had an unpopular task that was at times dangerous. Most of the prophets shrank from accepting the responsibility and felt inadequate to carry the burden. Moses at the burning bush pleaded and offered excuses, but Adonai insisted, so he reluctantly accepted. Isaiah, Jeremiah, Ezekial, and Jonah all tried to evade the responsibility. However, once the prophets began, they were fearless in carrying out their mission. They attacked the rich and the privileged and fought for the poor and underprivileged. Their preaching fell mostly on deaf ears. But their opinions aroused the anger of the ruling classes, the priests, and the powerful.

Hosea sums up the attitudes of the populace to his calling:

> *The prophet is a fool,*
> *the man of spirit is mad.* **9:7**

Text   Hosea realizes that his life's problems are symbolic of Adonai's relationship with the nation of Israel.

Hosea portrays the Israelites as the children of prostitute Gomer and urges them to condemn her for her infidelity.

> *Accuse your mother; accuse her*
> *for she is not My wife, and I am not her husband;*
> *tell her to remove the makeup from her face,*
> *and the pushup bra from her breasts.* **2:4**

If Israel does not change her ways and rid herself of her idolatries:

> *If not I will strip her naked*
> *like the day she was born;*
> *and she will live in the wilderness,*
> *in a dry land,*

and she will die of thirst.
I will have no pity on her children. **2:5–6**

Israel will suffer because of her sins and faithlessness. But Israel will pay the penalty, and punishment and exile will in the end purify Israel and bring her back. In the end there will be a renewal of faith:

On that day, Adonai says,
you will call Me "Ishi" (my Husband)
instead of "Baali" (my Master).
For I will erase the names
of the pagan idols from her lips,
and their memory will forever disappear. **2:18–19**

Our reconciliation will be complete.

I will accept you (Israel) as My faithful bride;
and then you will know the real Me. **2:22**

Connection The sidrah includes a census of the Israelites during their wanderings in the desert.

In the haftarah, Hosea characterizes the Israelites as living in an idol-worshipping desert devoid of Torah teaching. But Adonai the Merciful will transform the desert into a door of hope.

Haftarah for Bamidbar בַּמִדְבָּר
(Hosea 2:1–22)

2 Soon, the children of Israel will prosper
and be as numerous as the sands of the sea,
which are impossible to measure or number.
Then, instead of saying to them, "You are not my children,"
I will tell them, "Yes, you are the children of Adonai."
2 Then the kingdoms of Judah and Israel will be united
under one ruler, and they will return from exile; it will be a
great and momentous occasion for Jezreel (Israel).
3 Now you can call all your brothers "Ammi" (My relative),
and all your sisters "Ruchamah" (pitied).
4 Accuse your mother; accuse her,
for she is not My wife, and I am not her husband;
tell her to remove the makeup from her face,
and the adultery from her breasts;
5 If not, I will strip her naked,
like the day she was born;
and she will live in the wilderness,
in a dry land,
and she will die of thirst.
6 I will have no pity on her children;
for they are children of unfaithfulness.
7 Their mother was a prostitute,
and gave birth to them shamelessly.
She said: "I will chase after my lovers,
who will give me food to eat
and clothing to wear."
8 So I will block your roads with thorns,
and build a wall around her,
so she will not lose her way.
9 She will race after her lovers
but will not be able to catch up to them,
and she will search
but will be unable to find them.

Then she will decide:
"I will go and return to my first husband;
life was better with him than it is now."
10 She did not realize
that I was the one
who gave her the food and wine;
and I gave her much silver and gold,
which was used to worship the idol Baal.
11 But then I will take back
the harvest of corn and wine in its season,
and snatch away My clothing
which I gave to cover her nakedness.
12 Now, all of her lovers will see her nakedness,
and no one will save her from My punishment.
13 I will stop Israel's celebrations,
her New Moons,
and her Sabbaths,
and her festivals.
14 I will ruin her grapevines and fig trees,
of which she thought,
"This is what my lovers gave me";
but I will make them into fields of weeds,
and wild animals will eat their rotten fruit.
15 Adonai says,
I will punish her
for the years she worshipped idols,
and brought offerings to them,
and decorated herself with earrings and jewels,
and went searching for lovers,
and forgot to worship Me.
16 But I will persuade her to return,
and I will take her to the wilderness,
and gently speak to her.
17 I will return your vineyards from there,
and transform the Valley of Achor (trouble)
into a door of hope.
There she will accept Me,

as in the days of her youth
when she came out of the land of Egypt.
18 On that day, Adonai says,
you will call Me "Ishi" (my Husband)"
instead of "Baali" (my Master).
19 For I will erase the names
of the pagan idols from her lips,
and their memory will forever disappear.
20 On that day, I will make a treaty for you
with the wild animals,
and with the birds of the air,
and with the small animals that creep on the ground,
and I will destroy the bow, the sword,
and all weapons of war,
and you will live in peace.
21 I will accept you as My wife forever;
yes, you will be My bride,
and we will live a life of righteousness,
justice, kindess, and compassion.
22 I will accept you as My faithful bride;
and then you will know the real Me.

INTRODUCTION TO
HAFTARAH for NASO
Judges 13: 2–25

Book of Judges   See haftarah Beshallach, page 127.

History   A time of great peril came upon the Israelites. Their most formidable enemies, the Philistines, were on the march.

The Philistines had come from far away. Their long trek had led them through Crete, across the Aegean Sea by ship, and through Asia Minor on foot and by oxcart. Their ambitious plan of conquest even included mighty Egypt.

The Philistines marched into Canaan victoriously, for the inhabitants were helpless before them. They conquered the rich coastal cities and established five powerful city-states: Askelon, Ashdod, Ekron, Gaza, and Gath. Each of these cities was in the southern part of the fertile coastal plain and was ruled by an independent Philistine prince, but all five were united as allies in peace and in war. Next the Philistines began to subject the land of Israel to their power. They drove the tribe of Dan out of its territory. The Danites were forced to move on and settle in the far north of the land.

Text   This haftarah deals with the beginning of Samson's life. Samson's parents, Manoach and his wife, were a childless couple from the tribe of Dan living in Zorah, close to the Philistine town of Timnah.

An angel appeared and told them that they would soon have a son and that the child must be brought up as a Nazirite.

> *"You will become pregnant and give birth to a son; you must not drink any wine or liquor, or eat anything forbidden by the Torah; your son will be a Nazirite dedicated to Elohim from the day of his birth to the day of his death."* **13:7**

The angel also informed the parents that their son would save the Israelites from the Philistines.

When the child was born, they named him Samson. As a Nazirite, he was to drink no alcoholic beverages or shave or cut his hair.

> *"The woman gave birth to a son, and called him Samson; and the child grew, and Adonai blessed him. The spirit of Adonai began to control him in Machaneh-Dan, which is located between Tzorah and Eshtaol."* **13:24–25**

Samson grew up and became a man of enormous physical strength, admired by the Israelites and feared by the Philistines. Samson was a military hero and a judge. He died a hero's death, killing many thousands of Philistines.

Connection The connection between the sidrah and the haftarah are the Nazirites. The Torah portion details the rules for the Nazirites. The haftarah tells about the beginning of Samson's life and how he became a Nazirite.

Haftarah for Naso נָשֹא
(Judges 13:2-25)

13 **2** Manoach from the tribe of Dan lived in the village of Tzorah. His wife could not have any children. **3** One day, an angel of Adonai appeared and said to the woman, "You are barren and have no children; but you will soon become pregnant and give birth to a son. **4** Be careful; do not drink wine or whisky, and do not eat anything forbidden by the Torah. **5** You will become pregnant and give birth to a boy. Do not allow a razor to touch his head; your child from the time he is born will be a Nazirite dedicated to Elohim, and he will begin to rescue Israel from the hand of the Philistines."

6 So the wife went to Manoach and told him, "A messenger of Elohim came to me, and he looked like an angel. I was so terrified I did not ask him where he was from, and he did not tell me his name; **7** he said to me, 'You will become pregnant and give birth to a son; you must not drink any wine or liquor, or eat anything forbidden by the Torah; your son will be a Nazirite dedicated to Elohim from the day of his birth to the day of his death.'"

8 So Manoach prayed to Adonai and said, "Please let the messenger of Elohim whom You sent come to us again and instruct us what to do with the child who will be born." **9** Elohim answered Manoach; and the angel once again appeared to the woman as she sat in the field; but her husband Manoach was not with her. **10** So she quickly ran and told her husband, "The man who came to me the other day has once again appeared to me."

11 So Manoach arose and followed his wife to the man, and asked him, "Are you the man who spoke to my wife?"

"Yes!" he replied, "I am."

12 Manoach asked, "When your promise becomes true, how shall we bring him up, and what rules shall we obey?"

13 The angel of Adonai said to Manoach, "Tell her to carefully follow my instructions. **14** She must not eat of anything made from grapes, nor drink wine or liquor, or eat anything forbidden by the Torah. Tell her to follow all my instructions."

15 Manoach said to the angel of Adonai, "Please, stay with us, and we will prepare a young goat for your feast."

16 The angel of Adonai said to Manoach, "I will stay for a while but I will not eat your food. However, if you like you can prepare a burnt offering; you must offer it to Adonai." Manoach did not realize that the man was Adonai's angel.

17 Manoach asked the angel of Adonai, "What is your name, so that we can honor you when our son is born?"

18 Then the angel of Adonai said to him, "Why must you ask my name? My name is unknowable."

19 So Manoach took a young goat and a grain offering, and offered a sacrifice upon the rock to Adonai. Something amazing happened as Manoach and his wife looked on. **20** The flames from the altar blazed heavenward, and the angel of Adonai ascended the flames. Manoach and his wife looked on and they fell to the ground. **21** But Adonai's angel did not reappear to Manoach or to his wife. Then Manoach realized that he was truly an angel of Adonai.

22 Manoach said to his wife, "We will surely die because we have seen Elohim."

23 But his wife said to him, "If Adonai had wanted to kill us, He would not have accepted our burnt offering and grain offering, nor appeared to us, nor told us we would have a son."

24 The woman gave birth to a son, and called him Samson; and the child grew, and Adonai blessed him. **25** The spirit of Adonai began to control him in Machaneh-Dan, which is located between Tzorah and Eshtaol.

HAFTARAH for BEHA'ALOTECHA
Zechariah 2:14–4: 7

Book of Zechariah Zechariah was the next to last prophet. His visions were filled with mystical sights and riddles. He was a major factor in reenergizing the exiles after their degrading defeat and exile. His visions of a divine deity lifted the spirits and rebuilt the esteem of the once proud people.

History In 573 B.C.E. King Cyrus of Babylon permitted the Israelites to return to Jerusalem and rebuild the Temple. The Samaritans sought to hinder the Jews from rebuilding the Temple, and work was postponed. In despair, the Judeans appealed to the prophets. The prophets assured the people that the Temple would be rebuilt. For several years no work was done, but when Darius (522–486) became king, he encouraged the people to resume building the Temple.

During these years the prophets Haggai and Zechariah were a source of life and strength to the community.

Text Zechariah's task is to give an urgent message to rise up and rebuild the Temple:

> *Adonai says, O city of Zion, sing*
> *and celebrate; for I am coming,*
> *and I will live in your midst.* **2:14**

The text continues with the ordination of the High Priest Joshua:

> *This is what Adonai the Almighty says: If you will observe My commands and obey Me, then I will place you in charge of My house, and My courts, and you will be allowed to communicate with angels who are standing beside Me. Joshua the High Priest, listen closely.* **2:7–8**

Now the vision continues and Zechariah sees a golden menorah with seven lighted lamps flanked by two live trees.

An angel explains the significance of the symbols. According to some commentators, the burning candlestick represents the Judeans supported by the two olive trees, which represent the governor Zerubbabel and the High Priest Joshua.

The prophets encouraged the people and promises that Zerubbabel will succeed.

> *Adonai the Almighty says you will succeed not by might, not by power, but by My spirit. Nothing, not even a great mountain, can defeat Zerubbabel. The mountain will flatten into a plain, and Zerubbabel will set the Temple cornerstone with shouts of "Adonai is great!"* **4:6–7**

Connection   The sidrah contains the lighting of the Temple menorah by Aaron, and the haftarah contains Zechariah's vision of the rebuilt and relit Temple menorah.

Haftarah for Beha'alotecha בְּהַעֲלֹתְךָ
(Zechariah 2:14-4:7)

2 **14** Adonai says, O city of Zion, sing and celebrate; for I am coming, and I will live in your midst. **15** When Adonai comes, many nations will join Adonai and will become My people, and I will live among you; and you will know that Adonai has sent me to be your prophet. **16** And then the kingdom of Judah will be Adonai's inheritance in the holy land, and Jerusalem will be His chosen city.
17 Everyone be still;
Adonai is here;
Adonai is coming down from His holy place.

3 I saw the vision of Joshua, the High Priest, standing before the angel of Adonai, and Satan standing at Joshua's right side to accuse him.
2 And Adonai said to Satan, "Satan, Adonai criticizes you; Adonai, who has chosen Jerusalem, rejects your accusation. This man, he is like a burning coal plucked from the fire."
3 Joshua was standing before the angel, dressed in dirty clothes.
4 So the angel instructed those who stood before him, "Remove his dirty clothing." Then the angel said to Joshua, "See, I stripped your sins from you and I will clothe you with new clothing."
5 And I spoke up, "Let them also place a clean turban on his head." So they placed a clean turban on his head, and dressed him in new clothes; and the angel of Adonai stood by and watched.
6 Then the angel of Adonai instructed Joshua, saying,
7 This is what Adonai the Almighty says: If you will observe My commands and obey Me, then I will place you in charge of My house, and My courts; and you will be allowed to communicate with angels who are standing

beside Me. **8** Joshua the High Priest, listen closely, you and your fellow priests who sit before you; they are a good sign of things to come. Soon I will bring My servant Tzemach, "the Branch," a future king who will bring peace. **9** Look carefully, for the jewel that I have placed before Joshua has seven sides. I will engrave inscriptions on it, Adonai the Almighty says; in one day I will forgive the sins of the land. **10** Adonai the Almighty says, On that day, every person will invite his neighbor to come in his vineyard and under his fig tree.

 The angel who spoke to me returned and woke me, like a person who was in a deep sleep.

2 The angel asked me, "What do you see?" And I answered, "I saw a golden menorah, with a bowl on top of it, and seven lamps on it, each lamp with seven flames.

3 There was one olive tree on the right side of the bowl, and another olive tree on its left side." **4** Then I asked the angel that spoke with me, "What do those trees mean?"

5 Then the angel who spoke with me asked, "Don't you know what these are?" And I said, "No, my lord."

6 He explained, "This is God's message to Zerubbabel: Adonai the Almighty says you will succeed not by might, not by power, but by My spirit. **7** Nothing, not even a great mountain, can defeat Zerubbabel. The mountain will flatten into a plain, and Zerubbabel will set the Temple cornerstone with shouts of "Adonai is great!"

HAFTARAH for SHELACH LECHA
Joshua 2:1–24

Book of Joshua   The Book of Joshua is the sixth book in the *Tanak* and the first text in the section called *Nevi'im Rishinim*, meaning First Prophets.

Joshua, son of Nun, from the tribe of Ephraim, was an assistant to Moses and was chosen by Moses to defeat the Amalekites in Sinai.

History   As the Israelites drew close to the Promised Land, Moses gave the order for the march to halt, for he wanted time to map his strategy for the conquest of Canaan. Scouts were sent across the border, among them Caleb son of Yafunal and Joshua son of Nun, Moses' able young assistants. The scouts were ordered to find out all they could about the condition of the land, the number of troops, and the strength of the fortifications. They returned with conflicting reports. Joshua and Caleb spoke in glowing terms of the land's fertility and brought back luscious fruits as proof. Other scouts spoke in more somber, cowardly terms of well-armed soldiers and heavily fortified cities.

Moses realized that the Israelites lacked the faith and courage necessary for a successful invasion. He led them back into the desert, where they wandered for the next 40 years.

Moses, the great teacher, had grown old. The time had come to choose a leader to take his place after he had gone. Moses' choice fell on Joshua, a man loved and respected by the people and devoted to the laws of Sinai—a man, too, with a gift for military strategy. Into Joshua's capable hands Moses placed the task of invading Canaan

Text   The first obstacle to the invasion of Canaan was the capture of the heavily fortified city of Jericho, situated about five miles west of the Jordan River.

Joshua the son of Nun secretly sent two spies from Shittim, saying, "Scout the land, especially the city of Jericho." **2:1**

Two spies slipped into Jericho and, when the gates were closed, found shelter for the night with a prostitute named Rahab. Her rooms were located in one of the houses built into the city wall.

Rahab hid the two spies on the flat roof of her house under some stalks of flax and told the authorities that the spies had left before the gates were closed. In return for her bravery, Rahab asked the spies to guarantee the safety of her family.

The men said to her, "We cannot guarantee our promise which you made us swear unless you bind this scarlet cord in the window through which you let us down, and unless you bring into your house your father and mother, your brothers and sisters, and all your father's family. **2:17–18**

The spies escaped and, when they returned to Joshua, they told him that the inhabitants were terrified of the Israelites, who had already conquered the Trans-Jordan kingdoms of Sihon and Og.

They said to Joshua, "Truly Adonai has delivered the whole land into our power; and all the inhabitants of the land are scared to death of us." **2:24**

They also told Joshua that they had promised Rahab that she and her family would be saved. Her house would be identified by a red cord hanging from her window.

Connection The connection between the sidrah and the haftarah are the stories of the spies sent to Canaan by Moses and Joshua, respectively.

2 Joshua the son of Nun secretly sent two spies from Shittim, saying, "Scout the land, especially the city of Jericho." So they went, and came to the house of a prostitute named Rahab, and slept there that night. **2** Someone told the king of Jericho, "Israelites have come here tonight to spy out our land." **3** So the king of Jericho sent soldiers to Rahab, saying, "Bring out the men who came to you, who slept in your house, because they have come to spy out our whole land."

4 But Rahab took the two men and hid them; and she said, "Yes, the men came to my house, but I did not know where they were from; **5** and at sunset, as the gates were about to close, the men left; I do not know where they went. Pursue them; quickly chase and catch them, for you will overtake them."

6 But she had taken them up to the roof, and hidden them under the stalks of flax which were spread out. **7** So the soldiers chased the spies along the Jordan as far as the shallow crossing place; and as soon as the soldiers left, the city gate was shut. **8** Before the spies went to sleep, she went up to them on the roof.

9 She said to the men, "I know that Adonai has given the land to you, and all of us are afraid of you, and all the inhabitants of the land are shivering with terror because of you. **10** For we heard how Adonai made a path through the water of the Red Sea, when you came out of Egypt and how you defeated and destroyed Sihon and Og, the two kings of the Amorites, east of the Jordan River, whom you totally destroyed.

11 When we heard it, we shivered in fear; now, because of you, there is no courage remaining in any man; for Adonai is with you, He is your Elohim in heaven above, and on earth beneath. **12** Now, please swear to me in the name of Adonai that since I have shown you kindness, that you will also deal kindly with my family and give me a guarantee **13** that you will spare my father and mother, my brothers and sisters, and all that they have, and save us from death."

14 The spies assured her, "Our lives are your guarantee. If you do not tell anyone of our mission, we will deal kindly and faithfully with you when Adonai gives us the land." **15** Then she let them down by a red rope through the window; for her house was on the other side of the city, so that she lived within the wall.

16 She said to them, "Run to the mountains, or the soldiers will find you; hide there three days, until the soldiers return, and then you may go your way."

17 The men said to her, "We cannot guarantee our promise which you made us swear **18** unless you bind this scarlet cord in the window through which you let us down, and unless you bring into your house your father and mother, your brothers and sisters, and all your father's family. **19** If anyone leaves your house into the street, he will be responsible for his own death, and we will be innocent; however, if anyone in your house is harmed, it will be our fault. **20** But if you tell anyone of our mission, then we will be released from the promise which you made us swear."

21 She answered, "I accept your terms." Rahab sent them away, and they left; and she fastened the scarlet cord to her window. **22** They left for the mountains, and hid for three days until the soldiers returned. The soldiers searched for them all along the road but could not find them. **23** Then the two men came from the mountains, and crossed the river, and reported to Joshua the son of Nun all that had happened to them.

24 They said to Joshua, "Truly Adonai has delivered the whole land into our power; and all the inhabitants of the land are scared to death of us."

HAFTARAH for KORACH
1 Samuel 11:14–12:22

Books of Samuel I and II   See haftarah Shemini, page 174.

History   Judge and prophet Samuel realized that if Israel was to survive, its people had to be united and inspired. Like the priests and Levites of earlier times, he began traveling through the land, encouraging the people everywhere to hold fast to their faith.

On his travels, Samuel attracted many followers, men who were uplifted by his words and, like himself, felt called upon to talk to the people about Adonai and hope. Samuel's disciples would sing and play the harp, tell the stories of Israel's past, and expound the laws of the Torah.

When Samuel grew old, the elders of the tribes became fearful about the future. The tribes were worn out by the constant warfare with their enemies. They felt the need for a central authority which could mold them into a unified, strong nation. The people appealed to Samuel, "Appoint us a king who will rule us, like the other nations." Samuel was deeply troubled when the tribal elders asked him to select a king to rule over them.

Text   Samuel (ca. 1040–1010 B.C.E.) realized that life under a king would be different in many ways. The people would have to maintain a grand style of living for the king. A king would require a royal palace and servants. Hitherto the people had defended the land of their own free will, but with a king, a regular army would be needed, with men from each tribe to guard and serve in the armed forces. Taxes would have to be levied to meet the government's civil and military expenses. One by one, Samuel presented these arguments against the establishment of a kingdom, but the elders refused to be discouraged. The people had set their hearts on having a king. Reluctantly, Samuel bowed to their wishes.

Then Samuel said to the people, "Come, let us go to Gilgal and choose a king."

So all the people went to Gilgal; and there they crowned Saul king. They sacrificed peace offerings to Adonai; and there Saul and all the people of Israel celebrated. **11:14–15**

Connection The sidrah recounts the story of Korach, from the tribe of Levi, and Abiram and Dathan from the tribe of Reuben, who assembled 250 tribal leaders and challenged the leadership of Moses and Aaron.

Korach was jealous of the special privileges and power of Moses and Aaron. Dathan and Abiram were discouraged and frightened by the desert hardships.

Like Moses, Samuel was under constant pressure for a change in leadership and policies. Like Moses, Samuel took a loosely knit group of tribes and created a united nation.

Both Moses and Samuel consulted Adonai and under his guidance chose a new leadership.

Haftarah for Korach קֹרַח
(1 Samuel 11:14–12:22)

11 **14** Then Samuel said to the people, "Come, let us go to Gilgal and choose a king."

15 So all the people went to Gilgal; and there they crowned Saul king. They sacrificed peace offerings to Adonai; and there Saul and all the people of Israel celebrated.

12 Samuel said to the Israelites, "Behold, I have listened to everything you have said to me, and given you a king. **2** And now you have a king to lead you. Now I am old and gray; and my sons are with you; and I have been your leader from my youth until this day. **3** Here I am; can anyone tell me in the presence of Adonai and his chosen king: Whose ox have I taken? Or whom have I cheated? Or whom have I mistreated? Or from whose hand have I taken a bribe to shut my eyes? I will make it right."

4 They answered, "No! You did not cheat or mistreat us, and you accepted no bribes from anyone."

5 He said to them, "Adonai is against you, and his chosen king is my witness this day, that I have not done anything evil." And they answered, "Yes! That is true."

6 Samuel said to the people, "It is Adonai who appointed Moses and Aaron, who brought your ancestors out of the land of Egypt.

7 "Now stand while I plead with you before Adonai and remind you of all the great things that Adonai did for you and your ancestors.

8 "Jacob went down into Egypt, and your ancestors cried to God; then God sent Moses and Aaron, who brought your ancestors out of Egypt, and they settled in this land. **9** But they forgot Adonai, and he let them be defeated by Sisera, captain of the army of Hatzor, and by the Philistines, and by the king of Moab.

10 "Again, your ancestors cried to Adonai, and said, 'Yes! We have sinned! Yes, we have turned away from Adonai, and have worshipped the idols of Baal and the Ashtaroth; now please save us from our enemies, and we will worship only you.'

11 "Adonai send the judges Jerubbaal, Bedan, Yiphtach, and Samuel, and rescued you from the enemies around you, and you lived in safety.

12 "When you saw that Nachash the Ammonite king was advancing to attack, you insisted upon having a king, even though Adonai was your king. **13** Now here is the king whom you have asked for and chosen. Adonai has granted your request and set a king over you.

14 "If you fear Adonai and worship Him, and listen to Him, and do not rebel against Adonai's commandment, and if both you and the king who reigns over you follow Adonai . . . **15** But if you are stubborn and do not listen to Adonai's voice, but rebel against Adonai's commandments, then Adonai will punish you as He did your ancestors.

16 "Now stand and see the great thing, which Adonai will perform before you. **17** Today is the wheat harvest. I will pray to Adonai; He will send thunder and rain; and you will understand that your wickedness was great when you asked Adonai for a king."

18 So Samuel prayed to Adonai; and that day Adonai sent thunder and rain, and all the people were terrified of God and Samuel.

19 And the Israelites cried to Samuel, "Pray for us to Adonai your Lord or we will die; now we have added to our sins by asking for a king."

20 And Samuel said to the people, "Do not be afraid, because you have done this evil; you must always follow Adonai, and worship Him with all your hearts. **21** Do not turn and follow useless idols. **22** Adonai will never abandon His people, because that would dishonor His great name, because Adonai has chosen you as His special nation."

INTRODUCTION TO
HAFTARAH for CHUKKAT
Judges 11: 1–33

Book of Judges   See haftarah Beshallach, page 127.

History   In the beginning of the eleventh century B.C.E. the Ammonites were raiding Gilead and threatened to drive out the Israelite population. The Israelites prepared to resist and called upon an outcast named Yiphthach to lead them. He was the son of a prostitute and was known as a bandit chief in the desert area near the Sea of Galilee.

Yiphthach was from Gilead near the Jabbok river, a branch of the Jordan. It was a well-watered land with wooded hills and lush pasture land. The tribes of Reuben and Gad had settled the area. During the period of the Judges the Israelite inhabitants (1128–1100 B.C.E.) were oppressed by the Ammonites.

Text   The leader of Gilead asked Yiphthach to command the Israeli forces.

First Yiphthach sent emissaries to the Ammonites and tried to settle the conflict peacefully, but the offer was refused.

About this time, the Ammonites declared war against Israel, so the leaders of Gilead went to Yiphthach in the land of Tov. They said to Yiphthach, "Come and become our leader, and help us defend ourselves against the Ammonites." **11:4–6**

The Ammonites claimed that the land was theirs and had been forcefully seized by the Israelites.

To improve his prospects in the approaching battle, Yiphthach swore:

Yiphthach swore a vow to Adonai and said, "If you help me defeat the Ammonites, then whatever comes out of my house to meet me when I return in peace from the Ammonites shall belong to Adonai, and I will sacrifice it as a burnt offering." **11:30–31**

233

Yiphthach assembled his army and defeated the Ammonites. When he returned victorious, he was met by his only daughter. She accepted her father's decision and was sacrificed.

Connection   The connection between the sidrah and the haftarah are the battles for survival. In the sidrah the Israelites try to negotiate a peaceful settlement with the Ammonites, who refuse to allow the Israelites to pass through their territory. Sihon, king of the Ammonites, attacks the Israelites, but is defeated.

In the haftarah the Israelites of Gilead also try to negotiate a peaceful settlement. The Ammonites refuse and are defeated by Yiphthach.

Haftarah for Chukkat חֻקַּת
(Judges 11:1-33)

11 Now Yiphthach the Gileadite was a mighty warrior, but he was the son of a prostitute; and Gilead was Yiphthach's father. **2** Gilead's wife gave birth to sons, and when the sons grew up, they drove out Yiphthach, saying to him, "You shall not inherit anything in our father's house; for you are the son of a prostitute."

3 Then Yiphthach fled from his brothers and settled in the land of Tov, and outlaws joined Yiphthach and they went out raiding with him. **4** About this time, the Ammonites declared war against Israel, **5** so the leaders of Gilead went to Yiphthach in the land of Tov. **6** They said to Yiphthach, "Come and become our leader, and help us defend ourselves against the Ammonites."

7 Yiphthach replied to the leaders of Gilead, "Didn't you hate me, and drive me away from my father's house? Now you come to me because you are under attack?"

8 The leaders of Gilead said to Yiphthach, "We need you now to help us fight the Ammonites; if you do, you will become the ruler of all the inhabitants of Gilead."

9 Yiphthach replied to the leaders of Gilead, "If I return home to fight against the Ammonites, and Adonai makes me victorious, I will be your ruler."

10 The leaders of Gilead said to Yiphthach, "Let Adonai be a witness between us; we promise to do whatever you say."

11 So Yiphthach went with the leaders of Gilead, and they made him ruler and commander of the army. Yiphthach repeated the terms of the agreement before Adonai in Mitzpah. **12** Then Yiphthach sent a message to the king of the Ammonites, saying, "What is the problem between us, that you have come to fight against my land?" **13** The king of the Ammonites answered the messengers of Yiphthach: "When Israel came out of Egypt, they took away my land, from the Arnon even to the Jabbok, and to the Jordan; now I want them to return the cities."

14 Yiphthach sent messengers again to the king of the Ammonites. **15** And he said to him, "Yiphthach says, Israel did not take the land of Moab or the land of the Ammonites. **16** But when they came out of Egypt, and Israel marched through the wilderness to the Red Sea, and returned to Kadesh, **17** then Israel sent messengers to the king of Edom, saying, 'Please let us pass through your land'; but the king of Edom refused to listen. They also asked permission from the king of Moab, but he also refused to listen; Israel remained in Kadesh.

18 "Next, they marched through the wilderness, and avoided the lands of Edom and Moab, and came to the eastern border of the land of Moab, and they camped on the other side of the Arnon, but they did not cross the border of Moab, for the Arnon was the border of Moab. **19** Then the Israelites sent messengers to Sihon the king of the Amorites, the king of Heshbon; and Israel said to him, 'Please allow us to pass through your land to our country.' **20** But Sihon did not trust Israel to pass through his border; so Sihon mobilized all his army, and camped in Yahatz, and attacked Israel. **21** But Adonai, the Savior of Israel, gave Sihon and his army into the hand of Israel, and they defeated them; so Israel took possession of all the land of the Amorites, and its inhabitants. **22** They conquered all the land of the Amorites, from the Arnon to the Jabbok, and from the wilderness to the Jordan River.

23 "Now Adonai, the Savior of Israel, has driven out

the Amorites from before His people Israel; what right do you have to take it over? **24** Will you not take what your god Chemosh gives you? Everything Adonai has given us, we will hold onto. **25** Do you think that you are better than Balak the son of Zippor, king of Moab? Did he ever quarrel with Israel, or did he ever declare war against them? **26** Israel dwelt in Heshbon and its villages, and in Aroer and its villages and in all the cities on either side of the Arnon, for three hundred years. Why did you not retake them during all that time? **27** I have not harmed you, but you are the one who does wrong by waging war against me. Let Adonai be the judge between the children of Israel and the children of Ammon."

28 But the king of the Ammonites ignored Yiphthach's message.

29 At that time, the spirit of Adonai entered Yiphthach, and he passed through Gilead and Manasseh, then he passed on to Mitzpeh of Gilead, and from Mitzpeh of Gilead he passed through the land of the Ammonites. **30** Yiphthach swore a vow to Adonai and said, "If you help me defeat the Ammonites, **31** then whatever comes out of my house to meet me when I return in peace from the Ammonites shall belong to Adonai, and I will sacrifice it as a burnt offering."

32 So Yiphthach led his army against the Ammonites, and Adonai helped him, and he was victorious. **33** He pursued them from Aroer to Minnith, twenty cities, as far as Abel-Cheranim, and won a great victory. So the Ammonites were defeated by the children of Israel.

INTRODUCTION TO
HAFTARAH for BALAK
Micah 5:6–6:8

Book of Micah The Book of Micah is the sixth volume of *Trey Asar*, the Twelve Minor Prophets. Micah was a young man of humble birth from the small village of Moresheth-Gath in the Judean hills.

History After Israel's fall in 722 B.C.E. Merodach-baladan, king of Babylon, tried to form a coalition with Judah and organize the nations of western Asia to defy Assyria. The prophet Isaiah warned King Hezekiah (715–687 B.C.E.), son of Ahaz, that he would be trapped in the middle of a power struggle.

Isaiah was joined by the prophet Micah. Micah had also warned the ruler of Israel not to rely on the false promises and the power of foreign allies.

Text Micah grieves and weeps for the sufferings of the people of Israel. He warns the people of Judah not to forsake the Torah, just as the prophet Amos had done before him. Micah reminds the people that Adonai wants more of them than just sacrificial offerings.

The prophet Isaiah and Micah shared the same ideas of faith and peace. Their voices were heard throughout Judah, and these two prophets left a deep impression.

Predicting the destruction of the northern kingdom of Judah by the Assyrians (722–721 B.C.E.), Isaiah and Micah wrote prophecies of comfort and compassion during these dark days.

Micah in his opening prophecy sends a message of hope and renewal. He predicts that Israel will become like a lion and destroy its enemies.

Your victorious hand will be lifted over Your enemies,
and all Your enemies will be devastated. **5:8**

Micah preached:

> *O mortal,*
> *Adonai has told you what is right,*
> *and what Adonai expects from you;*
> *He only wants you to act justly,*
> *be good,*
> *and walk humbly with Adonai.* **6:8**

Connection   The connection between the sidrah and the haftarah is the story Balak, king of the Moabites, who hires the prophet Balaam to curse the Israelites.

> *"My people,*
> *remember Balak,*
> *king of Moab,*
> *and remember what Balaam,*
> *the son of Beor answered him.* **6:5**

Haftarah for Balak בָּלָק
(Micah 5:6–6:8)

5 **6** The remnant of Jacob
will be surrounded by many peoples;
but they will be sent by Adonai,
like dew to cover the earth,
like showers upon the grass,
which do not look to any person
or place their hopes in humans.
7 And the remnant of Jacob
will be surrounded by many peoples;
Jacob will be like a lion
among the animals of the forest,
like a young lion among the flocks of sheep,
which when he passes through
and tears them to shreds,
there is no one to save them.
8 Your victorious hand
will be lifted over Your enemies,
and all Your enemies will be devastated.
9 Adonai says,
On that day, I will wipe out your horses
and demolish your chariots.
10 I will destroy your cities
and level your strongholds.
11 I will remove the fortunetellers,
and you will have no more false prophets.
12 I will destroy your idols
and stone images
from your midst;
you will no longer worship idols and images.
13 I will remove the Asherim poles
from your midst
and demolish your enemies.
14 I will become furious,

and I will take revenge against the nations,
because they have not obeyed.

6 Now listen what Adonai says:
Plead your case to the mountains,
and let the hills hear your voice.
2 Pay attention,
mountains and rocks,
the foundations of the earth.
Adonai has a problem with His people,
and He will quarrel with Israel.
3 My people, how have I harmed you?
How have I wronged you?
Please tell Me.
4 Didn't I bring you out of the land of Egypt,
and free you from the house of slavery?
Didn't I send you Moses,
Aaron, and Miriam
to lead and teach you?
5 My people,
remember the evil plans of Balak
king of Moab,
and remember what Balaam
the son of Beor answered him;
remember what happened
on your journey from Shittim
to Gilgal,
and you will remember Adonai's righteous deeds.
6 With what offering
shall I come before Adonai,
and bow down before Him?
Shall I bring Him burnt offerings
of young calves?
7 Will Adonai be pleased with me
if I offer thousands of rams,
and ten thousands of rivers of oil?
Shall I sacrifice my firstborn,

the fruit of my body
for the sin of my soul?
8 O mortal,
Adonai has told you what is right,
and what Adonai expects from you;
He only wants you to act justly,
be good,
and walk humbly with Adonai.

HAFTARAH for PINCHAS
1 Kings 18:46–19:21

Book of Kings I and II   See haftarah Vayera, page 68.

History   The prophet Elijah was beloved by the people of Israel and was feared and hated by Queen Jezebel.

When Omri, king of Israel, died, Ahab became king. Intent on cementing his pact with Phoenicia, Ahab married a Phoenician princess, Jezebel. She brought her idols and priests to her new home in Samaria. Strongly influenced by Jezebel, Ahab set up shrines to Baal, the most popular Phoenician god.

Jezebel, with the priests of Baal, set about teaching the Phoenician way of life to the people of Israel, persecuting anyone who defied her. Many of the prophets were killed at her command. Many others escaped, for the people protected them.

Elijah's finest miracle took place on the slopes of Mount Carmel, where he challenged the Phoenician priests to a contest. They both prepared sacrifices on wood. The 450 priests, using music, prayers, and dancing, urged Baal to set the wood on fire, but nothing happened. Elijah prayed to Adonai, and the wood burst into flame.

Elijah then ordered the 450 priests of Baal to be seized and killed. Several hours later another miracle occurred: a rainstorm soaked the drought-stricken land of Israel.

Enraged, Queen Jezebel forced Elijah to flee. He fled into the city of Beersheba in the desert. There an angel appeared and ordered him to walk to the Mount of Adonai in the wilderness of Sinai. There Adonai appeared and instructed him to find Elisha and call him to prophecy.

Adonai also told Elijah to return to Damascus and appoint Hazael to be king of Aram and Jehu the son of Nimshi to be king of Israel.

Text   After the prophets of Baal were killed, Jezebel threatened Elijah.

*Let the gods punish me if by tomorrow I do not take
your life as you took the lives of the prophets.*   **19:2**

So Elijah fled to Beersheba and rested under a broom tree.
There Adonai appeared to him and sent him to Mount Sinai.
There in a great storm, a voice spoke to him and told him to
return to Damascus.

*When you get there, crown Hazael king over Aram,
crown Jehu the son of Nimshi to be king of Israel, and
anoint Elisha son of Shaphat of Abel-mehola to be the
prophet after you.*   **19:15-16**

Elijah left and found Elisha plowing with a team of oxen.
There Elijah placed his mantle on him. Then Elisha, without
hesitation, asked permission to kiss his parents goodbye and
then left to join Elijah.

Connection   The connecting link between the sidrah and
the haftarah are the passions and devotion to Adonai of
Pinchas and Elijah.

Haftarah for Pinchas פִּנְחָס
(1 Kings 18:46–19:21)

(Until the 17th of Tamuz)

18 **46** And Adonai inspired Elijah; and he wrapped his cloak around him, and ran alongside Ahab's chariot all the way to the entrance of Jezreel.

19 Ahab told his wife Jezebel everything Elijah had done, how he had killed all the prophets of Baal. **2** Then Jezebel sent a messenger to Elijah, saying, "Let the gods punish me if by this time tomorrow I do not take your life as you took the lives of the prophets." **3** When Elijah read the message, he arose, and fled for his life to the town of Beersheba in Judah, and left his servant there. **4** Then he walked all day, deep into the desert, and came and rested under a broom tree. He prayed that he might die; he said, "Adonai, I have had enough. Just take away my life, for I am no better than my ancestors."
5 Then he lay down and slept under the broom tree. Suddenly, an angel awakened him and said, "Get up and eat." **6** He looked, and there was a cake of bread on hot stones, and a jar of water at his head. So he ate and drank and lay down again.
7 Then Adonai's angel appeared again and said to him, "Get up and eat, because you will be going on a long journey."
8 So he got up again, and ate and drank, and the food gave him strength to walk forty days and nights to Horeb (Sinai), the mountain of Adonai. **9** There he found a cave, and slept in it; Adonai spoke to him: "What are you doing in there?"
10 Elijah replied, "All-powerful Adonai, I have faithfully served You, Adonai Tzvaot, but the Israelites

have abandoned Your covenant, destroyed Your altars, and killed Your prophets. I am the only one left alive, and now they are trying to kill me too."

11 And He said, "Go, and stand on the mountain before Me." And Adonai passed by, and a strong wind shook the mountain, and shattered the rocks in pieces; but Adonai was not in the wind. Then an earthquake followed the wind, but Adonai was not in the earthquake. **12** Now a fire followed the earthquake, but Adonai was not in the fire; and a still, small voice came. **13** When Elijah heard it, he covered his face in his robe and stood in the entrance of the cave. And then a voice spoke to him: "Elijah, what are you doing here?"

14 He said, "I have faithfully served Adonai, the Almighty Adonai Tzvaot. The Israelites have abandoned Your covenant, smashed down Your altars, and killed Your prophets. I am the only one still alive, and they are trying to kill me."

15 Adonai said to Elijah, "Go back and return to the desert near Damascus; and when you get there, crown Hazael to be king over Aram. **16** Crown Jehu the son of Nimshi to be king of Israel; and Elisha the son of Shaphat of Abel-meholah to be the prophet instead of you. **17** Anyone that escapes from the sword of Hazael will be killed, and anyone who escapes from the sword of Jehu will be killed by Elisha. **18** However, I will save seven thousand in Israel who have never prayed to Baal or embraced him."

19 So Elijah left, and found Elisha the son of Shaphat, who was plowing with a team of oxen. There were eleven other men, each with a team of oxen, and Elisha and his team was the twelfth; Elijah went over to him and placed his mantle on him.

20 So Elijah left his oxen and ran after Elijah, saying, "Before I leave, please let me kiss my father and mother goodbye, and then I will follow you." He said to him: "Go back; and think about the responsibilities I have placed upon you."

21 Elisha returned to his oxen, killed them, and built a fire and roasted their flesh, and everyone ate. Then he got up and followed Elijah and assisted him.

HAFTARAH for MATTOT
Jeremiah 1:1–2:3

Book of Jeremiah   See haftarah Bo, page 122.

History   The first of the month of Av is preceded by Three Haftarot of Rebuke. This is the first of the three, which deals with the destruction of Jerusalem.

Jeremiah continually placed his life in danger by criticizing the ruling class and the sins of the populace.

In 597 B.C.E. Nebuchadnezzar's troops stormed Jerusalem and carried King Jehoiachin, who was 18 years old, as well as many important females into captivity.

The conqueror left Mattaniah the son of King Josiah as a puppet ruler on the throne. Mattaniah changed his name to Zedekiah. After ten years of Babylonian rule, Judah revolted a second time, refusing to heed Jeremiah's warnings to rely on Adonai and to refuse any alliance that involved military action.

As Jeremiah predicted, the Babylonians furiously attacked and in 587–586 B.C.E. captured Jerusalem and leveled the Temple. They killed the sons of Zedekiah before his eyes and blinded the king and removed him to Babylon. The sovereign state of Judah was no more.

Text   As a young man, Jeremiah received the call to prophecy. Adonai informed him:

> *Before you were born,*
> *I made you holy.* **1:5**

Then Jeremiah said:

> *"Adonai, Adonai!*
> *Just look at me;*
> *I can hardly speak,*
> *for I am only a small boy."*

> *But Adonai answered me,*
> *Do not say, "I am just a youngster."*
> *You will go wherever I send you.* **1: 6–7**

In addition, Jeremiah never had a family. Adonai instructed him not to marry because a terrible fate would await them, and they would die gruesome deaths.

At the end of the haftarah, Jeremiah consoles the nation. Adonai says:

> *Israel was holy to Adonai.*
> *Israel was the first of my children.*
> *Anyone that attempted to harm Israel was punished,*
> *And calamity overtook them.* **2:3**

Connection This haftarah from Jeremiah precedes the fast of Tisha B'av. The particular reading was chosen because Jeremiah is believed to be the author of the Book of Lamentations, which is read on Tisha B'av.

Haftarah for Mattot מַטּוֹת
(Jeremiah 1:1-2:3)

1 This is the message of the priest Jeremiah the son of Hilkiah, living in Anathoth in the land of Benjamin. **2** Adonai spoke to him during the reign of Josiah the son of Amon, king of Judah, in the thirteenth year of his rule. **3** It came also during the reign of Jehoiakim, the son of Josiah, king of Judah. He continued to speak to him until the end of the eleventh year of Zedekiah the son of Josiah, king of Judah, until the capture of Jerusalem in the fifth month.

4 Adonai gave me this message, saying,

5 Before you were born,
I knew you were special,
and before you were born,
I made you holy;
I appointed you a prophet
to the world.

6 Then I said,
"Adonai, Adonai!
Just look at me;
I can hardly speak,
for I am only a small boy."

7 But Adonai answered me:
Do not say, "I am just a youngster."
You will go wherever I send you
and speak to whomever I command you.

8 Do not be afraid of anybody,
for I will be at your side.

9 Then Adonai reached out
and touched my mouth,
and said to me,
Now I have placed My words into your mouth.

10 Today you begin;
I have sent you to uproot and destroy,

and then to start over,
and to build and to plant.

11 Adonai spoke to me again and said, Jeremiah, what do you see? I replied, "I see a branch of an almond tree."

12 Then Adonai said, That is right, and it means that I intend to carry out my threats of punishment.

13 Then Adonai spoke to me a second time and said, Jeremiah, what do you see? I answered, "I see a boiling pot of water facing toward the north."

14 Then Adonai continuing, said to me, Terror will pour from the north and scald all the inhabitants of Judah. **15** I will summon all the armies of the kingdom of the north. They will come, and each one will place his throne at the entrance of the gates of Jerusalem and all along its walls, and all the cities of Judah. **16** Then I will pronounce judgments against the inhabitants of Judah for their wickedness; for the people have deserted Me, and worshipped idols, and worshipped manmade idols. **17** Now, get up and tell them everything that I told you. Do not be afraid of them, or else I will make you look foolish before them. **18** My power will make you as strong as a fortified city, as solid as an iron pillar and bronze walls. You will oppose the kings of Judah, its princes, its priests, and the people of Judah. **19** They will attack you, but they cannot win. Jeremiah, I am with you.

2 Then Adonai said to me,
2 Go out and shout in the streets of Jerusalem,
and say,
"This is what Adonai says:
I remember
when you were just a newlywed;
you loved as a bride,
and you followed Me
through the sandy wilderness.
3 In those days,
Israel was holy to Adonai.

Israel was the first of my children.
Anyone that attempted to harm Israel
was punished,
and calamity overtook them.

HAFTARAH for MASSAY
Jeremiah 2:4–28, 3:4, 4:1–2

Book of Jeremiah See haftarah Bo, page 122.

History Jeremiah criticized the Judeans for their alliances of protection with Assyria and Egypt against the powerful Babylonian war machine.

Jeremiah asked: What have you gained with your alliances with Assyria and Egypt? You drank the waters of the Nile and became stupefied. You swallowed their promises, hook, line, and sinker, and you have become a sacrificial pawn in a powerful chess game.

Text Jeremiah angrily criticizes the Judean nation for its lack of faith and gratitude and for its idol worship.

> *I brought you into a fruitful land,*
> *to enjoy its foods and its beauty*
> *but when you came in*
> *you corrupted My land,*
> *and made My heritage an abomination.* **2:7**

Even though Judah disobeyed Adonai, Adonai says:

> *Despite everything,*
> *I still care for you, . . .*
> *and I will continue*
> *to care for your children and grandchildren.* **2:9**

In conclusion, Adonai is forgiving. Jeremiah pleads with the Judeans and brings a message of hope.
Adonai says:

> *Israel, if you return to Me,*
> *and if you remove your idols*
> *from My sight, and do not waver,*
> *if you swear,*
> *"As Adonai lives,"*

in truth, in justice, and in righteousness,
you will be a blessing to nations. **4:1–2**

Connection   The haftarah is read two weeks before the sad holiday of Tisha B'av.

It is a Jewish tradition not to end a haftarah on a note of despair and gloom, so verses have been added from chapters 3 and 4 which depict the recognition of Adonai as the Father of the nation and of better times when Israel does teshuvah and returns to Adonai.

Haftarah for Massay מַסְעֵי
(Jeremiah 2:4-28, 3:4, 4:1-2)

2 **4** House of Jacob,
and all the families of Israel.
Listen closely to Adonai's message,
5 This is what Adonai says:
What weakness did your ancestors find in Me,
that they deserted Me,
and followed worthless idols,
and then they themselves became worthless?
6 They do not even ask,
"Where is Adonai who freed us
from the land of Egypt;
who led us through the wilderness,
through a land of deserts and rocks,
a waterless land of death,
a land where no one dares to travel
and where no one lives?"
7 I brought you into a fruitful land,
to enjoy its foods and its beauty;
but when you came in,
you corrupted My land,
and made My heritage an abomination.
8 The priests did not ask,
"Where is Adonai?"
The priest ignored My commandments,
and the rulers rebelled against Me.
The prophets worshipped the idol Baal,
and wasted their time with mumbo jumbo prayer.
9 Despite everything,
I still care for you,
Adonai says,
and I will continue
to care for your children and grandchildren.
10 Sail to Cyprus,

to the isles of the Kittites and check;
travel the deserts to Kedar and ask,
"Has anything like this ever happened?
11 Has a nation ever abandoned its gods,
even though they are false gods?"
But my people have exchanged
their true and glorious god
for a worthless idol.
12 Adonai says,
the heavens were astonished;
were horrified;
were shocked.
13 My people have committed two evils:
they have rejected Me,
the fountain of living waters,
and they have built leaking reservoirs
which cannot collect water.
14 Is Israel a servant?
Why has Israel become a nation of slaves?
Why is Israel a slave?
Why has Israel become a captured nation?
15 Lions have roared and growled
over Israel's carcass;
they have destroyed his land,
and his cities are in ruins,
without living souls.
16 The Egyptians from the cities of Noph and Tachpanches
have destroyed the crown of Israel.
17 You brought all of this upon yourself;
Adonai was your leader,
but you deserted Adonai the Almighty.
18 And now,
what have you gained in your alliances
with Egypt and Assyria,
in your drinking the water of the Nile
and becoming her slave?
19 Adonai the Almighty says,

Your own sins will punish you,
and your mistakes will harm you.
I want you to understand
that you have committed a grave error because
you have rejected Adonai the Almighty;
neither is the fear of Me in you.
20 Years ago,
you freed yourself away from your yoke,
and threw away your restraints,
and you said,
"I will not worship idols":
But now on every mountaintop
and under every large tree
you prostituted yourself
by worshipping idols.
21 I planted you as a healthy vine,
from a perfect seed;
and you changed into a wild plant
which produces only sour grapes.
22 Even though you wash yourself with strong soap,
the stain of your corruption
is still before Me,
says Adonai the Almighty.
23 How dare you say,
"I have not sinned,
I have not worshipped idols"?
Go search any valley,
and see the sins you have committed;
you are like a wild young camel
used to the desert mating;
24 a wild donkey used to the wilderness,
who sniffs up the wind.
Who can control it?
Those who seek you
will not grow tired;
they will find her.
25 Save your feet from bareness,

and your throat from thirst.
But you say,
"No, there is no hope,
for I have fallen in love with strangers,
and I cannot stop loving them."
26 Just as the thief is ashamed when he is caught,
so will your kings, your princes,
your priests, and your prophets
of the house of Israel be ashamed;
27 you who pray to a piece of wood and say,
"You are my father,"
and to a statue,
"You gave birth to me,"
they turned their backs to Me,
But in times of their trouble,
they will cry,
"Arise! Save us."
28 Where are those idols
that you made?
Let them rise up;
see if they can save you
in the time of trouble;
Judah, you have as many idols
as your cities.

(*Ashkenazim add*)

3 **4** Now you say,
"My Father,
You are the friend of my youth."

(*Sephardim add*)

4 Adonai says,
Israel, if you return to me,
and if you remove your idols
from My sight, and do not waver,

2 if you swear,
"As Adonai lives,"
in truth, in justice, and in righteousness;
you will be a blessing to nations.

INTRODUCTION TO
HAFTARAH for DEVARIM
Isaiah 1:1–27

Book of Isaiah   See haftarah Bereshit, page 51.

History   The days between the seventeenth of Tammuz and the ninth of Av are considered days of mourning, for they witnessed the destruction of Jerusalem, beginning with the breaching of the walls on the seventeenth of Tammuz and the burning of the Temple on the ninth of Av. Since exactly three weeks passes between the two events, this period is known as the "three weeks."

The sad mood of the "three weeks" is accentuated by three special haftarot called Haftarot of Admonition. On the first Saturday, we recited Jeremiah 1:1–2:3; on the second Saturday, Jeremiah 2:4–28; and on the third Saturday the haftarah of Devarim, Isaiah 1:1–27.

The third Saturday is called Shabbat Chazon, from the first Hebrew word of the haftarah.

Isaiah lived in the latter part of the eighth century. He witnessed the fall of Jerusalem in 734 B.C.E. and the fall of Israel in 722 B.C.E. In 722 he witnessed the siege of Jerusalem by Sennacherib of Assyria.

Throughout this time Isaiah provided counsel in time of war. In times of peace he was the conscience of society, fighting for the rights of the weak and providing a vision that the future could bring.

Text   In the prophecy, Isaiah severely criticizes the Judeans. He says:

Israel, you are a sinful nation,
a people loaded with guilt;
you are descendants of evildoers,
children who know only corruption.
They have rejected Adonai;
they despised the Holy One of Israel;
they are completely cut off. **1:4**

Then he says that Adonai is interested not in ceremony, but in ethics and morality. He says:

> *Remove the evil of your deeds*
> *from My sight.*
> *Do only good deeds;*
> *work for justice,*
> *help the unfortunate,*
> *relieve the homeless,*
> *defend the widows.* **1:16–17**

The haftarah ends with an upbeat message:

> *First, I will restore your good judges*
> *as in days of old, and restore honest leaders.*
> *Then Jerusalem will once again be called*
> *the City of Justice, the Faithful City.*
> *Zion and her people*
> *will be reformed with justice and faith.* **1:26–27**

Connection   This haftarah is chanted with sad notes and is read before Tisha B'av as a warning to future generations about the consequences of the lack of morality.

Haftarah for Devarim דְּבָרִים
(Isaiah 1:1–27)

1 During the reigns of Uzziah, Jotham, Ahaz, and Hezekiah, kings of Judah, Isaiah the son of Amotz had a vision in which he saw what was going to happen to Judah and Jerusalem.

2 Adonai has spoken:
O heavens and earth,
I cared for and raised children,
but they rejected Me.

3 Even the ox recognized his master,
and the donkey the master
that feeds him;
but Israel has not learned;
My people still do not understand.

4 Israel, you are a sinful nation,
a people loaded with guilt;
you are descendants of evildoers,
children who know only corruption.
They have rejected Adonai;
they despised the Holy One of Israel;
they are completely cut off.

5 Why do you continue to ask for punishment?
Why do you continue to rebel?
Your brain is injured,
and your heart is weak.

6 From head to toe
you are covered in cuts, bruises,
and infected sores filled with pus;
they have not been cleaned
or bandaged, or medicated with olive oil.

7 Your country is in ruins;
your cities burned to ash.

While you watch,
foreigners destroy your land;
and it is abandoned.
8 And beautiful Jerusalem
is left like a hut in a vineyard,
like a shack in a field of dead cucumbers,
like a city under siege.
9 If Adonai the Almighty
had not saved a few survivors,
Zion would have been completely destroyed
like Sodom and Gomorrah.
10 You rulers of Sodom,
listen to the word;
you people of Gomorrah,
listen to the law of Adonai.
11 Adonai says,
Your sacrifices mean nothing to Me.
Do not bring Me any more offerings of rams and cattle.
I take no joy
in the sight of the blood of bullocks, lambs, or he-goats.
12 Why do you continue
to crowd My Temple with your sacrifices?
13 Stop bringing worthless sacrifices;
your offering of incense is disgusting to Me.
New Moon, Sabbath, and the Festivals—
I cannot stand the hypocrisy of your celebrations.
14 I detest your New Moon Festival,
and all other feasts.
To Me, they are a heavy burden
that I am tired of carrying.
15 When you spread out your hands and pray,
I will hide My eyes
and not listen to you.
No matter how much you pray,
I will not hear; you are violent;
your hands are full of blood.

16 Cleanse yourselves.
Remove the evil of your deeds
from My sight.
17 Do only good deeds;
work for justice,
help the unfortunate,
relieve the homeless,
defend the widows.
18 Adonai says,
come, and let us get together
and reach an agreement.
Now your sins are blood red,
I can turn them as pure as snow;
though your sins are scarlet red,
they shall be as white as pure wool.
19 If you are willing to obey,
you will have plenty to eat;
20 but if you are stubborn
and refuse to obey,
you will die by the sword.
I, Adonai, have spoken.
21 Alas, the holy city of Jerusalem
has become a prostitute!
She was once full of justice and righteousness,
but now she is filled with criminals.
22 Your silver coins
are now counterfeit;
your strong wine
is now diluted with water.
23 Your leaders are rebelling,
and there are gangs of crooks.
Your leaders take bribes,
and hunt for rewards.
They do not defend the homeless,
or support the widows.

24 So Adonai the Almighty promises:
Now, I will remove My adversaries,
and take revenge against My enemies.
25 I will punish you,
and remove all your impurities.
26 First, I will restore your good judges
as in days of old, and restore honest leaders.
Then Jerusalem will once again be called
the City of Justice, the Faithful City.
27 Zion and her people
will be reformed with justice and faith.

INTRODUCTION TO
HAFTARAH for VA'ETCHANAN
Isaiah 40:1–26

Book of Isaiah   See haftarah Bereshit, page 51.

Halachah   Just as the weeks before Tisha B'av are marked by practices that accentuate the sorrowful moods of the period, so the seven weeks following are marked by practices that encourage a mood of comfort and consolation. The first Sabbath after Tisha B'av is called Shabbat Nachamu, meaning Sabbath of Consolation, because the haftarah begins with the words "Nachamu, Nachamu."

History   The Babylonians had destroyed Jerusalem in 586 B.C.E. and deported most of the inhabitants to Babylon. Their exile lasted 42 years and now Babylon was to be defeated by Cyrus, the founder of the Persian Empire. The Israelites saw Cyrus as a redeemer and willing to restore the exiles to their own land.

Text   Chapters 40–53 are usually attributed to the prophet known as Second Isaiah, who wrote in about 539 B.C.E.

At this moment, Adonai's prophet is commanded to comfort Israel and proclaim the Restoration of Zion.

The prophet hears Adonai commanding him to revive Israel's spirit:

Adonai said to Isaiah:
Go, encourage and comfort My people.
Speak gently to Jerusalem,
and tell her that
her punishment is ended,
that her sins have been forgiven. **40:1–2**

Now the command is given to make ready for Israel's deliverance from exile. The return from captivity is pictured as a march of Adonai.

Listen! I hear a shout:
Adonai is coming;
clear a road in the wilderness;
smooth a highway for Adonai. **40:3**

When Adonai appears, He will act:

Like a shepherd,
He will feed His flock,
He will gather the lambs
and carry them in His arms. **40:11**

Now Isaiah talks about the stupidity of idol worship:

To whom can we compare Adonai?
Is there any image that resembles Him?
An idol that a craftsman molds
and a goldsmith gilds,
and a silversmith decorates with silver chains?
A person chooses a tree wood that is not rotten.
He looks for a sculptor
to carve an idol
that will not fall down. **40:18–20**

The prophet shows that the idols are ridiculous compared with the Creator of the world.

Raise your eyes,
look up at the sky.
Who created the heavenly bodies?
He brings out all of them
giving each one a name.
Then He counts them,
to see if any are lost or astray.
He calls each of them
stars, planets, quasars, the sun,
the moon, unknown galaxies. **40:26**

Connection The haftarah Nachamu nachamu is the first Haftarah for Consolation after Tisha B'av.

Haftarah for Va'etchanan וָאֶתְחַנַּן
(Isaiah 40:1-26)

40 Adonai said to Isaiah:
Go, encourage and comfort My people.
2 Speak gently to Jerusalem,
and tell her that
her punishment is ended,
that her sins have been forgiven;
Adonai has punished
you more than enough for your transgressions.
3 Listen! I hear a shout:
Adonai is coming;
clear a road in the wilderness;
smooth a highway for Adonai.
4 Fill in the valley;
level the mountain,
and straighten the hill.
The rugged will become level,
and the rocky places smooth.
5 Adonai's glory will appear,
and all mankind will see it,
just as Adonai has promised.
6 Listen!
I hear someone say, "Shout!"
And I ask,
"What shall I shout?"
"Shout that mankind is like the grass,
and its beauty fades
like the flower of the field;
7 when Adonai's just spirit blows on it,
the grass dries up;
flowers fade;
people are just like grass.
8 Grass dries,
the flowers fade;

but God's power exists forever."
9 Messengers of joy,
climb up to the mountaintops of Zion;
raise your voices
toward Jerusalem's
messengers of good news.
Shout; do not be afraid.
Say to the cities of Judah,
"Adonai is here!"
10 Yes, Adonai the Almighty
is coming with power;
He will rule with strength.
See, He brings His reward with Him,
and He rewards those obeying Him.
11 Like a shepherd,
He will feed His flock.
He will gather the lambs
and carry them in His arms.
He will gently lead the mothers.
12 Who else can hold the oceans in His hand?
Who else measured the heavens
with a ruler?
Who else can weigh the earth,
the mountains, and the hills?
13 Is there anyone who can advise the spirit of Adonai
or act as His advisor?
14 Does Adonai consult for advice?
Does he ask for anyone
to teach Him justice and wisdom?
Does anyone show Him
the difference between right and wrong?
15 Compared to Adonai,
the nations are like a drop
in the bucket, or dust on the scales;
He moves islands
as though they are weightless.
16 All the cedars of Lebanon

do not contain enough wood,
nor enough animals for burnt offerings.
17 Nations are nothing to Him;
in His eyes they are just a lot of hot air
and make believe.
18 To whom can we compare Adonai?
Is there any image that resembles Him?
19 An idol that a craftsman molds
and a goldsmith gilds,
and a silversmith decorates with silver chains?
20 A person chooses a tree wood that is not rotten.
He looks for a sculptor
to carve an idol
that will not fall down.
21 Do you not know?
Haven't you heard?
Haven't you been told
that Adonai created the universe
from its beginnings until now?
22 He is the One
who exists above the circle of the earth,
and to Him,
its inhabitants look like crawling insects.
He is the one who stretches out the heavens
like a curtain which covers the world like a tent;
23 who reduces world leaders to dust.
24 They are like newly planted flowers,
their roots just starting to grow.
When He just breathes on them,
they shrivel up,
and the wind blows them away like straw.
25 The Holy One asks,
To whom can you compare Me?
Who is My equal?
26 Raise your eyes,
look up to the sky.
Who created the heavenly bodies?

He brings out all of them
giving each one a name.
Then He counts them,
to see if any are lost or astray.
He calls each of them
stars, planets, quasars, the sun,
the moon, unknown galaxies.

INTRODUCTION TO
HAFTARAH for EKEV
Isaiah 49:14–51:3

Book of Isaiah   See haftarah Bereshit, page 51.

Halachah   This haftarah, the second Haftarah of Consolation, is recited on the second Sabbath after Tisha B'av, on the ninth of Av.

History   Tisha B'av is the saddest day in Jewish history. On that day in 581 B.C.E. the Babylonians destroyed the First Temple, the Romans destroyed the Second Temple in 70 C.E., and the Jews were driven out of Spain in 1492.

Text   The exiles had lost hope of material restoration. This haftarah brings a message of hope and consolation to the exiled Babylonian Jews.

Throughout the haftarah, Isaiah preaches trust and faith in Adonai. Soon the exiles will stream back to Jerusalem. The prophet tells the Israelites that they will be rewarded with restitution. He says:

> *For Adonai has protected Israel.*
> *He was protected in the desert*
> *and has made her wilderness bloom*
> *like the Garden of Eden,*
> *and her desert grow like Adonai's garden.*
> *Israel will celebrate;*
> *it will be thankful with gladness and joyful songs.* **51:3**

Connection   The link between the sidrah and the haftarah is the vital duty of Israel to remain spiritually steadfast in the face of Canaanite idol worship. The haftarah says that those who participate in the idolatrous ceremonies conducted with flaming torches will lie down in sorrow:

But those who live in your light,
who surround yourselves with flaming torches,
and walk in the light of your fire,
and among the sparks
which you have kindled,
this is the reward you will receive from Me.
You will soon lie down in sorrow. **50:11**

49

14 But the nation of Zion complained:
"Adonai has abandoned me;
Adonai has forgotten me."
15 Impossible!
Can a mother forget her nursing child?
Can a mother not love the child she gave birth to?
Perhaps humans may forget;
but I will never forget you.
16 As a reminder,
I have written you on the palms of my hands;
the ruined walls of Jerusalem
are constantly in my sight.
17 Your descendants are hurrying back;
Those who destroyed it will flee.
18 Look, look around you
and see; your descendants
will stream back to you.
As surely as I live,
Adonai promises:
your descendants will beautify Jerusalem
with ornaments,
and decorate Jerusalem with jewels like a bride.
19 Your most desolate places
of your devastated land
will be crowded with your descendants,
and the enemies who tried to destroy you
will retreat.
20 Your descendants who were born in exile
will again return and complain,
"Jerusalem is now too crowded for us;
build settlements for us in which to live."
21 Then you will think to yourself,
"Who has blessed me with such descendants?

I had lost my children,
and generations were born in exile,
and wandering from land to land.
Who gave birth to them?
I was left alone.
Now these children, where did they come from?"
22 This is what Adonai Almighty says:
With My hand, I will signal the nations,
and they will return with your sons in their arms,
and your daughters they will carry on their shoulders.
23 Heads of government
will supply you politically and militarily.
They will bow down to you
with their faces to the ground,
and lick the dust of your feet;
then you will realize
that I am Adonai.
Those who wait for Me
will not be disappointed.
24 Is it possible
that the weak shall be rescued from the mighty
or the captives be freed from the jails of tyrants?
25 But this is what Adonai says:
Even the prisoners in the land of the mighty
will be freed,
and the victims of the tyrants
will be rescued;
for I will save your descendants.
26 Your enemies will eat their own flesh;
and they will be drunk
with their own blood,
and all mankind will know that I, Adonai,
am your Savior and your Redeemer,
the Mighty One of Jacob.

50 This is what Adonai asks:
Where is your mother's bill of divorce

with which I dismissed her?
Or, did I sell you to My creditors?
I sold you
because of your sins,
and your mother was taken away
because of your evils.
2 Why was there no one when I came,
and no one to answer when I called?
Isn't My power strong enough?
Or do you think I am powerless?
At my command, I dry up the seas,
and turn rivers into deserts
so that their fish die
for lack of water, and thirst.
3 I clothe the heavens
with darkness,
and cover them with sackcloth.
4 Adonai the Almighty
has given me the words of wisdom,
so I can know to encourage the weary ones.
Every morning,
He awakens me to hear His wisdom.
5 Adonai the Almighty has encouraged me,
and I did not rebel,
and I did not run away.
6 I allowed them to whip me,
and gave my cheeks
to those who pulled out the hair of my beard.
They spit in my face;
I never hid my face from shame.
7 Because Adonai Almighty will help me.
I will never be discouraged.
Therefore, I steeled my face like a rock,
and I know that I will not be ashamed.
8 He who defends me is near.
Now who will dare to challenge me?
Where are my enemies?

Who are my accusers?
I dare them to face me.
9 I know
that Adonai the Almighty will defend me;
who will dare accuse me?
They will all become tattered
like a threadbare garment.
Moths will feast on them.
10 Which of you fear Adonai,
or obey His messenger.
Such people who stumble in the darkness with no
light should rely on Adonai's name
and trust in Elohim.
11 But those of you who live in your light,
who surround yourselves with flaming torches,
and walk in the light of your fire,
and among the sparks
which you have kindled,
this is the reward you will receive from Me.
You will soon lie down in sorrow.

51 Listen to Me,
all of you who are righteous,
all of you who seek Adonai.
Look to the rock from which you were mined,
and to the quarry from where you were taken.
2 Think of your ancestor Abraham,
and of Sarah who gave birth to you.
He was the only one I chose;
I blessed him and he grew into a great man.
3 For Adonai has protected Israel.
He was protected in the desert
and has made her wilderness bloom
like the Garden of Eden,
and her desert grow like Adonai's garden.
Israel will celebrate;
it will be thankful with gladness and joyful songs.

HAFTARAH for RE'EH
Isaiah 54:11–55:5

Book of Isaiah   See haftarah Bereshit, page 51.

Halachah   This is the third Haftarah of Consolation. It is recited on the third Sabbath after Tisha B'av.

History   Isaiah ben Amoz spoke to the people of Judah over a period of forty years during the reign of four kings: Ahaz, Hezekiah, Manasseh, and Amon During that period, the Assyrian empire was on the ascent and nations joined together to fight the colossus. After much bloodshed, Assyria conquered Israel and the surrounding countries.

Scholars divide the Book of Isaiah into three parts, which some believe are by three different prophets: chapters 1 to 39, 40 to 54, and 55 to 66. Isaiah provides hope to the discouraged Judeans in Babylon. He preaches that if the people turn back to Adonai, He will rescue them from Babylon and the other nations where they have been dispersed. Soon they would return to their own land and live in peace and prosperity.

Text   Isaiah starts by promising the exiles that they will return and Jerusalem will be rebuilt if they keep the faith.

> *I will rebuild walls with precious stones*
> *on a foundation of sapphires.*
> *I will build your tower with rubies,*
> *your city gates with jewels,*
> *and all your walls with precious gems.* **54:11–12**

But the fulfillment of the promises, and the rewards, are dependent on the exiles.

> *Adonai says:*
> *I promise*
> *no weapon that is created to destroy you*
> *shall ever succeed;*

everyone who tells lies about you
will be proved wrong.
These are the rewards of Adonai. **54:17**

Now Isaiah calls upon the rich and poor to take part in a new covenant and in the blessings of a new era.

Pay attention and come close to Me.
So listen closely, and your soul will be revived;
I am going to make
an everlasting covenant with you,
the same which I made with David. **55:3**

Isaiah asks the Israelites to have faith. Adonai promised that the House of David would continue to rule Israel for generations to come. Zarubbabel, the leader of the returning exiles, was a distant descendant of David.

I made him [Zerubbabel] a leader of peoples,
a prince and a commander of the people. **55:4**

Connection In the sidrah, Adonai offers the Israelites two choices, right or wrong, a blessing or a curse.

The haftarah also offers the exiles a choice. Adonai offers them deliverance if the Israelites choose lives of justice and righteousness.

Haftarah for Re'eh רְאֵה
(Isaiah 54:11–55:5)

54 **11** Israel, you are a troubled nation,
storm-battered and crushed;
I will rebuild walls with precious stones
on a foundation of sapphires.
12 I will build your tower with rubies,
your city gates with jewels,
and all your walls with precious gems.
13 Adonai will teach all your children,
and they will live in peace and happiness.
14 You will be planted in righteousness.
Your enemies will not oppress you,
and you will not be afraid,
and devastation will not touch you.
15 Enemies may gather to attack you,
but it will not be a punishment from Me;
whoever comes to attack you will be defeated.
16 I created the blacksmith
who flames the burning coals beneath the forge,
and who makes deadly weapons.
I also created armies which destroy.
17 Adonai says,
I promise
no weapon that is created to destroy you
shall ever succeed;
everyone who tells lies about you
will be proved wrong.
These are the rewards of the servants of
Adonai,

55 Attention!
Let everyone who is thirsty come
and drink.
Let anyone who has no money

come and eat.
Come, buy wine and milk
without money;
it's all free.
2 Why do you waste your money
on what is just junk food,
and your earnings on worthless schemes?
Carefully listen to me: only eat what is nutritious.
Let your soul delight in healthy and abundant foods.
3 Pay attention and come close to Me.
So listen closely, and your soul will be revived;
I am going to make
an everlasting covenant with you,
the same which I made with David.
4 I made him a leader of peoples,
a prince and commander of the people.
5 You will issue commands to nations
that you do not know
and a nation that did not know,
and they will run to obey you
because Adonai Almighty,
Holy One of Israel, has honored you.

HAFTARAH for SHOFTIM
Isaiah 51:12–52:12

Book of Isaiah   See haftarah Bereshit, page 51.

Halachah   This is the fourth Haftarah of Consolation and is read on the fourth Sabbath after Tisha B'av.

History   Second Isaiah urges the Israelites to draw comfort from past history and to look forward to return to a new Jerusalem. There is wonderful news. Now is the time to shake off sadness and lethargy. Adonai is about to bring the exiles home.

Text   The haftarah starts by asking a question and answering it:

> *I am your source of peace.*
> *So why are you afraid of mere mortals?*
> *They are just humans who will dry up like grass.* **51:12**

Do not be afraid; the oppressor, meaning Babylon, will be defeated. Adonai assures Zion that they are His chosen people. Now it's time to rejoice:

> *Jerusalem, awake,*
> *awake and stand tall!*
> *You have drunk too much from Adonai's*
> *cup of anger.*
> *You have drunk the last drop.* **51:17**

Now the prophet consoles the exiles and says:

> *I have taken from your hand*
> *the cup that made you drunk,*
> *that cup filled with My anger.*
> *You will never drink from it again.* **51:22**

Isaiah tells the exiles that Adonai promises that Jerusalem will once again rise up. Everyone, including the mountains and the deserts, will rejoice:

> *Jerusalem, wake up,*
> *stand up,*
> *and show your strength.*
> *Dress in your majestic clothing.*
> *Foreigners and the sinners*
> *will no longer attack you;*
> *you are Jerusalem, the holy city.* **52:1**

Isaiah informs the Israelites that freedom is at hand, and Cyrus the Persian has given them permission to return:

> *Leave, go out from there [Babylon],*
> *do not touch anything unclean.*
> *Go out from her midst,*
> *purify yourselves,*
> *all of you who carry back*
> *the vessels of the Holy Temple.*
> *Do not leave in a hurry,*
> *or run for your life,*
> *for Adonai is leading you,*
> *and Adonai will protect you.* **52:11–12**

Connection   The connection of the haftarah is with time. Four weeks ago, on Tisha B'av, the saddest period in Jewish history was celebrated; our sorrow at this horrific occasion is still with us. The prophet Isaiah consoles the exiles and reminds us that Adonai has not forgotten those of us who are living in exile, that redemption is coming.

Haftarah for Shoftim שׁוֹפְטִים
(Isaiah 51:12–52:12)

51

12 I am your source of peace.
So why are you afraid of mere mortals?
They are just humans who will dry up like grass.
13 You have forgotten Adonai, your Maker,
who spread out the sky,
and created the planet Earth.
So why are you in continual terror
of the enemy as he prepares to destroy you.
And now where is the enemy?
14 Everyone who is enslaved
will speedily be freed.
The oppressed will not go down into the grave,
nor will they lack food.
15 I am Adonai the Almighty,
who stirs up the sea
so that its waves roar;
Adonai Tzvaot is His name.
16 I have placed my teachings in your mouth,
and sheltered you in My hand,
placed the stars in place,
created planet Earth's foundation;
I have assured Zion,
"You are My people."
17 Jerusalem, awake,
awake, and stand tall!
You have drunk too much from Adonai's
cup of his anger.
You have drunk the last drop
and you cannot see or walk straight.
18 Among all the children to whom she gave birth
there is no one to guide her,
or anyone to lead her by the hand.
19 These two calamities have befallen you;

Does anyone care what happens to you?
Desolation and destruction,
hunger and death;
who can help you?
20 Adonai poured out His anger on them.
Your sons have fainted;
they lie in every street
like an animal caught in a net.
21 Now hear this;
you are in trouble
and drunk, but not with wine.
22 This is what Adonai Almighty,
who cares for His people, says:
I have taken from your hand
the cup that made you drunk,
that cup filled with my anger.
You will never drink from it again.
23 I will put the cup hand of your tormentors
who said to you,
"Lie down, so we can walk all over you";
and you made your back like the ground
and like the street,
to be walked upon by those who go over.

52 Jerusalem, wake up,
stand up,
and show your strength.
Dress in your majestic clothing.
Foreigners and the sinners
will no longer come attack you;
you are Jerusalem, the holy city.
2 O captive daughter of Zion.
O, Jerusalem, rise up from the dust.
Remove the chains around your neck.
3 Adonai says,
You were sold for nothing
and you will be redeemed with nothing.

4 This is what Adonai Almighty says:
First My people went down to Egypt to live there,
and then Assyrians were also cruel to them
without cause.
5 Adonai says, And now,
seeing that My people are
being enslaved once again,
hearing the tyrants howl,
and My name is constantly cursed,
6 I will reveal Myself to My people;
people will know My name,
and on that day they will know
who I am and the strength of My name.
7 Upon the mountains
the messenger brings good news;
he announces peace,
he announces salvation;
who says to Zion,
"Your Adonai rules!"
8 Listen! Hear the watchmen raise their voices
and sing together;
for with their own eye they will see
Adonai's return to Zion.
9 Ruins of Jerusalem,
break into joyous song.
Adonai has comforted His people,
He has freed Jerusalem.
10 Adonai has demonstrated His might
before all the nations;
and the four corners of the earth
shall see Adonai's victory.
11 Leave, go out from there [Babylon],
do not touch anything unclean.
Go out from her midst,
purify yourselves,
all of you who carry back
the vessels of the Holy Temple.

12 Do not leave in a hurry
or run for your life,
for Adonai is leading you,
and Adonai will protect you.

HAFTARAH for KI TETZE
Isaiah 54:1–10

Book of Isaiah See haftarah Bereshit, page 51.

Halachah This is the fifth Haftarah of Consolation and is recited five weeks after Tisha B'av.

History It is believed that chapters 40–66 were written by an unknown prophet referred as Second Isaiah (ca 550 B.C.E.), at the end of the Babylonian exile. Some experts divide chapters 40–66 into two sections, suggesting a Third Isaiah.

In chapters 40–54 Adonai, through His spokesman Second Isaiah, addresses the discouraged exiles in Babylonia and offers them hope. If the Israelites abandon their idol worship and return to Adonai, then He will rescue the exiles and return them to their own land. The return will signal a renewal of Adonai's blessing and an age of prosperity.

Text Adonai promises that His love for the people of Israel is unswerving. This message of hope promises that the exiles will once again be restored to the Holy Land.

Israel's cities will be repopulated. Jerusalem was once like a rejected woman, but now that the exiles have returned en masse, it is again a large, united family which needs more space:

> *Do not waste time:*
> *Enlarge your tent,*
> *and stretch the cords to the pegs of your tent.*
> *Soon you will expand*
> *until your descendants repossess the land*
> *and once again revive the desolate cities.* **54:2–3**

Adonai's anger was only temporary:

> *For a brief moment,*
> *I abandoned you,*
> *but with great compassion*
> *I will take you back.* **54:7**

Adonai's love for His people is unshakable:

Adonai promises:
Mountains may disappear,
and hills may be flattened;
but My love for you will never cease.
My covenant of peace will never be broken,
who has mercy on you. **54:10**

Connection   This Haftarah of Consolation helps comfort the Judeans. It is also an assurance for the modern state of Israel that Adonai will never abandon it.

Haftarah for Ki Tetze כִּי תֵצֵא
(Isaiah 54:1–54:10)

54 Adonai says,
Sing, O childless woman.
Break into song,
and shout aloud,
you who have never given birth;
for your children
will be more numerous
than those who have been married for a long time.
2 Do not waste time:
Enlarge your tent,
and stretch the cords to the pegs of your tent.
3 Soon you will expand
until your descendants repossess the land
and once again revive the desolate cities.
4 Do not be afraid
and do not be ashamed.
Do not be discouraged,
for you will not forget the shame of your youth
and the sadness of your widowhood.
5 The Creator is your husband;
His name is Adonai Tzvaot.
The Holy One of Israel will rescue you;
He will be called
the Elohim of the whole earth.
6 For Adonai will remove your grief
as an abandoned wife.
Adonai your Redeemer asks,
Should a wife of youth be rejected?
7 For a brief moment,
I abandoned you,
but with great compassion
I will take you back.

8 Adonai, your Redeemer, says,
In a moment of anger
I rejected you;
but with great love,
I will have pity on you.
9 I promised Noah
that I would never again flood the earth;
now I also swore
that I would never again be angry with you
and would never again punish you.
10 Adonai promises: Mountains may disappear,
and hills may be flattened;
but My love for you will never cease.
My covenant of peace will never be broken,
who has mercy on you.

INTRODUCTION TO
HAFTARAH for KI TAVO
Isaiah 60:1–22

Book of Isaiah   See haftarah Bereshit, page 51.

Halachah   This haftarah is the sixth of the Haftarot of Consolation.

History   This haftarah is from the third section of the book of Isaiah (chapters 55–66). The prophet addresses the despondent, exiled Judeans, and promises a bright and successful future for those who follow and are faithful to Adonai. The prophet announces that all people who respect Adonai are welcome to worship Adonai.

The promises are like windows, which foretell a future time when Adonai will create a world filled with joy and gladness.

Text   To Jerusalem, sinking deeper in depair, Isaiah reassures that Adonai is coming to transform the world and to establish His rule over all the earth. The prophet exultantly announces to Jerusalem that a new day is coming and salvation is at hand:

Jerusalem, arise and shine,
let your light be seen,
for Adonai's glory shines upon you. **60:1**

When you see your children returning for their exiles, then:

Your eyes will see and glow,
and your heart will beat
and overflow with joy. **60:5**

The whole world will applaud and assist your return. Even

The descendants
of your oppressors will come
and bow down to you,
and all who hated you will kneel at your feet.
They will call Jerusalem
"The City of Adonai. . . ." **60:14**

The haftarah ends in a rhapsody of mystic joy.
You will succeed because Adonai's holy presence will shine upon Jerusalem:

> *You will not need the sun*
> *to be your light by day;*
> *you will not need the moon*
> *for light at night.*
> *Now Adonai will be your eternal light.* **60:19**

Connection   This is the sixth of the seven Haftarot of Consolation. Isaiah consoles the suffering and sad exiled Israelites in Babylon. He says,

> *Nations will be delight in your light*
> *And royalty will see*
> *the brightness of your new day.* **60:3**

The Torah portion is part of the second discourse of Moses. In it Moses promises that Adonai will raise Israel above all the nations on earth.

> *You will be blessed when you come in.*
> *You will be blessed when you go out.*
> **Devarim 28:6**

Haftarah for Ki Tavo כִּי תָבוֹא
(Isaiah 60:1–22)

60 Jerusalem, arise and shine,
let your light be seen,
for Adonai's glory shines upon you.
2 Thick darkness will cover the people of earth;
but Adonai's glory will shine upon you.
3 Nations will delight in your light,
and royalty will see
the brightness of your new day.
4 Open up your eyes
and look around and see;
marvel at the multitudes
that are returning to you;
your children from distant lands,
and your daughters are carried home in your arms.
5 Your eyes will see and glow,
and your heart will beat
and overflow with joy.
They will bring treasures from across the ocean,
and the wealth of nations will flow to you.
6 From Sheba,
streams of camels will travel to you;
young camels will come from Midian and Ephah.
The merchants will bring gold and spices
and will praise Adonai.
7 The sheep of Kedar
will be given to you,
the rams of Nebaioth will also be yours.
They will become offerings on My altar;
they will bring glory to My Temple.
8 Who are those who fly among the clouds,
like doves flying back to their nests?
9 The ships from the isles of Tarshish
are returning your children from distant lands.

They are coming with gold and silver,
in honor of Adonai Almighty,
the Holy One of Israel,
because He has glorified Jerusalem
in the eyes of the world.
10 Foreigners will come to rebuild your walls,
and their kings will assist you.
Even though in My anger I punished you,
now I will have mercy on you.
11 Your gates will always be open,
day and night and will never shut
to receive the wealth of nations,
brought by their kings.
12 Any nation and kingdom
that will not live in peace
will be completely destroyed.
13 The best of Lebanon forests
will come to you:
the cypress, the maple, and the pine,
to beautify the Temple;
My Temple will be glorious.
14 The descendants
of your oppressors will come
and bow down to you,
and all who hated you will kneel at your feet.
They will call Jerusalem
"The City of Adonai,
Zion, the city of the Holy One of Israel."
15 Once you were forsaken and hated,
no one passing through you,
but now I will make you into an eternal majesty,
a joy forever.
16 Nations will bring you the best of products;
then you will know
that I, Adonai, am your Savior,
and I, the Mighty One of Jacob, am your Redeemer.
17 I will replace your brass with gold,

your iron with silver,
your wood with brass,
your stones with iron.
Peace and justice
will rule the land.
18 In your land, there will be no violence.
Within your borders,
there will be no ruins
nor destruction;
your walls will be named Yeshua, meaning Salvation,
and your gates will be called Tehillah, meaning Praise.
19 You will not need the sun
to be your light by day;
you will not need the moon
for light at night.
Now Adonai will be your eternal light,
And glory.
20 Your sun will no longer set,
and your moon will continually shine.
Adonai will be your eternal light,
and your days of mourning will be ended.
21 Your people will be righteous;
they will always possess the land;
they are the trees
that I planted with My own hands,
so that I can be praised.
22 The smallest family
will become a tribe,
and a group will become a mighty nation;
I, Adonai, will make it happen.

HAFTARAH for NITZAVIM
Isaiah 61:10–63:9

Book of Isaiah   See haftarah Bereshit, page 51.

Halachah   This haftarah is the last of the seven Haftarot of Consolation and is read on the Sabbath before Rosh Hashanah.

History   Having followed political developments closely, Second Isaiah realized that even greater events were in the making, and in the swift rise of Persia he sensed the promise of imminent deliverance for Israel. In poetic utterances he compared the Babylonian Exile to Israel's bondage in Egypt, and he declared that even the Exodus would be surpassed by the new liberation and return, a triumph that would be consecrated in a renewed covenant between Adonai and His people Israel. The one necessary condition, the unknown prophet of the Exile warned, was that the Judean exiles have complete faith in the ability and desire of Adonai to accomplish the restoration.

More than any other prophet since the days of Elijah, Second Isaiah emphasized and reiterated the uniqueness and omnipotence of Adonai. He set himself the task of convincing his fellow Jews that the heathen were no more than the rod of His anger and chastisement. Adonai was the one ruler in the entire universe, and there was no one else beside Him.

Text   Isaiah consoles the exiles in Babylon and pictures a transformation. The prophet appears in the role of a messenger, bringing good news and words of comfort to the Israelites in Babylon.

Isaiah compares the rebirth of Israel to the earth and the miracle of seed.

Just as the earth bursts with vegetation,
and as the garden causes its seeds to grow,
so Adonai Almighty
will cause justice and adoration
to spring up among the nations. **61:11**

Jerusalem will burst forth in brilliance and majesty.

Never again
will you be a ruined city,
and never again
will Israel be called a desolate city.
Your new name will be Hefzi Bah,
meaning "City of Adonai's delight."
And your land will be called Beulah,
meaning "married,"
because you will be embraced. **62:4**

Now the prophet envisions a long line of return of the exiles.
He says:

Go out! Walk through the gates,
smooth the highway,
remove the stones,
clear the road for people;
so people will see it and come. **62:10**

Adonai promises that He will never again leave them. He
Himself will come down and revenge Himself against Israel's
enemy Edom. The nation of Edom represents the type of
enemy who was always untrustworthy and cruel in their deal-
ings with Israel. Adonai says:

In My anger, I stepped on My enemies
and furiously trampled My enemies.
Their blood has spurted on My clothing,
and I have stained all My clothes.
The time for revenge was in My heart,
and the time of deliverance has come. **63:3–4**

Adonai also needed consolation, as He was aware of the suffering of His people.

During their suffering,
He also suffered. **63:9**

Connection   This haftarah is recited on the Sabbath before Rosh Hashanah. The New Year is a joyful holiday and a time for a new beginning and spiritual revival. The haftarah celebrates the coming rejuvenation and redemption of Israel and a spiritual revival.

Haftarah for Nitzavim נִצָּבִים
(Isaiah 61:10–63:9)

61 10 I will rejoice;
my whole being acclaims Adonai;
for He has clothed me
with the garments of salvation.
Just as a bridegroom
puts on a white robe,
and a bride
adorns herself with her jewels,
Adonai has covered me
with the robe of righteousness.
11 Just as the earth bursts with vegetation,
and as the garden causes its seeds to grow,
so Adonai Almighty
will cause justice and adoration
to spring up among the nations.

62 For the sake of Zion
I will not keep silent;
and for the sake of Jerusalem,
I will not rest,
until her righteousness
blazes with radiance,
and her deliverance flames like a burning torch.
2 Nations will see your righteousness,
and leaders will see your majesty.
Adonai will give you a new name.
3 In the hand of Adonai you will be a crown of
beauty, and you will be a halo in the palm of Adonai.
4 Never again
will you be a ruined city,
and never again
will Israel be called a Desolate city.
Your new name will be Hefzi Bah,
meaning "City of Adonai's delight."

And your land will be called Beulah,
meaning "married,"
because you will be embraced.
5 Just as a young man marries a bride,
so will your children wed you;
and just as the bridegroom
celebrates with his bride,
so will Adonai celebrate with you.
6 O Jerusalem, I have posted watchmen on your walls.
They will never remain silent day or night:
"They keep praying."
7 Keep reminding Him,
until He establishes Jerusalem
and makes her the wonder of the world.
8 With His right hand,
and with His strong arm,
Adonai has sworn:
I will no longer allow your enemies
to steal your grain and wine
and strangers will never again drink your wine,
which you labored to produce.
9 Only those who raised it will eat it
and thank Adonai;
only those who made the wine
will drink it in the courts of My Temple.
10 Go out! Walk through the gates,
smooth the highway,
remove the stones,
hoist a flag;
clear the road for people;
so people will see it and come.
11 Adonai has sent a message to the ends of the world
and said,
Tell the people of Israel:
your Deliverer is coming to reward you.
12 They will call you "The Holy People,"

redeemed by Adonai,
and you will be called
"Looked For," a city full of people.

63 Who is this person
dressed in red garments
who comes from Edom,
from the city of Bozrah?
Who is this person in splendid apparel,
marching with power?
It is I who speak righteously;
I am ready to save.
2 Why are you dressed in red,
like someone who squeezes red grapes?
3 I have trodden on the grapes alone,
and no one was there to help me.
in My anger, I stepped on My enemies
and furiously trampled My enemies.
Their blood has spurted on My clothing,
and I have stained all My clothes.
4 The time for revenge was in My heart,
and the time of deliverance has come.
5 I searched, but there was no one to help;
I was amazed
because there was no one to volunteer.
So My own arm brought Me victory,
and My anger encouraged Me.
6 In my anger I trampled peoples,
and crashed them in My fury.
I made their blood soak the earth.
7 I will tell about Adonai's kindness
and good deeds
that Adonai has done for us,
and His great goodness
which He bestowed on Israel
with His mercy and love.

8 He said,
They are My people,
they are My children;
they will never again be false.
So He became their Deliverer.
9 During all their suffering,
He also suffered,
and His angel saved them.
With His love and mercy
He rescued them;
He held them in His arms
and carried them all those years.

INTRODUCTION TO
HAFTARAH FOR VAYELECH
HAFTARAH for SHABBAT SHUVAH
Hosea 14:2–10, Micah 7:18–20, Joel 2:15–27

Book of Hosea   See haftarah Vayetze, page 84.

Book of Micah   See haftarah Balak, page 238.

Book of Joel   We know almost nothing about the prophet Joel, whose book consists of only four chapters. In very descriptive language, he tells of a plague of locusts sweeping over Judah and destroying its fields and vineyards. He calls upon the people to fast in repentance. Joel predicts that one day Judah will again be glorious and blessed with abundance by Adonai.

> *I will give you corn,*
> *wine and oil*
> *to satisfy your hunger.* **2:19**

Halachah   The Sabbath between Rosh Hashanah and Yom Kippur is called Shabbat Shuvah because the haftarah (Hosea 14:2–10) starts with the phrase *shuva yisrael*, meaning "Israel return." The haftarah is read on this Sabbath because the prophet Hosea appeals to Israel to "return" to Adonai.

There is a custom that a haftarah should have at least twenty-one verses. Therefore the authorities added twelve verses (Joel 2:15–27) from Joel to complete the required twenty-one.

In addition, two verses from Micah were added because the reading from Hosea ends on a discouraging note:

> *But sinners stumble and fall.* **14:10**

Text   The haftarah consists of selections from three prophets: Hosea, Micah, and Joel.

Hosea prophecies against the corruption and decay he saw in the kingdom. He warns his countrymen of the disaster that awaits them unless they repent and reform. He says:

> *O Israel,*
> *return to Adonai the Almighty;*
> *for your sins have been your downfall.* **14:2**

Hosea continues and urges them to change, saying that Adonai is loving and merciful and there is hope in the coming calamity:

> *I will cure you of idolatry,*
> *I will love you without limit,*
> *for My anger is at an end.*
> *To Israel, I will be like the dew;*
> *he will blossom like the lily.* **14:5–6**

The prophet *Micah* thunders against elaborate Temple rituals and sacrifices as a substitute for true, heartfelt faith. Here Micah comforts the people and says that Adonai is aware:

> *You will again have mercy upon us.*
> *He will suppress our indignities.*
> *And You will drown their sins*
> *in the depths of the ocean.* **7:19**

The prophet *Joel* predicts the coming of Adonai and calls upon the people to repent and return:

> *Blow the shofar on Mount Zion,*
> *gather the people and declare a fast.*
> *Gather everyone,*
> *assemble the elders.* **2:15–16**

> *Tell the priests,*
> *the servants of Adonai,*
> *to cry at the altar, and let them pray:*
> *"Spare Your people. . . ."* **2:17**

Then if they truly return, Adonai will answer their prayer.

> *I will give you corn,*
> *wine, and oil*
> *to satisfy your hunger.* **2:19**

Israel will know
that I am in their midst. **7:27**

Connection   The theme of the three prophets is *teshuvah*, repenting and returning to become once more a "holy nation" based upon the teachings of the Torah. The text is ideal for the Shabbat Shuvah, the Shabbat of Return.

Haftarah for Vayelech וַיֵּלֶךְ
(Hosea 14:2–10, Micah 7:18–20, Joel 2:15–27)

Haftarah Shabbat Shuvah (Sabbath between Rosh Hashanah and Yom Kippur, Vayelech or Ha'azinu)

14 **2** O Israel,
return to Adonai the Almighty;
for your sins have been your downfall.
3 Listen to me,
and return to Adonai.
Say to Him,
"Forgive all our sins,
and be compassionate;
so we will offer You the praise of our lips
instead of bullocks.
4 Assyria will not save us;
horses will not bring us victory;
never again will we worship idols;
in you the orphan finds forgiveness."
5 I will cure you of idolatry,
I will love you without limit,
for My anger is at an end.
6 To Israel I will be like the dew;
he will blossom like the lily,
and grow deep roots
like the cedars of Lebanon.
7 Your branches will spread;
you will be beautiful like the olive tree,
and your fragrance like the forest of Lebanon.
8 Those who live near Him
will grow like grain,
and blossom like the grapes,
and become as fragrant as the wine from Lebanon.
9 Ephraim (Israel) will say,
"I will have nothing to do with idols."

I am the one;
I listen and care for him;
I am like a tree that is always in season;
your fruit comes from Me.
10 Whoever is wise
will understand these things;
whoever is intelligent, let him know them.
Adonai's commandments are true,
and the righteous follow them.
But sinners stumble and fall.

(*Sephardim add*)

7 **18** Adonai, who can compare with You,
who wipes away sin
and pardons the misdeeds
of the survivors of His people?
You do not stay angry forever,
because You delight in mercy.
19 You will again have mercy upon us;
He will suppress our iniquities.
And you will drown their sins
in the depths of the ocean.
20 You will keep Your promise
to Jacob and Abraham,
as You promised our ancestors
from the days of old.

(*Ashkenazim add*)

2 **15** Blow the shofar on Mount Zion,
gather the people and declare a fast.
16 Gather everyone,
assemble the elders,
the children, and even the infants.
Call the bridegroom
and his bride from the honeymoon.

17 Tell the priests,
the servants of Adonai,
to cry at the altar, and let them pray:
"Spare Your people,
do not make Your nation
into a laughingstock among the nations.
Why should nations sneer and ask,
'Where is Adonai?'"
18 Then Adonai became concerned
for His land of Israel,
and he had pity on His people.
19 Adonai answered their prayers
and said to His people,
"I will give you corn,
wine, and oil
to satisfy your hunger.
And I will no longer make you an undesirable
among the nations.
20 Adonai performs great miracles:
I will remove enemies on your northern border,
far away from you,
and chase them into a barren and desolate desert,
toward the Dead Sea,
and toward the Mediterranean.
His stink will rise to high heaven.
21 O Israel, do not be afraid,
be glad and rejoice;
for Adonai has done great things.
22 Do not be afraid,
wild animals of the field,
for the pastures of the desert
will turn green;
trees will be filled with fruit,
and fig trees and vines
will produce large crops.
23 Children of Zion,
celebrate in honor of Adonai the Almighty;

He sends you
the autumn and spring rains
in their right time.
24 Your granaries will be full of corn,
and the barrels will overflow with wine and oil.
25 I will make up your losses
during the years of the locusts,
the worms, the caterpillar, and the culler worm,
which I sent among you.
26 Man will have plenty to eat,
and be filled,
and you will praise Adonai the Almighty,
who did wondrous things for you.
And never again
will My people be put to shame.
27 Israel will know
that I am in their midst,
and that I am Adonai the Almighty,
and there are no other gods;
never again will My people be put to shame.

HAFTARAH for HA'AZINU
2 Samuel 22:1–51

Books of Samuel I and II   See haftarah Shemini, page 174.

History   Saul had met Israel's dire need for a courageous and clever military leader; but Samuel was disappointed in the new king. Saul's spiritual values did not always meet the high standards set by the Torah. A rift developed between Samuel the spiritual leader and Saul the warrior king. In his last years, Samuel refused even to meet with Saul.

Saul's advisors had heard about David's outstanding musical talent. Soon after these events, they brought the young shepherd to Saul's court to play his harp and sing his songs for the troubled king.

The king took a fancy to the young singer and later gave David his daughter Michal in marriage. David and Jonathan, Saul's eldest son, became very good friends.

David had proven himself as capable in battle as he was with his harp and song. He had slain Goliath, the Philistine giant, who had terrified the Israelite army. Up and down the land went the stories of David's valiant deeds. "Saul has slain his thousands," the people sang, "but David his ten thousands!" Saul became jealous of David. The king began to plot to destroy the popular young hero.

Samuel, the aged seer, began to look about secretly for a new king. Inspired by Adonai, his choice fell on David, a shepherd, the youngest son of Jesse of Bethlehem, a farmer of the tribe of Judah. Samuel anointed David in secret and proclaimed him the next king of Israel.

Early on, Jonathan, the heir to the throne, recognized David's gifts of bravery and leadership. He told David, "You are going to be king over Israel, and I shall be your second."

Jonathan's friendship with David alienated him from his father, King Saul. He secretly warned David when he learned that Saul was planning to kill David. David, accompanied by his most trusted warriors, fled into the mountains of Judah.

Saul tracked him down and David realized that he would be safe nowhere in Israel. He was forced to seek refuge in the land of Israel's Philistine enemies.

The Philistine army, encouraged by news of King Saul's troubles, prepared for all-out attack. Saul and his army were overwhelmed by the Philistine onslaught.

The battle at Mount Gilboa was a disastrous defeat for Israel. Many thousands were slain, among them the sons of Saul, including the valiant Jonathan. Saul, dreading the fate of being taken captive, died by his own hand.

The Philistines carried the bodies of Saul and his sons in triumph to their temple at Beth-She'an, where they exhibited them on the temple walls. The loyal men of Jabesh-Gilead, remembering how Saul had once so bravely defended them, removed the bodies in the night to save them from further shame.

David took the bones of Saul and Jonathan and buried them in the tomb of Saul's father, Kish.

Then the Philistines declared war against Israel, but David defeated them.

Text   In gratitude for his victory, David composed the Song of Thanksgiving. In the song, David credits Adonai for his deliverance, and safety, and victories.

> *Adonai takes revenge for me,*
> *and places nations in my power.*
> *He gives me victories over my enemies.*
> *You raise me above my enemies;*
> *You save me from violent enemies.*
> *Adonai, for this I will praise You;*
> *I will joyfully sing praises*
> *to Your name among the nations.*   **22:48–49**

Connection   The sidrah contains the Farewell Song of Moses. In his song of joy, Moses praises Adonai for His goodness, and credits Adonai for his success and victories.

David's song of thanksgiving is sung to Adonai, whom he calls the rock, and he too praises Adonai for his own escapes from death and his accomplishments.

Haftarah for Ha'azinu הַאֲזִינוּ
(2 Samuel 22:1-51)

22 And David sang this song to Adonai on the day after Adonai saved him from his enemies,
and from king Saul;
2 He sang:
Adonai is my rock,
my fortress,
and my deliverer;
3 I find safety with Adonai,
who is my rock,
He is my shield,
my champion, my fortress,
and my shelter:
and my Savior; You rescue me from evil.
4 I pray, "Praised is Adonai,"
and You save me from my enemies.
5 Tremors of death surrounded me,
the floods of destruction attacked me.
6 The chains of the Sheol (netherworld) encircled me;
death traps blocked my escape route.
7 In my agony I called to Adonai.
I called to Adonai,
and from His heavenly place
He heard my pleas,
and He heard my cry.
8 Then the earth quaked and shivered,
and the heavens thundered with anger.
9 His nostrils breathed flames,
and burning coals came out from His mouth.
10 He opened the heavens
and came down;
thick, dark clouds were under His feet.
11 He rode on the back of an angel
and soared on the wings under His feet.

313

12 He wrapped himself in dark thunderclouds
and hid His presence.
13 Coals of fire blazed
in the brightness of His presence.
14 Adonai thundered from heaven
and the Most High gave a mighty shout.
15 He shot arrows,
and scattered the enemy;
He sent lightning,
and confused them.
16 At Adonai's command,
at the blast of breath from His nostrils,
the depths of the sea were revealed,
and the foundations of the world appeared.
17 He reached down from heaven;
He lifted me;
He rescued me from the angry waters.
18 He rescued me from powerful enemies
who hated me.
19 They attacked me
when I was weak,
but Adonai saved me.
20 He brought me to a refuge of safety;
He rescued me, because He loved me.
21 Adonai rewarded me for my righteousness;
He rewarded me because of my innocence.
22 I have been faithful to Adonai,
and have never turned to do evil.
23 I obeyed all of Your commandments
and I did not deviate from Your teaching.
24 I obeyed Him completely,
and I kept myself from sin.
25 So Adonai has rewarded me
for my righteousness,
and for my innocence.
26 You are loyal to those who are loyal;
You are ethical to those who are ethical.

27 You show Your sincerity
with those that are sincere,
and with the unfaithful
You show your distrust.
28 You rescue the humble people;
but Your eyes humiliate the arrogant
and humble them.
29 Adonai, You are my lamp;
Adonai, you lighten my darkness.
30 Because of You
I can charge the enemy troops;
because of You I can scale a barrier.
31 Adonai, Your way is perfect;
Adonai's word is truth;
Adonai is a shield
to all who trust in Him.
32 Adonai is unique.
Elohim is a rock.
33 Adonai is my fortress,
and He has made my life safe.
34 He makes me as swift as a deer,
and leads me safely onto mountaintops.
35 He strengthens my arms for battle,
so that my arms can bend a bow of brass.
36 You are my saving shield;
and Your support has made me famous.
37 You cleared the path for me,
and I did not stumble.
38 I chased my enemies and destroyed them;
I did not stop until they were annihilated.
39 I destroyed them with my sword;
they fell under my feet.
40 For You have given me strength for battle;
You defeat enemies who attack.
41 You also made my enemies retreat in panic
and destroyed those who hated me.
42 They cried for help,

but there was no one to save them;
they cried to Adonai,
but He ignored them.
43 I smashed them to dust;
I stamped and stepped on them,
just like mud in the streets.
44 You rescued me from the quarrels with my people;
You made me into a leader of nations;
people whom I did not know now bow down to me.
45 Strangers now obey me;
as soon as they hear me,
they obey me.
46 Strangers will lose courage
and come trembling from out of their hidden caves.
47 Adonai lives!
Blessed be my Rock:
Exalted be Adonai,
my Rock who gives me victory.
48 Adonai takes revenge for me
and places nations in my power.
49 He gives me victories over my enemies.
You raise me above my enemies;
You save me from violent enemies.
50 Adonai, for this I will praise You;
I will joyfully sing praises
to Your name among the nations.
51 He gives great victories
to His king,
and shows great kindness
to His anointed,
to David and his descendants forever.

INTRODUCTION TO
HAFTARAH for VEZOT HA'BERACHAH
Joshua 1:1–18

Book of Joshua   The Book of Joshua belongs to the section of the Torah known as *Nevi'im Rishonim*, meaning First Prophets. The Book of Joshua chronicles one of the most important eras in Jewish history: the conquest of the Promised Land, the division of land among the tribes, and Joshua's farewell address.

History   After the death of Moses, Adonai affirmed to Joshua that He supported him in the efforts. Before the invasion, Joshua spoke to the two and a half tribes that settled in Transjordan and reminded them of the promise they gave Moses to cross the Jordan and assist the tribes in the conquest of Canaan.

Text   The taking of Canaan is accomplished in a single spectacular invasion with Joshua defeating thirty-one kings. The tribes led by Joshua cross the Jordan near the Dead Sea and take the key city of Jericho, "whose walls came tumbling down."

The next objective was the city of Ai in the hills about ten miles from Jericho.

The tribes of Reuben, Gad, and half of Menasseh occupied Transjordan, while the other half of Menasseh settled on the Plain of Sharon. The remainder of the tribes shared in the partition of Canaan according to the population.

Adonai says to Joshua:

Now that Moses My servant is dead, now is the time to lead My people across the Jordan River, to conquer the land which I am giving to them. **1:2**

Then Joshua sets the strategic plans and the schedule for the invasion, and the Israelites enthusiastically respond.

*They answered Joshua, saying, "All that you have com-
manded us, we will do, and everywhere you send us,
we will go.* **1:16**

Connection   In the sidrah, Joshua assumes the leadership
of the Israelites, and in the haftarah he continues his role as
dynamic leader. At first he is rewarded with amazing suc-
cesses, but after a while there is a long period of struggle that
continues after Joshua's death.

Haftarah for Vezot Ha'berachah וְזֹאת הַבְּרָכָה
(Joshua 1:1–18)

1 After Adonai's servant Moses died, Adonai spoke to Joshua the son of Nun, Moses' assistant:

2 Now that Moses My servant is dead, now is the time to lead My people across the Jordan River, to conquer the land which I am giving to them. **3** As I promised to Moses, I have given you all the land on which you will tread. **4** Your border will be from the Negev Desert to the mountains of Lebanon to the great river, the Euphrates River, over the land of the Hittites to the Mediterranean Sea toward the west. **5** No power will be able to oppose you all the days of your life. As I was with Moses, I will be with you. I will not fail or abandon you.

6 Be strong and brave, for you will lead the people to conquer the land which I swore to their ancestors to give them. **7** So be strong and brave and observe and obey all the laws which Moses My servant gave you. You must not turn away from them either to the right or to the left, and you will succeed wherever you go.

8 Study the Torah continually; do not turn away from its teachings; think about them day and night, and observe everything that is written in it; if you do, you will be prosperous and succeed. **9** I have commanded you: be strong and brave; do not be afraid or discouraged, for Adonai will be with you wherever you go.

(*Sephardim conclude here*)

10 Then Joshua commanded the leaders of the people, **11** "Go through the camp, and command the people to prepare food for themselves, because within three days we will cross the Jordan River and invade and conquer the land, which Adonai has given you."

12 Joshua said to the Reubenites, the Gadites, and half

the tribe of Menasseh, **13** "Remember what Moses, Adonai's servant, commanded you: 'Adonai is giving you this land.' **14** Your wives, your children, and your cattle may remain on the land which Moses gave you on the east side of the Jordan; but all your warriors will lead your tribesmen and will help them, **15** until Adonai has given your kinsmen land, as you have, and they also have taken possession of the land which Adonai has given them. Only then can you return to your land, which Adonai's servant Moses gave you on the eastern side of the Jordan."

16 They answered Joshua, saying, "All that you have commanded us, we will do, and everywhere you send us, we will go.

17 "We will obey you, just as we obeyed Moses, and may Adonai be with you, just as He was with Moses.

18 "Whoever rebels against your orders and refuses to obey your commands will be put to death. So be strong and brave."

HAFTARAH for MACHOR CHODESH
1 Samuel 20:18–42

Books of Samuel I and II   See hafatarah Shemini, page 174.

History   See the Introduction to Ha'azinu, page 311.

Text   Early on, Jonathan, the heir to the throne, recognized David's gifts of bravery and leadership. He told David, "You are going to be king over Israel, and I shall be your second."

Jonathan's friendship with David alienated him from his father, King Saul. He secretly warns David when he learns that Saul is planning to kill David.

> *Jonathan said to David, "We will celebrate the New Moon festival tomorrow, and you will be missed, because your place at the ceremony will be empty."*
> **20:18**

Jonathan tells David to hide near the stone of Ezel and says he will warn David if he is in danger. When the feast begins,

> *Saul asked his son Jonathan, "Why has not the son of Jesse come to eat with us yesterday or today?"* **20:27**

Saul is so infuriated at Jonathan that he shouts:

> *"As long as the son of Jesse lives on this earth, neither you nor your kingdom will be safe. Send for him and have him brought to me, so I can kill him."* **20:31**

The next morning Jonathan meets David and warns him to escape.

In parting, Jonathan tearfully says to David:

> *"Go in peace. We have made an agreement in Adonai's name. We asked Adonai to make sure that our descendants forever live in peace with each other."*
> **20:42**

Connection   The connection between the sidrah and the haftarah reading is the theme of the New Moon.

Haftarah for Machor Chodesh
(1 Samuel 20:18–42)

20 **18** Jonathan said to David, "We will celebrate the New Moon festival tomorrow, and you will be missed, because your place at the ceremony will be empty. **19** By the third day, you will be greatly missed; go down to the place where you hid before, and hide by the stone pile. **20** I will shoot three arrows to the side of the stone pile as if aiming at a target. **21** And then I will send a servant, saying, 'Go and find the arrows.' If I say to the servant, 'Find the arrows on this side; go and get them,' then you are safe, and as Adonai lives, there is nothing to fear. **22** But if I say this to the servant, 'Look, the arrows are behind you,' then you must leave, for Adonai is warning you to run away.

23 "Adonai is the witness of the promises which you and I have made between us forever."

24 So David hid himself in the field; and when the festival of the New Moon began, the king sat down to eat his meal. **25** The king sat in his usual seat near the wall, and Jonathan sat opposite him. Abner sat beside Saul, but David's seat was empty. **26** That day, Saul did not say anything, because he thought "something has happened to him; perhaps he is ceremonially unclean." **27** But after the festival of the New Moon, when David's seat was still empty, Saul asked his son Jonathan, "Why has not the son of Jesse come to eat with us yesterday or today?"

28 And Jonathan replied to Saul, "David begged me to let him go to Bethlehem. **29** He asked, 'Please allow me to leave, for our family is having a sacrificial ceremony and my brother has commanded me to attend. So now, if you approve, please let me go and see my brothers.' That is why he has not eaten at the king's table."

30 Saul was angry at Jonathan, and yelled at him,

"You son of the rebellious woman, I know that you have chosen to be loyal to that son of Jesse; your mother should be ashamed of you. **31** As long as the son of Jesse lives on this earth, neither you nor your kingdom will be safe. Send for him and have him brought to me, so I can kill him."

32 And Jonathan answered his father, and said to him, "Why do you want to kill him? What has he done?" **33** And Saul threw a spear at Jonathan and tried to kill him. Now Jonathan was sure that his father was determined to kill David. **34** Jonathan left the table in anger and refused to eat at the king's table on the second day of the Festival of the New Moon; for he was sorry for David because his father had insulted David.

35 The next morning, Jonathan went out into the field at the prearranged time with David, and a servant came with him.

36 Jonathan said to his servant, "Run, find the arrows which I shoot." The servant ran, and he shot an arrow beyond him. **37** As the servant reached the place where Jonathan had shot the arrow, Jonathan said to him, "Isn't the arrow behind you?" **38** And Jonathan shouted after the servant, " Hurry, be quick, do not just stand there." So Jonathan's servant gathered up the arrows and came to his master. **39** But the servant did not understand the warning; only Jonathan and David knew the secret. **40** Jonathan gave his bow and arrow to his servant and told him, "Go and carry them back to town."

41 As soon as the servant had gone, David came out of his hiding place and bowed three times. They hugged each other and wept with one another, but David wept longer. **42** Then Jonathan said to David, "Go in peace; we have made an agreement in Adonai's name. We asked Adonai to make sure that our descendants forever live in peace with each other."

HAFTARAH for SHABBAT ROSH CHODESH
Isaiah 66:1–23

Book of Isaiah   See haftarah Bereshit, page 51.

History   This haftarah is situated in the period after the Judean exiles in Babylon have been given permission by King Cyrus in 538 B.C.E. to return to Jerusalem. The native population of Palestine and the Samaritans did not want to accept the form and the kind of worship brought in at the return of Zerubbabel and later at the time of Ezra in 458 B.C.E.

In ancient Israel, the day after the appearance of a new moon was celebrated as a festive occasion with special offering at the Temple. The new moon on the seventh of Tishrei was observed as a Sabbath in addition to the usual worship of the day of a new moon. This celebration assumed the character of the New Year festival Rosh Hashanah.

People watched for the emergence of the new moon and when it appeared, the Sanhedrin pronounced the word *mekuddosh*, meaning "sanctified." The proclamation of the new moon was signaled from mountaintop to mountaintop throughout Israel by the lighting of fires.

Text   The haftarah has a variety of prophecies ranging from condemnation to consolation. It starts with the statement that Adonai is the supreme architect of the cosmos:

> *The heaven is My throne,*
> *and the earth My footstool;*
> *can any man ever build Me a temple*
> *as great as that?* **66:1**

Then the prophet relays the words of Adonai and says:

> *You who sacrifice an ox*
> *are more like a murderer;*
> *you who sacrifice a lamb to Me*
> *is like one who breaks a dog's neck;*

when you offer a grain offering
it is like one who offers pig's blood;
when you burn incense to me
it is like one who has prayed to an idol. **66:3**

Now the tone dramatically changes and the haftarah rhapsodies with hope and salutation:

All you who love Jerusalem,
celebrate with her,
and be happy with her;
all who mourned over her,
rejoice with her in joy. **66:10**

Adonai will punish the enemies of Jerusalem and many will be killed. Now Jerusalem will become a city of joy and hope for Judeans and people of all faiths. Exiles will arrive in wagons, upon mules, and in swift boats

Adonai says,
I promise,
just as the heavens and the earth which I created
will remain forever,
so will your descendants never be forgotten. **66:22**

Connection The sidrah and haftarah both refer to the New Moon and to the Sabbath:

And from one New Moon to another.
and from one Sabbath to another,
all mankind will come to worship before Me. **66:23**

66 This is what Adonai says:
The heaven is My throne,
and the earth My footstool;
can any man ever build Me a temple
as great as that?
2 Adonai says, I, with My hand,
made everything;
that is how it was created.
I will bless
the person who is humble and contrite
in spirit,
and who obeys when I speak.
3 You who sacrifice an ox
are more like a murderer;
you who sacrifice a lamb to Me
is like one who breaks a dog's neck;
when you offer a grain offering
it is like one who offers pig's blood;
when you burn incense to Me
it is like one who has prayed to an idol.
For they have chosen their own god,
and they enjoy their sinful practices.
4 I will also choose their punishments
and surround them with fear;
because when I called,
you did not answer;
when I spoke,
you did not listen.
But you in My eyes did evil,
and chose what I despise.
5 You who tremble at Adonai's word
listen to the message from Him:
Your relatives who hated you,
who rejected you,

because you listened to Me
have said,
"Honor Adonai, let us see His power."
But they will be put to shame.
6 Do you hear the noise of victory
from the city,
the shouts from the Temple?
That is Adonai shouting
as He takes revenge on His enemies.
7 She gives birth
before a woman goes into labor;
she gives birth to a child
before her pain came.
8 Who has ever heard such a thing?
Who can imagine such a happening?
Can a country be born in one day?
Can a nation
be brought into existence in one moment?
Yes, the moment Jerusalem began labor,
she gave birth to children.
9 Adonai says,
I am the one who makes birth happen.
10 All you who love Jerusalem,
celebrate with her,
and be happy with her;
all who mourned over her,
rejoice with her in joy.
11 She will nurse and comfort you,
and you will drink deeply
and be filled with her love.
12 Adonai promises,
I will flood Jerusalem,
and the wealth of the nations
will prosper with Jerusalem;
then you will nurse,
be carried on her hips,
and dandled on her knees.

13 I will comfort you
just as a mother comforts her child,
and you will be comforted in Jerusalem.
14 When this happens,
your heart will be happy,
and your strength will grow
like newly planted grass;
and Adonai's hand
will reward His servants,
and He will punish His enemies.
15 Adonai will descend with fire like a storm.
His flaming chariots will be very angry
and send punishment with flames of fire.
16 Adonai will dispense punishment
with fire, death upon all mankind,
and many will be killed.
17 Adonai says,
Those who go into the garden to sanctify
and purify themselves
and eat detestable foods
and pig's flesh, and mice
will die together.
18 I am aware of what they do
and how they think;
now is the time that I will unite nations
who speak different languages,
and they will come and see My glory.
19 And I will set a sign
among them;
I will send the survivors to Tarshish,
to Pul, to the archers of Lydia,
to Tubal, and to Javan,
and to the distant isles
that have not heard about Me
or about My fame; and
they will publicize My deeds among the nations.
20 Adonai says,

And they will gather to Jerusalem
all your relatives
from all the nations as an offering to Me.
They will arrive in chariots,
in wagons, upon mules,
and upon swift beasts,
to My holy mountain, Jerusalem.
It will be
as the Israelites are bringing an offering
in a clean vessel to the House of Adonai.
21 Adonai says, And I will also appoint some of them
to be priests and Levites.
22 Adonai says,
I promise,
just as the heavens and the earth which I created
will remain forever,
so will your descendants never be forgotten.
23 Adonai says,
From one New Moon to another,
and from one Sabbath to another,
all mankind will come to worship before Me.
24 Adonai says,
They will go out
and see the dead bodies of the people
who rejected Me;
the worms that eat their flesh
will never die,
and the fire that burns them
will never go out,
and they will be a disgusting warning sight
to all mankind...
And from one New Moon to another,
and from one Sabbath to another,
all mankind will come to worship before Me,
Adonai says.*

---

* According to tradition, verse 3 is read a second time, so as to conclude the reading with words of comfort.

INTRODUCTION TO
HAFTARAH for the FIRST DAY
OF ROSH HASHANAH
1 Samuel 1:1–2:10

Books of Samuel I and II   See haftarah Shemini, page 174.

History   In the period after Samson's death, the sanctuary at Shiloh was tended by Eli, who served as both priest and judge.

Samuel became well known for his knowledge and great wisdom. In time he was revered as a man of divine inspiration, a judge, and a prophet in Israel. Samuel became the national leader and head of the tribes.

Text   Eli noticed that a woman named Hannah was a frequent visitor to the sanctuary at Shiloh. When the kindly priest learned that Hannah was there to pray for the birth of a son, he comforted her and told her to be of good faith, promising that Adonai would soon answer her prayer.

As she prayed, she swore, "Adonai Tzvaot, see my misery and suffering, and please remember me and answer my prayer; give Your handmaid a son; then I will dedicate him to Adonai, and all the days of his life, he will never cut his hair." **1:11**

Soon thereafter a son was born to Hannah.

In due time, Hannah became pregnant and gave birth to a son, whom she named Samuel, meaning, "I asked Adonai for him." **1:20**

The word *Shmuel* (Samuel) comes from two Hebrew words: *shmu* meaning "to hear" and *El* meaning *Elohim*.

As soon as Samuel was old enough to leave home, Hannah brought him to Shiloh and asked Eli to make the boy his assistant in the service of Adonai. The priest was delighted to grant Hannah's request, and Samuel proved an apt and eager pupil.

Eli was very pleased with Samuel, for the youngster seemed truly worthy to be a future leader and judge of Israel, even though he was not a descendant of the priestly family of Aaron. Eli instructed Samuel in the ways of the Torah and the faith of Israel.

Connection The connection between the Torah portion and the haftarah is the birth of children to two childless couples. Despite Sarah's old age, she finally gives birth to twins, Jacob (Isaac) and Esau.

Hannah, also childless for a long time, eventually gives birth to a son, Shmuel (Samuel).

According to the Talmud, Sarah and Hannah both gave birth on Rosh Hashanah.

Haftarah for
the First Day of Rosh Hashanah
(1 Samuel 1:1–2:10)

1 There was a certain man named Elkanah, son of Jerocham, the grandson of Elihu, the great grandson of Tohu, from the clan of Tzuph, from the tribe of Ephrath, who lived in Ranathaim-Tzophim, in the hill country of Ephraim.

2 Elkanah had two wives, one named Hannah and the other Peninnah. Peninnah had children; Hannah had no children.

3 Each year, Elkanah traveled from his city to worship and to offer sacrifices to Adonai Tzvaot in Shiloh. At that time, the two sons of Eli, Chophni and Pinchas, served as priests to Adonai. **4** When Elkanah sacrificed, he would give portions of the meat to his wife Peninnah, and also all her sons and daughters. **5** But to Hannah, because he loved her very much, he would give a double portion though Adonai had denied her children. **6** But Peninnah teased her mercilessly because Adonai had made her childless. **7** Continually, year after year, when they traveled to Shiloh, Peninnah would tease Hannah so much that she cried and would not eat.

8 Elkanah her husband asked her, "Hannah, why are you crying? Why are you not eating? Why is your heart so sad? I love you more than ten sons."

9 One time, while the family was feasting at Shilo, Hannah left and went to the tabernacle to pray. At that time, Eli the priest was sitting in his usual place near the entrance of Adonai's Tabernacle. **10** Hannah was brokenhearted as she cried bitterly and prayed to Adonai.

11 As she prayed, she swore, "Adonai Tzvaot, see my misery and suffering, and please remember me and answer my prayer; give Your handmaid a son; then I will dedicate him to Adonai, and all the days of his life, he will never cut his hair."

12 Eli watched her lips as she continued to pray to Adonai. **13** Now Eli thought that Hannah was drunk because she was praying silently; only her lips were moving and no sounds could be heard.

14 So Eli asked her, "How long will you stay drunk? It's time for you to stop drinking."

15 But Hannah answered, "No sire, I am not a drunk, I am a deeply wounded woman, and I have poured my sorrows to Adonai. **16** I am not an evil person; my actions are caused by my great sorrow and misery."

17 Then Eli answered, "Go in peace. May Adonai answer your petition that you made to Him."

18 She said, "Thank you for your good wishes." Then Hannah returned to the feast, and ate, and she was no longer sad.

19 The family rose early in the morning, prayed to Adonai, and returned to their home in Ramah. Elkanah slept with his wife Hannah; and Adonai remembered her prayer. **20** In due time, Hannah became pregnant and gave birth to a son, whom she named Samuel, meaning, "I asked Adonai for him."

21 Elkanah and his whole household went to Shiloh to offer the yearly sacrifice to Adonai. Elkanah brought a gift he had promised to Adonai. **22** But Hannah did not go with the family, for she told Elkanah, "I cannot travel until Samuel stops nursing, and only then will I bring him. Then I will bring him to Adonai at Shiloh and he will forever live there."

23 Elkanah agreed with her: "Do what you think is best for you; remain here until he stops nursing, then I am sure Adonai will help you keep your promise." Hannah stayed home and nursed her son until he stopped nursing. **24** When he stopped nursing and the family went to Shiloh, Hannah and Elkanah took Samuel to Adonai's Tabernacle at Shiloh. They also brought a gift of a bull, 20 pounds of flour, and a bottle of wine. **25** Hannah and

Elkanah sacrificed the bull and then brought Samuel to Eli.

26 She said to Eli, "Sire, do you remember? I am the woman who was standing near you, praying to Adonai. **27** I prayed for a child, and Adonai has answered my prayer which I made to Him. **28** Now I will carry out my promise; as long as he lives he will be dedicated to Adonai." Then Hannah and Elkanah worshipped and thanked Adonai.

2 Then Hannah prayed:
Adonai's salvation makes my heart rejoice;
Adonai, my spirit
is bursting with goodness,
my spirit gets high!
I laugh at my enemies;
I rejoice in You.
2. There is no Holy One like Adonai.
There is no one besides You.
There is no rock like our Savior.
3 Stop putting on a ritzy act;
remove the sneer from your face.
Adonai knows everything;
He will judge by your deeds.
4 The strength of the mighty is now weakened,
while those who were weak
are now with new strength.
5 Those who once were rich
now slave for their daily bread,
while those who were starving
now will feast.
Those who had no children
have given birth,
and she who had many children
is lonely.
6 Adonai takes away life
and brings life;

He sentences people to the grave;
Adonai raises people from the depths.
7 Adonai makes people poor
and Adonai makes people wealthy;
Adonai brings disgrace
and Adonai brings honor.
8 Adonai rescues the poor from the dust,
and rescues the beggar
from the garbage dump.
Adonai is seated among princes
in a seat of honor.
Adonai created the foundations of the earth,
and He has anchored the world on them.
9 He will protect those who obey Him,
and the wicked will die in darkness,
for no man can be victorious just by strength.
10 The enemies of Adonai
will be crushed;
thunder from heaven will destroy them.
Adonai will judge the whole world;
He will give strength to His king
and glorify the power of His chosen one.

HAFTARAH for the SECOND DAY OF ROSH HASHANAH
Jeremiah 31:2–20

Book of Jeremiah   See haftarah Bo, page 122.

History   Traditional and Conservative Jews celebrate two days of Rosh Hashanah. Israeli and Reform Jews celebrate only one day.

The theme of this haftarah is *teshuvah*, meaning "repentance" or "return." The theme of *teshuvah*, returning to Adonai, was a favorite theme of the prophets of Israel. The worst sinners are encouraged to believe that they can improve their conduct, since their sins are a temporary obstacle rather than a permanent sentence. The prophets preached that *teshuvah* required a determined effort by the sinners to break with their past. The gates of *teshuvah* are never closed, even when a person is in danger of death.

By the middle of the sixth century, two generations of Judeans had grown up in exile. Many had lost touch with their heritage, and the memory of the Temple and the Covenant had faded. They were content to earn a living and live in peace. However, a minority maintained the will to resist assimilation.

Text   The haftarah is dominated by Adonai's concern for the people of Israel and brings a message of life for the exile in Babylon:

> *I have always loved you*
> *and will never stop.*
> *I have drawn you close to me.*
> *Beautiful maid of Israel,*
> *I will revive you again*
> *and you will be strengthened;*
> *you will again take your tambourines*
> *and join in the dances of the merrymakers.* **31:3–4**

Exile was bitter, and the Israelites struggled to keep the dream of restoring the Temple and the nation of Judah.

To them, Jeremiah says:

> *Once again you will plant vineyards*
> *on the hills of Samaria;*
> *you will plant*
> *and enjoy the fruits of your harvest.* **31:5**

Jeremiah recalls the matriarch Rachel who was buried on the roadside near Ramah. She weeps for her homeless children, meaning the exiles in other countries, and she cries for their return.

Jeremiah urges the people Israel to repent:

> *"Please take me back*
> *so that I may return to Your good graces."* **31:18**

Connection *Teshuvah*, repentance, and return are the major themes of Rosh Hashanah.

Haftarah for the
Second Day of Rosh Hashanah
(Jeremiah 31:2-20)

31

2 This is what Adonai promises: The Israelites who survived the killing will find peace as they travel through the wilderness, and I will give them a place to rest.

3 Adonai, with lovingkindness,
said to them,
I have always loved you
and will never stop.
I have drawn you close to Me.

4 Beautiful maid of Israel,
I will revive you again
and you will be strengthened;
you will again take your tambourines
and join in the dances of the merrymakers.

5 Once again you will plant vineyards
on the hills of Samaria;
you will plant
and enjoy the fruits of your harvest.

6 Soon the day will come
when the watchmen in the hills of Ephraim
will joyously shout,
"Rise up, get on your feet
and let us go up to Jerusalem,
to meet Adonai our Almighty."

7 Now this is what Adonai says:
Sing with joy for Israel,
and shout from the hilltops;
cry out, sing praises and say,
"Adonai has saved His people,
the remnant of Israel."

8 I will bring them back from the north country,
and gather them from the four corners of the earth;

I will gather the blind and the lame,
the pregnant women and women in labor;
I will bring them all back.
9 They will come with prayers of joy,
and I will lead them with prayer;
and I will lead them beside the streams of water
on smooth roads
so they will not stumble;
I will do this
because I am the parent of Israel,
and Ephraim is My firstborn child.
10 Nations, listen to Adonai's message,
and announce it to the world:
"He who exiled Israel will gather them,
just as a shepherd watches over his flock."
11 Adonai has saved Jacob
and freed him from the strength of Babylon.
12 The children of Israel will return home
and sing with joy on the hills of Jerusalem
and thank Adonai for his numerous gifts:
the grain, the wine, the olive oil,
and for the young of the flocks and the herds;
their lives will be like a watered garden;
and their sorrows will disappear.
13 The women will dance for joy,
young men and old will celebrate;
I will change their mourning into joy,
and I will comfort them.
After their mourning
I will make them rejoice.
14 Adonai says,
I will supply the priests
with abundance of offerings.
My people will have many sacrifices.
15 This is what Adonai says:
Listen: bitter weeping and mourning
is heard in Ramah;

the matriarch Rachel is weeping for her children
and refuses to be comforted,
for her children are gone.
They are in exile.
16 This is what Adonai says:
Stop weeping and hold back your tears.
Adonai says, I will reward you,
and your children will return from the land of exile.
17 I promise there is hope for your future,
and your children
will safely return to their own country.
18 I have surely heard Israel blaming himself:
"Adonai, you have disciplined me,
and punished me like a wild calf;
Adonai the Almighty,
please take me back
so that I may return to Your good graces.
19 After I abandoned Adonai,
I was sorry;
and after I understood,
I cried to myself in sorrow;
I was ashamed and sorry,
because of my youthful stupidity."
20 Adonai says,
Isn't Israel My favorite child?
Isn't he still My beloved child?
I remember him,
I often speak of him with love.
My heart aches for him,
and I will always have mercy on him.

HAFTARAH for SHACHARIT OF YOM KIPPUR
Isaiah 57:14–58:14

Book of Isaiah See haftarah Bereshit, page 51.

Some scholars are of the opinion that these chapters are the work of a Third Isaiah.

History Yom Kippur ends the Ten Days of Penitence. Worshippers observe the day by denying themselves in all aspects of daily life. The worshipper does not eat or drink and does not do any work. It is the time to review one's past and repent for last year's misdeeds.

Repentance will bring about a change of heart and regenerate a new personality. The haftarah calls for repentance and:

> *If you open your heart*
> *to the hungry*
> *and satisfy the afflicted soul;*
> *then your light*
> *will shine in the darkness,*
> *and your gloom*
> *as the noonday.* **58:10**

In Judaism, fasting is a sign of religious reverence. It emphasizes a desire for praiseworthy living with the ethical emphasis of the Torah. That is why Isaiah 58 was chosen as the haftarah for Yom Kippur.

Text The fifty-seventh and fifty-eighth chapters are condemnations of the ritual of fasting without justice for the poor. The Israelites complain that they worship daily and observe all the feasts, yet Adonai has not answered.

> *"Why have we fasted," they say,*
> *"and You do not see it?*

> *Why have we afflicted ourselves,*
> *and You take no notice?"* **58:3**

The prophet explains:

> *To bow down his head*
> *like a bulrush?*
> *To sit in sackcloth and ashes?*
> *Will you call this a fast,*
> *an acceptable day to God?*
> *Is not this the fast that I have chosen:*
> *to loosen the bonds of wickedness,*
> *to undo the bonds of oppression,*
> *to let the crushed go free,*
> *and to break every yoke?* **58:5–6**

So the prophet also reassures the people:

> *God will answer.*
> *You will cry, and He will say,*
> *Here I am.* **58:9**

And he adds:

> *If you open your heart*
> *to the hungry*
> *and satisfy the afflicted soul,*
> *then your light*
> *will shine in the darkness.* **58:10**

Connection The theme of the haftarah indicts the worthlessness and hypocrisy of ritual without genuine repentance. On Yom Kipppur, the most solemn day of the year, Jews are reminded that fasting, prayer and resolutions are not enough.

True repentance requires doing justice and walking humbly with Adonai.

Haftarah for
Shacharit of Yom Kippur
(Isaiah 57:14–58:14)

57 **14** It shall be said,
"Build up, build up,
prepare the way,
remove every obstacle from My people's way."
15 For thus says the high and lofty One
who inhabits eternity,
whose name is Holy:
I dwell in the high and holy place,
also with one
who is of a contrite and humble spirit,
to revive the spirit of the lowly,
and the heart of the humbled.
16 I will not quarrel forever,
nor will I always be angry.
If I did, everyone would pass away,
even the souls which I have made.
17 His sin of greed
has made Me angry;
I struck him,
I hid my face and was angry,
and he went astray in the way of his heart.
18 I have seen his doings,
but I will heal him.
I will guide him,
consoling him and his mourners.
19 I create the speech of lips;
peace, peace to the far and to the near,
says God,
and I will heal him.
20 But the wicked are like the restless sea,
which cannot be still,
whose water cast up with filth and dirt.

21 There is no peace for the wicked,
says my God.

58 Cry out, spare not,
raise your voice like a trumpet,
and show My people their transgression,
and Jacob's house their sins.
2 Yet they seek Me daily,
and delight in knowing My ways,
like an upright nation
that has not forsaken
the ordinances of their God.
They asked Me
about the righteous ordinances;
they delight in approaching God.
3 "Why have we fasted," they say,
"and You do not see it?
Why have we afflicted ourselves,
and You take no notice?"
Behold, on your fast day
you seek your own pleasure
and oppress your workers.
4 Behold,
you fast to quarrel and fight,
and to hit with the wicked fist.
You do not fast today
to make your voice heard on high.
5 Have I chosen such a fast?
A day for man to afflict his soul?
To bow down his head
like a bulrush?
To sit in sackcloth
and ashes?
Will you call this a fast,
an acceptable day to God?
6 Is not this the fast that I have chosen:
to loosen the bonds of wickedness,

to undo the bonds of oppression,
to let the crushed go free,
and to break every yoke?
7 Is it not to share your bread
with the hungry,
and to take the outcast poor
into your home?
To clothe the naked
and not to hide yourself from your own flesh?"
8 Then your light will break forth
like the dawn,
and your healing will come soon.
Your rightousness will go before you,
God's glory backing you.
9 Then you will call,
and God will answer.
You will cry, and He will say,
Here I am.
If you take away
the yoke of oppression from your midst,
the scornful finger and slanderous speech;
10 If you open your heart
to the hungry,
and satisfy the afflicted soul;
then your light
will shine in the darkness,
and your gloom
as the noonday.
11 God will always guide you,
and satisfy your soul in drought
and relieve your bones.
You will be like a water garden,
a never-ending spring of waters.
12 Your ancient ruins
will be rebuilt;
you will restore the foundations
of many generations;

you will be called the repairer of the breach,
the restorer of paths to dwell in.
13 If you turn away your foot from the Sabbath,
from doing your pleasure on My holy day,
but call the Sabbath a delight,
the holy of God,
honorable, and honor it,
not doing your business,
or seeking your own pleasure,
or speaking idle talk;
14 then you will find delight in God;
and I will cause you to ride on the high places
of the earth,
and feed you with the heritage
of your father Jacob;
for Adonai's mouth has spoken it.

INTRODUCTION TO
HAFTARAH for the MINCHA
OF YOM KIPPUR
(YOM KIPPUR AFTERNOON)
Jonah 1:1–4:11; Micah 7:18–20

Book of Jonah The Book of Jonah is the fifth book in the section of the *Tanak* called *Trey Aser*, meaning "twelve." It is read on the afternoon of Yom Kippur. The haftarah ends with three verses from the Book of Micah.

The story of Jonah is the biggest fish story of all time. Everybody knows that Jonah was swallowed by a whale. The Book of Jonah, however, says only that Jonah was swallowed by a huge fish. Second, there are not and were not any whales in the Mediterranean Sea.

There is nothing in the book to indicate the authorship of Jonah and no claim that it was written by Jonah. Scholars cannot agree when it was written. It must have been written after the fall of Nineveh, about 600 B.C.E. The style indicates that it may have been written between 400 and 200 B.C.E.

History The Book of Jonah has been described in some Jewish circles as a mystic parable of a period of Jewish history.

Each character represents a historical personage. Jonah is Israel, the sailors are the nations surrounding Israel; Nineveh is the center of idol worship; the ocean is the volatile and dangerous Near Eastern political scene; the storm is the rising violent danger of Babylon.

In the synagogue the Book of Jonah is read during the afternoon service on Yom Kippur.

Text Adonai instructs Jonah to go to the Assyrian capital of Nineveh and warn the inhabitants that Adonai will destroy the city because of their immorality.

> *I want you to go to the great city of Nineveh, and tell the people: Adonai has seen your sins, and He will punish you.* **1:2**

Jonah hates Assyria because, in 722 B.C.E., it destroyed the Ten Tribes of Israel.

Jonah rejects his mission and instead takes a boat to the city of Tarshish in Spain. Suddenly Adonai sends a violent storm which threatens to sink the ship. The sailors believe that they are being punished because someone on the boat is a bad luck person.

> *Then the sailors were frightened, and said to him, "What have you done to us?" Then he told them that he was running away from Adonai. Then they asked him, "What shall we do to you, so that the sea will stop storming?"* **1:10–11**

To save themselves, the sailors throw Jonah into the sea, where he is swallowed by a large fish.

> *So the sailors picked up Jonah and threw him into the sea; and the sea ceased its raging.* **1:15**

The sailors are amazed at the miracle so they immediately offer a sacrifice to Adonai and pledge to serve Him. After three days the fish spits Jonah onto dry land.

Once again, Adonai instructs Jonah to prophesy in Nineveh. This time Jonah realizes that flight is useless, so he goes to Nineveh and prophesies. To his amazement, the inhabitants believe Adonai and repent. The Hebrew word for repentance is *teshuvah,* meaning "return."

> *When Adonai saw their deeds, how they stopped their evil way, Adonai changed His mind about them; He did not do what He had threatened.* **3:10**

The cancellation of the destruction makes Jonah angry. So Jonah leaves the city. Adonai grows a plant next to Jonah to provide shade but then causes the shrub to wilt. Once again Jonah is upset and complains.

> *Then Adonai said, "You had pity on the bush, which you did not plant or help to grow; it grew up in one night and died the next.*

> *Shouldn't I take pity on the great city of Nineveh, in which are more than a hundred and twenty thousand humans who cannot tell the difference between right and left, and many cattle?"* **4:10–11**

Adonai points out that Jonah was sorry for the plant that grew one day and disappeared the next day and Jonah had done nothing to make it grow. How much more should Adonai the Creator have pity on Nineveh, which contained more than one hundred thousand humans?

The book ends with the real reason for Jonah's mission: to save the city and not destroy it. The text also reveals that Adonai is merciful not only to Jews but to all His creations.

Connection The reason we read the Book of Jonah on Yom Kippur is that it illustrates the power of repentance and that humans no matter where they are—even in the belly of a fish—cannot escape Adonai's presence.

Haftarah for
the Mincha of Yom Kippur
(Jonah 1:1–4:11; Micah 7:18–20)

1 Adonai appeared to Jonah the son of Amittai, saying, **2** I want you to go to the great city of Nineveh, and tell the people: Adonai has seen your sins, and He will punish you. **3** Instead, Jonah decided to run away from God's presence to the city of Tarshish. He went down to the port of Jaffa and found a ship bound for Tarshish. He paid for a ticket and boarded the ship to sail to Tarshish, far away from Adonai's presence.

4 But Adonai sent a strong wind and created such a heavy storm on the sea that the ship was about to break up. **5** The sailors were frightened, and every man prayed to his god. The sailors lightened the ship by throwing cargo overboard. But Jonah, fast asleep all this time, was below decks.

6 So the captain came and said to him, "How can you sleep during such a storm? Get up and pray; perhaps Adonai will remember us, and we will not drown."

7 The sailors said to each other, "Let's cast lots, so that we can find the guilty one who has caused this storm." They cast lots, and the guilty lot fell on Jonah.

8 Then they said to him, "Now tell us, why are we being punished. What is your occupation? Where do you come from? Where do you live? What is your nationality?"

9 He said to them, "I am a Hebrew; and I fear Adonai, the Creator of heaven, the sea, and the earth." **10** Then the sailors were frightened, and said to him, "What have you done to us?" Then he told them that he was running away from Adonai. **11** Then they asked him, "What shall we do to you, so that the sea will stop storming?"

12 He answered, "If you pick me up and throw me into the sea, the sea will calm down; I am sure that this great storm is my fault."

13 But the men rowed harder to bring the ship back to land; but the sea grew even more stormy. **14** So they prayed to Adonai and said, "Adonai, we beg You, do not let us perish for this man's sin; we do not want to be guilty of shedding innocent blood. Adonai, you sent the storm for your own reasons.

15 So the sailors picked up Jonah and threw him into the sea; and the sea ceased its raging.

16 The sailors were amazed at Adonai; so they offered a sacrifice immediately to Adonai and pledged to serve Him.

2 Now Adonai had sent a huge fish to swallow Jonah. Jonah lived in the belly of the fish for three days and three nights.
2 In the fish's belly,
Jonah prayed to Adonai,
3 and said,
"In my distress, I prayed to God,
and He answered me;
from inside the belly of the fish
I cried, and You heard my plea.
4 You threw me into the deep,
into the heart of the seas;
and the waves raged around me.
Your swells
and Your waves passed over me."
5 Then I said,
"I am evicted from your sight.
I thought I would never again see Your holy Temple.
6 The waters closed over me;
the depths surrounded me,
the seaweeds tangled around my head.
7 I sank to the bottoms of the mountains;
the earth closed above me forever;
but yet You have brought me up alive
from the grave,

O Adonai my Lord.

8 When I fainted, I remembered Adonai;
and my prayer reached You,
in Your holy Temple.

9 Those who pray to useless idols
forsake their true deliverer.

10 With a voice of gratitude
I will pray to You.
I will fulfill what I have sworn.
Deliverance comes from Adonai."

11 Then Adonai spoke to the fish,
and it spit Jonah out upon the dry land.

3 Then Adonai appeared to Jonah the second time, saying, **2** Get up, go to the great city of Nineveh, and give them my message.

3 So Jonah obeyed Adonai; he got up and went to Nineveh. Nineveh was such a huge city that it took three days to see it all.

4 Jonah entered the city and on the first day prophesied, "Forty days more, and Nineveh will be destroyed." **5** So the inhabitants of Nineveh who believed Adonai began to fast, and they put on sackcloth; all of them mourned in sackcloth.

6 Even the king of Nineveh stepped down from his throne, removed his royal robe, dressed in sackcloth, and sat on a pile of ashes. **7** Then he issued a proclamation and made it known throughout Nineveh. The king and his nobles issued a decree: "No man nor beast, or herd or flock may eat or drink water. **8** Every human and animal must put on sackcloth and pray to Adonai. Let everyone turn from their sinful ways and from the cruelty that is in their hands. **9** Who can tell, perhaps Adonai may change his mind and have mercy on us.

10 When Adonai saw their deeds, how they stopped their evil ways, Adonai changed His mind about them; He did not do what He had threatened.

4 But Jonah was very annoyed. **2** He prayed to Adonai, "Adonai, isn't this what I said when I was still in my country? This is the reason I fled to Tarshish. Adonai, I know that you are kind and merciful; you are slow to anger, of great kindness, and relenting of evil.

3 "Adonai, please, I beg You, take away my life, for it is better for me to die than to live."

4 Then Adonai asked, "Is there a reason for your anger?"

5 So Jonah left the city, and sat to its east side, and made a booth in which to rest. He sat under it in the shade waiting to see what would happen to Nineveh.

6 Then Adonai sent a bush and it grew around Jonah, and it grew over his head, and it protected him from the heat of the sun. Jonah was happy with the protection from the sun.

7 Early the next day, Adonai sent a worm, and it chewed up the bush and the bush lost its leaves. 8 Then at sunrise, Adonai prepared a scorching east wind; and the sun beat down on Jonah's head, so that he fainted, and Jonah was prepared to die. He said, "I am better dead than alive."

9 Then Adonai said to Jonah, "Do you have the right to be angry at the bush?" Jonah replied, "Yes! I am very angry, angry enough to die."

10 Then Adonai said, "You had pity on the bush, which you did not plant or help to grow; it grew up in one night and died the next.

11 Shouldn't I take pity on the great city of Nineveh, in which are more than a hundred and twenty thousand humans who cannot tell the difference between right and left, and many cattle?"

(*Some congregations stop here*)

7 **18** Adonai, who is like You, who pardons sins and overlooks the misdeeds against the remnant of Your chosen people? You are not angry forever, because You are

happy to be merciful. **19** You will once again take pity on us. You will stop our wrongs; and You will throw all our sins into the depths of the sea. **20** You will be faithful to Jacob, and have mercy on Abraham, just as you promised our ancestors from the centuries of old.

HAFTARAH for the FIRST DAY OF SUKKOT
Zechariah 14:1–21

Book of Zechariah   See haftarah Beha'alotecha, page 221.

History   Zechariah lived and prophesied during a very difficult period of Jewish history. Jerusalem was still in ruins and the construction of the Temple was not completed. The country was economically and politically fractured. During the first years of King Darius of Persia rebellions threatened the empire's existence.

Zechariah preached that the Persian Empire was strong and resistance was futile. He encouraged the Israelites to remain true to their religion and practice justice and kindness toward each other.

Zechariah had a vision of a heavenly empire with its capital in rebuilt Jerusalem.

Text   Chapter 14 is the last of Zechariah's prophecies. It describes the assault against Jerusalem:

> *I will gather all nations to battle against Jerusalem; the city will be captured, the house plundered, and the women raped; half of the city will be led into exile, but the rest of the city will remain.* **14:2**

Zechariah continues:

> *Then Adonai will rise and battle against those nations, as He fights on a day of war.* **14:3**

The victory of good against evil will be complete and Jerusalem will be restored to its former glory. Former enemies will stream to Jerusalem to celebrate the holiday of Sukkot.

> *Then the survivors of the nations that attacked Jerusalem will each year go to worship Adonai, and to celebrate the feast of Sukkot.* **14:16**

In the end, Jerusalem will become the city of holiness and Adonai will be the Ruler over all the earth.

Connection   The connection between the sidrah and haftarah is the holiday of Sukkot.

(Zechariah 14:1–21)

14 Watch for the judgment day when Adonai is coming and your possessions will be taken. **2** I will gather all nations to battle against Jerusalem; the city will be captured, the houses plundered, and the women raped; half of the city will be led into exile, but the rest of the people will remain.

3 Then Adonai will rise and battle against those nations, as He fights on a day of war. **4** On that day, He will stand on the Mount of Olives, east of Jerusalem, and the Mount of Olives will be split right down the middle, east and west, and form into a very wide valley; half of the Mount will shift north and the other half will shift south. **5** You will escape just as you escaped from the earthquake during the reign of Uzziah, king of Judah; Adonai and all the angels will appear.

6 It will be a spectacular day; there will be no sunlight or moonlight. **7** It will be one special day; no daytime and no nighttime; but at evening time there will be a light which will be known as God's. It will be a light that only Adonai can create. **8** On that day, fresh, pure water will flow out from Jerusalem; half toward the eastern, Dead Sea and half toward the western, Mediterranean Sea; the water will flow continuously in summer and in winter.

9 Adonai will rule over all the world; on that day Adonai will be One and his name One. **10** Then all the land from Giza to Rimmon, south of Jerusalem, will become flat, but Jerusalem will remain on its site, high up, from Benjamin's Gate to the place of the first gate, then to the Corner Gate, and from the tower of Hananel to the king's winepress in the south. **11** People will live there, and there will be no more destruction, and Jerusalem will be a safe place in which to live.

12 Adonai will send a plague which will infect all the nations who attacked Jerusalem; while they are standing, their flesh will rot, their eyes will fall out of their sockets, and their tongues will rot in their mouths. **13** On that day, Adonai will confuse them; every one will hold his neighbor's hand, but they will attack each other. **14** On that day, even Judah will attack Jerusalem; in the end, the treasure of all surrounding nations will be collected, mountains of gold, silver, and garments. **15** The plague will infect the horses, mules, camels, donkeys, and all the camp animals.

16 Then the survivors of the nations that attacked Jerusalem will each year go to worship Adonai, and to celebrate the feast of Sukkot. **17** However, if any of the nations of the earth do not go to Jerusalem to worship Adonai the King, I will send rain upon it. **18** If the people of Egypt refuse to go up to Jerusalem, then I will send no rain; there Adonai will punish with the plague the nations that do not come up to celebrate the feast of Sukkot. **19** This plague will be Egypt's punishment, and the punishment of all nations that do not go up to keep celebrating the feast of Sukkoth.

20 On that day, horse's bells will be inscribed with, "Adonai is holy." Even the pots in Adonai's house will be like the bowls before the altar. **21** Every cooking pot in Jerusalem and Judah will be sacred to Adonai the Almighty, and all who come to sacrifice will take of the pots and cook in them. On that day, there will be no need for merchants in the Temple of Adonai the Almighty.

HAFTARAH for the SECOND DAY
OF SUKKOT
1 Kings 8:1–21

Books of Kings I and II   See haftarah Vayera, page 68.

History   David's achievements laid a sound political foundation for the Solomonic era. Living in a period relatively free from the clashes of ambitious monarchs, Solomon was able to concentrate on his country's internal and religious welfare.

Text   Solomon's greatest achievement was the building of the Temple in Jerusalem. According to the *Tanak*, the construction of the Temple took seven years, from the fifth to the eleventh year of his reign. The bulk of the artisans were Phoenician, lent by Hiram, King of Tyre. Conscripted Israelites were the labor force. The Temple was constructed of hewn stone, cedar wood, and masonry, tied together by bronze.

When the Temple was finished, Solomon summoned all the leaders to help bring up the Ark from Mount Zion to the city of David. The priests carried the Ark and placed it in the Inner Sanctuary of the Temple.

They carried the Ark of Adonai, along with the tent of meeting, and all the holy vessels that were in the tent. The priests and the Levites carried everything up. **8:4**

The text tells us that the cloud with the Divine Presence (*Shechinah*) which in the days of Moses had covered the Meeting Tent now filled the new sanctuary.

When the priest left the inner Sanctuary, a cloud filled Adonai's Temple. The priests were unable to carry out their duties because of the cloud; Adonai's glory filled His Temple. **8:10–11**

The Israelites interpreted the cloud as an omen that Adonai had accepted the Temple as His new dwelling. Solomon said:

I have built a Temple for You, a place where You can live forever. **8:13**

Connection   The dedication of Solomon's Temple (Bet Hamikdash) took place in the tenth century B.C.E. The festivities lasted for fourteen days, the last seven days of which occurred during the festival of Sukkot.

Haftarah for
the Second Day of Sukkot
(1 Kings 8:1–21)

8 Then Solomon summoned all the elders of Israel, and all the leaders of the tribes, the heads of the families of Israel, before King Solomon in Jerusalem, to bring up the Ark of God's covenant from Mount Zion, in the city of David. **2** All the men of Israel assembled before King Solomon for the festival of Sukkoth in the month Ethanim, which is the seventh month. **3** When all the elders of Israel arrived, the priests picked up the Ark. **4** They carried the Ark of Adonai, along with the tent of meeting, and all the holy vessels that were in the tent. The priests and the Levites carried everything up. **5** King Solomon and all the people of Israel, who had assembled before him, paraded with him in front of the Ark. Along the route, they sacrificed untold numbers of sheep and oxen. **6** The priests carried in the Ark of God's covenant into the inner Sanctuary of the Temple, its most holy place, and placed it under the wings of the cherubim. **7** The cherubim spread out their wings over the Ark, and formed a covering over the Ark and its carrying poles. **8** The poles of the Ark were so long that the ends of the poles were seen from the holy place, at the entrance of the Sanctuary. The poles could not be seen outside. To this day, they are still there. **9** Nothing was in the Ark except the two tablets of stone with the Ten Commandments, which Moses placed there at Horeb (Mount Sinai), where Adonai made a covenant with the Israelites when they were freed from the land of Egypt.
10 When the priests left the inner Sanctuary, a cloud filled Adonai's Temple. **11** The priests were unable to carry out their duties because of the cloud; Adonai's glory filled His Temple.

12 Then Solomon said, "Adonai has promised that He would live in the darkness. **13** I have built a Temple for You, a place where You can live forever."

14 Then the king turned around, and all the community of Israel stood, and he blessed the whole community.

15 He said, "Blessed be Adonai, the Almighty of Israel, who spoke to my father David, and has fulfilled His promise, saying: **16** Since the day that I brought My people Israel out of Egypt, I never chose a city among the tribes of Israel to build a Temple to attach My name to; but I chose David to rule over My people Israel. **17** Now my father David wanted very much to build a Temple to honor the name of Adonai the Almighty of Israel. **18** But Adonai said to my father David, I know that you were eager to build a Temple to honor My name, and I appreciated your inentions. **19** However, you will not be the one to build the Temple, but your son will build the Temple to honor My name. **20** Now Adonai has made His promise come true; now I am the ruler in the place of my father David; now I sit on the throne of Israel, as Adonai predicted, and I have built the Temple to honor Adonai, the Almighty of Israel.

21 And I have made a place to house the Ark, which contains Adonai's covenant, which He made with our ancestors, when He freed them of the land of Egypt.

INTRODUCTION TO
HAFTARAH for SHABBAT CHOL HAMOED
OF SUKKOT
Ezekiel 38:18–39:16

Book of Ezekiel   See haftarah Vayigash, page 105.

History   After the Temple was destroyed and thousands of Judeans had been deported to Babylonia, Ezekiel's prophecy became a call to restoration. He brought renewed hope to the exiled Israelites that Adonai would renew them.

Some scholars believe that Ezekiel's prophecy was based on the Scythians, a barbaric tribe that lived in the Ukrainian steppes near the Black Sea. They were fierce horse warriors who rampaged through Assyria and the Fertile Crescent, plundering, looting, and destroying anything and everything that crossed their paths.

Text   Ezekiel conjures up a science fiction prophecy. He visualizes a mighty army led by evil leader Gog descending on a defenseless Israel. Gog represents the evil cosmic forces of Satan. The armed Gogian mythic enemies have landed from a satellite to battle Adonai's earthbound allies, the Israelites. Now Adonai descends and, using His supernatural power, single-handedly defeats the evil forces of Gog.

The weapons of Gog's evil army of unearthly Creatures is so humongous that it will provide Israel with a seven-year supply of fuel.

Then those who live in Israel will stream out of the cities and burn their weapons, their shields, bows and arrows, clubs and spears. The fires will burn for seven years, says Adonai the Almighty. There will be no need to find wood in the fields, or to chop down trees in the forests; weapons will keep the fires burning; . . .
39:9–10

The Gogian corpses are so numerous that:

It will take seven months for the people of Israel to cleanse the land and bury all the soldiers. **39:12**

Connection According to a midrash, this battle will be fought during the holiday of Sukkot.

Haftarah for Shabbat
Chol Hamoed of Sukkot
(Ezekiel 38:18–39:16)

38 **18** Adonai the Almighty says, I will become very angry on the day when Gog invades the land of Israel. **19** In My jealousy and in My anger I will send an earthquake in the land of Israel. **20** The fish in the sea, the birds in the sky, the wild animals, the reptiles that creep upon the earth, and all the humans in the world will tremble at My presence. Mountains will be flattened, cliffs will crumble, and walls will topple. **21** Adonai says, Then I will declare war against Gog throughout all My mountains; then every enemy soldier will battle his brother. **22** I will send torrents of rain, and I will punish his bands and his allies with disease and bloodshed and hailstones, fire, and sulphur.

23 I will show My greatness and holiness and I will make myself known to many nations. Then they will realize that I am Adonai.

39 Now, son of man, prophesy against Gog. Give him My message; this is what Adonai the Almighty says: Gog, chief prince of Meshech and Tubal, I am your enemy.

2 I will turn you around, and drag you from the north, and drive you around the mountains of Israel. **3** Then I will knock your bow from your left hand, and your arrows will fall from your right hand. **4** Adonai promises: You and your bands, and the nations who are with you will be defeated in the mountains of Israel. Your corpses will be eaten by the birds of prey and the wild animals. **5** Your dead bodies will pile up in the fields, for I have spoken.

6 I will rain down a fire on Magog, and on those who live along the coast; and then they will realize that I am God.

7 My people Israel will know My holy name, and never again will I allow My holy name to be disgraced; and the nations of the world will know that I am Adonai the Holy One in Israel. **8** Adonai the Almighty says, The day is coming; the time is near; everything will happen just as I told you.

9 Then those who live in Israel will stream out of the cities and burn their weapons, their shields, bows and arrows, clubs and spears. The fires will burn for seven years, says Adonai the Almighty. **10** There will be no need to find wood in the fields, or to chop down trees in the forests; weapons will keep the fires burning; they will plunder those who plundered them, and they will rob those who robbed them.

11 At that time, the Valley of the Travelers, east of the sea, will make a graveyard for the soldiers of Gog. The graveyard will block the travelers, for there they will bury Gog and his whole army. Now they will change the name of the Valley of Hamon—Gog (The Valley of Gog's Army). **12** It will take seven months for the people of Israel to cleanse the land and bury all the soldiers. **13** Adonai the Almighty says, Everyone in Israel will help bury them; and it will be a victorious day when I demonstrate My glory. **14** At the end of seven months they will hire specialists to search the land continually and bury those remaining bodies, so that the land will be cleansed. **15** When any of the travelers passing through the land find a human bone, he will mark it; so the burial crew buried it in the Valley of Hamon-Gog. **16** There will also be a city named Hamonah, meaning "Multitude." This is how they will finally cleanse the land.

INTRODUCTION TO
HAFTARAH for SHEMINI ATZERET
1 Kings 8:54–66, 9:1

Books of Kings I and II   See haftarah Vayera, page 68.

History   After seven years of labor and the expenditure of lots of assets, the magnificent Temple was finished. The treasury was bankrupt. The kingdom was heavily in debt to Hiram of Tyre for labor and materials, so Solomon paid by ceding some territory and villages to Tyre.

Text   When the Temple was finished, Solomon invited all the notables in Israel to the dedication. Afterwards the king blessed the congregation and made a feast for the guests. He sacrificed thousands of oxen and sheep for a celebration which lasted fourteen days: seven days for the dedication and seven days for the festival of Sukkot.

Connection   The Torah reading describes the three pilgrimage festivals: Passover, Shavuot, and Sukkot. During these three holidays, Israelites journeyed to the Temple in Jerusalem and brought sacrifices and tithes to support the Temple and the priests.

The haftarah reading deals with the dedication of the Temple. The reading also contains the specific reference to the eighth day, Shemini Atzeret:

On the eighth day, the king sent the people away; they blessed the king and returned home. **8:66**

Haftarah for Shemini Atzeret
(1 Kings 8:54-66, 9:1)

8 **54** Now when Solomon finished offering prayer and requests to Adonai at the altar, where he had been, he raised his hands up to heaven. **55** He stood, and in a loud voice, blessed the community of Israel and said, **56** "Blessed be Adonai, who has kept His promise and given His people Israel peace. He has delivered everything that He promised His servant Moses.

57 May Adonai the Almighty always be with us, just as He was with our ancestors, and never abandon us.

58 May He inspire us to walk in all His ways, and observe his commandments and statutes, which He gave to our ancestors. **59** May my word, with which I have prayed to Adonai day and night, be close to Adonai Almighty, to champion the cause of His servant, and the daily welfare of His people Israel.

60 There is no other; in this way, all the nations of the earth will be convinced that there is only one Adonai.

61 Let your hearts beat in tune with Adonai the Almighty, and observe His statutes, and follow His commandments, as on this day."

62 Then the king and the whole congregation Israel sacrificed to Adonai. **63** As peace offerings to God, Solomon offered 22,000 oxen and 120,000 sheep. So the king and all the Israelites dedicated Adonai's Temple. **64** On the very same day, king Solomon dedicated the area of the courtyard that was in front of the Temple. The king brought burnt offerings, grain offerings, and the fat of the peace offerings; because the bronze altar in front of the Temple was too small for all the burnt offerings, meal offerings, and the fat of the peace offerings. **65** At that time, Solomon celebrated a feast, and all Israel with him, a large gathering, from the city of Chamath to the bank of Egypt. The celebration of Adonai lasted fourteen days:

seven for the festival of Sukkot, and seven for the Temple dedication. **66** On the eighth day, the king sent the people away; they blessed the king and returned home, happy for all the blessings that Adonai had given His servant David and His people Israel.

(The following verse is said by some congregations.)

9 Solomon completed building God's Temple, and the king's palace, and everything that Solomon aspired to do.

INTRODUCTION TO
HAFTARAH for SIMCHAT TORAH
Joshua 1:1–18

Book of Joshua   See haftarah Shelach Lecha, page 224.

History   Each week we read another portion of the Torah. In the synagogue we go from the very first chapter of Bereshit to the very last chapter of Devarim. On Simchat Torah, the day right after Sukkot, the twenty-third day of Tishrei, Jews all over the world read the very last portion of the Torah's fifth book, Devarim, and then begin reading the Torah all over again from the beginning.

On Simhat Torah, everyone in the synagogue is called up to the Torah for an aliyah. For the last aliyah, all the children are called up. A worshipper spreads his tallit like a canopy under which the children stand and recite the first blessing. After the second benediction, the congregation recites the blessing, which Jacob gave to his grandchildren, the sons of Joseph.

The Torah reading ends with the death of Moses. Moses the leader was aware of his mortality and the need for a strong charismatic leader to succeed him. During the forty years in the desert, Moses carefully nurtured and taught Joshua how to take over the reins of leadership. Now Joshua, the capable pupil, steps into the shoes of Moses.

Text   The haftarah starts with Adonai's instructions to Joshua, the new leader. Adonai assures Joshua that he will be successful and He will support him just as He did Moses.

> *Be brave and courageous, because you will lead these people, and they will inherit the land which I swore to give to their ancestors. Only be brave and courageous, and follow all the commandments which My servant Moses commanded you to do.* **1:6–7**

Then Joshua, encouraged by Adonai, assumes the leadership. He sends his officers through the great throng of Israelites camped on the shore of the Jordan and instructs the people to prepare for the invasion of Canaan.

Joshua also reminds the tribes of Reuben, Gad, and half of Menasseh (who had already acquired land on the eastern side of the Jordan) that they promised Moses to help the tribes conquer their homesteads.

> *The warriors answered Joshua, saying, "We will do everything that you have commanded us, and we will go everywhere you send us.*

> *"Just as we obeyed Moses in all things, so we will listen to you; may Adonai Almighty be with you, as He was with Moses. Anyone who disagrees with your orders, and refuses to obey your commands, will be executed. We wish you strength and courage."* **1:16–18**

Connection   The sidrah ends with the death of Moses, and the haftarah seamlessly proceeds to Joshua, the new leader, and his preparations for the invasion of Canaan.

Haftarah for Simchat Torah
(Joshua 1:1–18)

1 After Moses, Adonai's servant died, Adonai spoke to Moses' assistant, Joshua, the son of Nun:

2 My servant Moses is dead. Now get up and lead the nation, the children of Israel, over the Jordan River, to the land which I am giving to them. **3** As I promised Moses, I will give them every piece of ground where you set your foot. **4** Your boundary will extend from the desert to Lebanon, and from the Euphrates River, all the way to the land of the Hittites to the Mediterranean Sea toward the west. **5** No person as long as you live will be able to defeat you. Just as I helped Moses, I will always be with you. I will not fail or abandon you.

6 Be brave and courageous, because you will lead these people, and they will inherit the land which I swore to give to their ancestors. **7** Only be brave and courageous, and follow all the commandments which My servant Moses commanded you to do. If you do not deviate from them, to the right hand, or to the left, you will be successful wherever you go. **8** Do not forget the Torah; study it day and night and remember to observe faithfully all the rules and laws in it. If you do, you will become prosperous and have success. **9** I have commanded you: Be brave and courageous; do not be afraid or discouraged; for Adonai Almighty will help you everywhere you go.

(Sephardim conclude here.)

10 Joshua commanded the officers, **11** "Go through the camp, and tell them, Prepare supplies for yourselves; In three days we will cross the Jordan River to enter and conquer the land, which Adonai the Almighty has given you to possess."

12 Joshua addressed the Reubenites, the Gadites, and half the tribe of Manasseh: **13** "Remember what Moses, Adonai's servant, commanded you: 'Adonai Almighty has given you land on this side of the Jordan; **14** your wives, your children, and your flocks may remain in the land that Moses gave you east of the Jordan River, but all your tough warriors must cross over the Jordan and lead your armed brothers, and help them. **15** Until Adonai has given your brother a place to rest, as He had given you, and they also have taken possession of the land which Adonai the Almighty has given them, only then can you freely return to the land which Moses, Adonai's servant gave you on the east side of the Jordan, and occupy it."

16 The warriors answered Joshua, saying, "We will do everything that you have commanded us, and we will go everywhere you send us.

17 "Just as we obeyed Moses in all things, so we will listen to you; may Adonai Almighty be with you, as He was with Moses. **18** Anyone who disagrees with your orders, and refuses to obey your commands, will be executed. We wish you strength and courage."

INTRODUCTION TO
HAFTARAH for the FIRST SABBATH
OF CHANUKAH
Zechariah 2:14–4:7

Book of Zechariah   See haftarah Beha'alotecha, page 220.

History   The story of Chanukah historically emphasizes the victory of the Hasmoneans over the Greek invaders. It was the struggle against the suppression of Judaism and resulted in the rededication of the Temple and the lighting of the rebuilt menorah. The rededication took eight days and the tiny cruse of oil miraculously burned for all eight days.

Talmudic sources stress the miracle of the cruse of oil and only casually mention the Hasmonean struggle. It seems that by talmudic times the Hasmonean victories had lost their glory. The Hasmoneans were guilty of the very crimes that Judah and his Maccabees had fought to eradicate.

Eighteen years had passed since Cyrus permitted the Israelites' return to Jerusalem. The returnees were living under difficult conditions, with no jobs, insufficient food, and poor harvests. Zechariah preached that these conditions were punishment for the failure to rebuild the destroyed Temple. The prophet pressured Zerubbabel, the governor, and Joshua, the high priest, to proceed with the building of the Temple.

Text   In his vision, the beginning of which is filled with symbolism, Zechariah sees angels riding horses and an angel with a measuring stick measuring the future walls of Jerusalem. The prophet sees Joshua the high priest dressed in rags, standing before Adonai and Satan. Satan accuses Joshua and his priests of being sinners and not worthy to rebuild the Temple.

Then Satan is rebuked and Joshua's rags, which represent the sins of the people, are replaced, and the priest is cleansed and clothed in new garments and crowned with a mitre. This transformation represents a symbolic removal of sins of the guilt of the people.

Then the angel of Adonai instructed Joshua: This is what Adonai the Almighty says: If you will follow My instructions and observe My commandments, then you will be in charge of My Temple and its courtyards; and I will permit you to speak with the angels who are standing here. **3:6–7**

Connection   The sidrah deals with the Tabernacle, its altar, and the gold and silver vessels used in the service.

In the haftarah, Zechariah has a vision of the golden Tabernacle menorah.

Both the sidrah and the haftarah have links to the menorah used on the holiday of Chanukah.

So the angel explained, "This is Adonai's message to Zerubbabel, saying, I am Adonai the Almighty. Do not depend on your strength but rely only on My spirit, says the Lord of Hosts. Mountains will stand in your way, then in front of you you will set the final stone of the Temple in place. And the people will shout, 'May Adonai bless it.'" **4:6–7**

Haftarah for the
First Sabbath of Chanukah
(Zechariah 2:14–4:7)

2 **14** Adonai says, daughter of Zion, sing and rejoice; for I am coming, and I will live among you. **15** When he comes, many nations will turn to Adonai and will become My people, and I will live in your midst; and you will know that the Adonai Almighty has sent me to you. **16** Adonai will choose Judah as His part in the holy land, and He will once again choose Jerusalem as His city. **17** Humanity, be silent before Adonai; for He is moving in action from His holy dwelling.

3 In another vision, the angel showed me Joshua, the High Priest, standing before the angel of Adonai. Satan was standing near the angel's right hand, accusing Joshua. **2** Then Adonai said to Satan, O Satan, I, Adonai, reject your accusation. Adonai, who has chosen Jerusalem, rebukes you. This man Joshua is a stick rescued from a flaming fire. **3** Now Joshua was dressed in dirty clothes. **4** So the angel said to the people who stood around him, "Remove his dirty clothes." And the angel said to Joshua, "See, I have forgiven and cleaned you from your sins and now I will dress you with new garments." **5** Then I said, "Put a clean turban on his head." So they placed a clean turban on his head, and dressed him with new garments; and the angel of Adonai stood by and watched. **6** Then the angel of Adonai instructed Joshua: **7** This is what Adonai the Almighty says: If you will follow My instructions and observe My commandments, then you will be in charge of My Temple and its courtyards; and I will permit you to speak with the angels who are standing here. **8** Joshua the High Priest, listen carefully, you and your fellow priests are symbols of good things that are coming; soon I will bring back the Branch, My servant. **9** Observe the jewel that I have placed before Joshua; it is a jewel with seven sides. Adonai the Almighty says, Watch Me, I will engrave inscriptions on it; in one day, I will remove the sins of this land.

10 Adonai the Almighty says, On that day, each of you will invite his neighbor to join you under your grape and fig trees.

4 Then the angel who talked to me returned, and woke me, like a person who is awakened from a deep sleep.

2 The angel asked me, "What do you see?" And I replied, "I saw a golden candlestick with a bowl of oil on top of it. Around the bowl of oil I saw seven lamps; each lamp had seven spouts with wicks.

3 "I also saw two olive trees nearby, one tree on the right side of the bowl, and the other tree on its left side." **4** So I asked the angel that spoke with me, "Sir, can you please explain the meaning of my vision?"

5 So the angel who spoke asked me, "Don't you understand the meaning?" And I answered, "No, sir, I do not understand the message."

6 So the angel explained, "This is Adonai's message to Zerubbabel, saying, I am Adonai the Almighty. Do not depend on your strength or rely only on My spirit, says the Lord of Hosts. **7** Mountains will stand in your way, then in front of you you will set the final stone of the Temple in place. And the people will shout, 'May Adonai bless it.'"

HAFTARAH for the SECOND SABBATH OF CHANUKAH
1 Kings 7:40–50

Books of Kings I and II   See haftarah Vayera, page 68.

History   King Solomon turned to the project that would demand his greatest effort, the one dearest to his heart and the hearts of his people—the building of the Holy Temple (*Bet Hamikdash*) on Mount Zion. Until now, Israel had worshipped Adonai in the simple sanctuary that housed the Holy Ark. Solomon wanted a more fitting house of Adonai, a magnificent Temple that would be the grandest structure in all Jerusalem, indeed in all the land of Israel.

From his close friend and ally, King Hiram of Tyre, Solomon obtained cedar wood of Lebanon for the Temple. He paid for this precious wood with the produce of Israel—grain and oil, olives and figs—and with copper from the mines of Ezion-Geber.

Text   King Hiram sent a metalworker, also called Hiram, to cast the brass metal objects for Hamikdash. Hiram was of mixed ancestry; his father was a Tyranian and his mother was from the tribe of Naphthali.

Gold, newly brought to the land of Israel from other countries in exchange for copper and olive oil, was lavishly used to make Solomon's Temple a dazzling sight to behold.

The altar, the menorah, the showbread table, the candlesticks, tongs, basins, and the doors both of the Holy of Holies and of the Temple were made of gold.

> *So Solomon made all the utensils for Adonai's Temple; the golden altar, the golden table for the showbread; the golden candlesticks, five for the right side, and five for the left, before the Sanctuary; the flowers, the lamps, and the tongs of gold; the cups, snuffers, basins, spoons, firepans, of pure gold; and the hinges, of gold;*

both for the doors of the inner house, the most holy place, and for the doors of the Temple. **7:48–50**

Connection This section of Kings is read on Chanukah because it contains a description of the golden menorah which had been destroyed and the vessels and menorah used in the First Temple.

Haftarah for the
Second Sabbath of Chanukah
(1 Kings 7:40–50)

40 Hiram also made the pans, the shovels, and the basins. Hiram finished all the work that King Solomon ordered for Adonai's Temple.
41 He made two pillars, the two bowls of the capitals that were on the top of the pillars; and the two strings of chains to cover the two bowls of the capitals that were on the top of the pillars; **42** the 400 pomegranates for the two strings of chains, two rows of pomegranates for each string of chains to cover the two bowls of the capitals on the top of the pillars; **43** the ten water wagons and the ten basins on the bases; **44** and the one sea, and the twelve oxen under the sea. **45** The pans, the shovels, and the basins, and all the utensils which Hiram made for King Solomon, in Adonai's Temple, were made of burnished brass. **46** The king cast the bronze utensils in the clay ground in the Jordan Valley between Succoth and Zerethan. **47** Solomon did not weigh all the utensils, because there were so many of them that the utensils could not be weighed.
48 So Solomon made all the utensils for Adonai's Temple; the golden altar, the golden table for the showbread; **49** the golden candlesticks, five for the right side, and five for the left, before the Sanctuary; the flowers, the lamps, and the tongs of gold; **50** the cups, snuffers, basins, spoons, firepans, of pure gold; and the hinges, of gold, both for the doors of the inner house, the most holy place, and for the doors of the Temple.

INTRODUCTION TO
HAFTARAH for SHABBAT SHEKALIM
2 Kings 11:17–12:17

Books of Kings I and II   See haftarah Vayera, page 68.

Halachah   In ancient days, every male Israelite twenty years and older had to contribute a half-shekel anually to the maintenance of the Temple in Jerusalem. This had to be paid before the first of Nisan. In order to remind the people of their duty, proclamations were made on the first day of Adar that the half-shekel was due.

Since Jews came to the synagogue on Shabbat, the Torah reading included the passage describing the proclamation of the half-shekel.

On that Shabbat, two Torahs were removed from the ark. From one, the sidrah of the week is read, and from the other, Shemot 30:11 is read, which contains the half-shekel passage.

History   King Ahab of the Northern Kingdom (876–869 B.C.E.) was successful in his military campaigns, establishing friendly relations with Israel's neighbors. Realizing the importance of obtaining allies against Assyria, Ahab gave his daughter Athaliah in marriage to Jehoram, crown prince of Judah, thus strengthening Israel's bond with the Southern Kingdom. When Ahab became involved in a war with Aram, Judah helped him to win the victory.

Ahab's pacts with Judah, Aram, Phoenicia, and Moab were well timed, for the Assyrian army, commanded by King Shalmaneser III, was drawing nearer. Ahab and his allies met the Assyrians in battle at Carcemish and succeeded in stopping the invasion.

Ahab was succeeded by his son Ahaziah, but he soon fell ill and died. He was followed by his brother Joram, the last king of the House of Omri.

With the support of the prophet Elisha, Jehu, one of the king's officers, led a revolt against Jehoram. Elisha was confident that Jehu, once he became king, would abolish idol worship and govern in accordance with the Torah. Jehu's revolt was successful but bloody. Among the victims were the foreign Queen Jezebel and all the members of the House of Omri. Jehu now ascended the throne.

Jehu's revolt in Israel had grave consequences for Judah. King Ahaziah of Judah was killed in ambush on his journey home from Samaria. Ahaziah's mother, the ambitious queen Athaliah, was a true daughter of Jezebel and Ahab. When Athaliah learned of her son's death, she saw her chance to become ruler of Judah. She had all the princes of the House of David killed, no matter how closely they were related to her. Ascending the throne, she was a ruthless and tyrannical ruler for six years.

Text   Unknown to Athaliah, one prince had escaped her henchmen: Joash (Jehoash), her grandson. The child had been saved by his aunt, the wife of Jehoiada, the high priest, and for seven years she kept him hidden.

When the time seemed ripe for revolt, Jehoiada brought the young prince before the elders of Judah, and Joash was anointed king. Athaliah's tyrannical reign came to an end, and the House of David was established in Judah once more.

Jehoash was seven years old when he began to rule in Judah. During Jehu's seventh year in Israel, Jehoash began his reign in Judah; Jehoash reigned in Jerusalem forty years. **12:1**

Jehoash instructed the priests:

Let the priests take the money and use it to repair the damages to the Temple, wherever they are needed. **12:6**

Jehoiada, the priest, took a chest, cut a hole in the lid, and placed it beside the altar for the contributions with which to pay the workers. When the repairs were finished, there was a surplus, which was used to purchase a new vessel for the Temple service.

Then King Jehoash summoned Jehoiada and the other priests, and said to them, "Why have you not repaired the damages of the Temple? From now on, do not accept any more money for yourselves, but use the money to repair the Temple." **12:8**

Connection   The connection between the sidrah and the haftarah is the contributions to building the Tabernacle in the desert and the description of the efforts to raise funds for the repair of the Temple.

Haftarah for Shabbat Shekalim
(2 Kings 11:17–12:17)

11 **17** And Jehoiada the priest made an agreement between Adonai, the king, and the Israelites, that they would be Adonai's people; he also made an agreement between the kings and the people. **18** All the people of the land marched to the temple of Baal and destroyed it; they smashed into pieces the altars and his idols, and they killed Mattan the priest of Baal in front of the altars. The priest Jehoiada stationed guards around Adonai's Temple. **19** And he took with him the commanders, the captains, the guards, and all the people of the land, and they escorted the king from Adonai's Temple, through the gate of the guards to the king's palace. And the king sat on the throne.

20 All the people of the land rejoiced, and the city was peaceful after they killed Athaliah in the king's palace.

(Ashkenazim begin here)

12 Jehoash was seven years old when he began to rule in Judah. **2** During Jehu's seventh year in Israel, Jehoash began his reign in Judah; Jehoash reigned in Jerusalem forty years. His mother's name was Tzivya of Beersheba. **3** And Jehoash as long as he lived did what was right in Adonai's eyes, just as Jehoiada the priest instructed him.

4 But he did not destroy the idol shrines, where the people continued to sacrifice and burn incense. **5** Jehoash said to the priest, "Collect all the money which is donated to Adonai's Temple, even the money which each person is assessed in the census, and all the money that a man generously contributes to the Temple. **6** Let the priests take the money and use it to repair the damages to the Temple, wherever they are needed." **7** But up to the twenty-third year of King Jehoash, the priests still had not repaired the damage to the Temple.

8 Then King Jehoash summoned Jehoiada and the other priests, and said to them, "Why have you not repaired the damages of the Temple? From now on, do not accept any more money for yourselves, but use the money to repair the Temple." **9** The priests agreed not to accept any more money from the people, and also would not repair the damage of the Temple.

10 Then Jehoiada the priest took a strongbox, bored a hole in its lid, and placed it on the right side of the altar in Adonai's Temple; and the priests who served as guards put in it all the money that was donated to Adonai's Temple.

11 When the strongbox was filled with money, the king's secretary and the High Priest came and counted the money and put it in bags. **12** They used the money to pay the building supervisors, and paid the carpenters and the masons who were repairing Adonai's Temple.

13 They gave money to the masons, and the stonecutters, to buy wood and stone to repair the damages to Adonai's Temple, and for other materials needed to repair the house.

14 The money that was brought into Adonai's Temple was not used to make bowls of silver, snuffers, basins, trumpets, or vessels of gold and silver. **15** The money was used to pay the workmen, who were repairing Adonai's Temple with it. **16** The men responsible for the money were honest, and they did not need to keep track of the expenditures. **17** The money that was contributed for guilt offerings and sin offerings was not used for repairing Adonai's Temple; it was given to the priests.

INTRODUCTION TO
HAFTARAH for SHABBAT ZACHOR
1 Samuel 15:1–34

Books of Samuel I and II   See haftarah Shemini, page 174.

History   The Sabbath preceding Purim is called Shabbat Zachor, meaning a Sabbath of Remembrance. Two Torah scrolls are used during the service. The weekly sidrah is read in the first Torah, and in the second Torah Devarim 25:17–19 is read. This portion tells of the battle with Amalek. The reading begins with the word *zachor*, meaning "remember." That is how Shabbat Zachor got its name.

When the Israelites invaded Canaan, they were a loose confederation of tribes. In time of trouble, the elders would turn to an individual, chosen by Adonai, to act as a military leader and save them. This leader was called *shofet*, meaning "judge." After the victory, the military savior served as a *shofet* for many years.

The prophet Samuel was unhappy with King Saul. He assumed that Saul would remain subservient to him and call upon him for advice. However, Saul was acquiring his own independent authority and initiated military attacks without consulting Samuel.

The Israelites were in a constant battle with the Philistines. They were also campaigning against the kingdoms of Edom, Moab, Ammon, and Zobar. Saul's campaign against the Amalekites led to a rupture between the religious and military leaders.

Text   Samuel calls for a holy war against the Amalekites and forbids the taking of prisoners or booty. Samuel brings the word of Adonai:

This is what Adonai Almighty says: I remember what Amalek did to Israel, ambushing him when he left Egypt. **15: 2**

Saul defeats the Amalekites but allows his soldiers to keep some of the animals for themselves. Saul also saves King Agag as his prisoner. When Samuel hears the news, he accuses Saul of disobeying Adonai's commands.

Adonai speaks to Samuel and says:

I am sorry that I made Saul king. He has disobeyed Me and has refused to obey My commands. **15:11**

The next morning Saul boasts to the prophet that he performed Adonai's command. So Saul asks:

"Then what is all this noise of sheep and of oxen which I hear?" **15:14**

Saul lamely explains that he brought the animals as sacrifice, to which Samuel replies:

"Adonai's commands are more important than burnt offerings and sacrifices. Obedience is more important than sacrifices and the fat of rams. . . . Since you have rejected Adonai's command, He has also rejected you as king." **15:22–23**

Saul begs Samuel for forgiveness. The prophet demands that the Amalekite king be brought to him. Samuel looks into Agag's eyes and says:

"Just as your sword has killed the children of mothers, now your own mother will lose her son." Then Samuel chopped Agag in pieces." **15:33**

Connection The haftarah is associated with Purim because according to tradition Haman the villain was a descendant of the Amalekites and he was called Agagite. Agag was a territory close to Media.

15

One day, Samuel said to Saul, "Adonai sent me to anoint you king over His people Israel. Now I want you to listen to Adonai's instructions.

(Ashkenazim begin here)

2 "This is what Adonai Almighty says: I remember what Amalek did to Israel, ambushing him when he left Egypt.

3 Now go and attack Amalek, and totally destroy them; do not pity them, but completely destroy all the Amalekites and all their oxen, sheep, camels, and donkeys."

4 So Saul mobilized 200,000 soldiers in Telaim, and 10,000 soldiers from Judah. **5** And Saul's army marched to the city of Amalek, and hid in the valley. **6** Saul warned the Kenites, "Go, move far away from the Amalekites, or else I may destroy you with them. We remember that you were helpful to the children of Israel, when they were freed from Egypt." So the Kenites hurriedly marched away from the Amalekites. **7** And Saul defeated the Amalekites from Havilah all the way to Shur, which is east of Egypt. **8** He captured Agag, the Amalek king, and with the edge of the sword completely destroyed all the people. **9** But Saul and his people spared Agag, and the best of the sheep, oxen, fatlings, and lambs. They did not destroy anything worth keeping. However, everything that was worthless they completely destroyed. **10** Then Adonai spoke to Samuel, saying,

11 I am sorry that I made Saul king. He has disobeyed Me and has refused to obey My commands. Samuel was troubled deeply; and all night he cried out to Adonai. **12** When Samuel awakened early in the morning to meet Saul, he was told, "Saul went to Carmel, and there he erected a monument to himself, and he went down to Gilgal." **13** And Samuel found Saul, who said to him, "May you be blessed by Adonai. I have fulfilled Adonai's commands."

14 And Samuel asked, "Then what is all this noise of sheep and of oxen which I hear?"

15 Saul answered, "The soldiers took them from the Amalekites; they saved the best of the sheep and oxen, to sacrifice to Adonai, and we completely destroyed the rest."

16 Then Samuel said to Saul, "Stop! Let me tell you what Adonai said last night." So Saul said to Samuel, "Please tell me."

17 And Samuel continued, "When you were just an ordinary Israelite, weren't you made the head of the tribes of Israel? Adonai appointed you as king over Israel. **18** Adonai sent you on a mission and specifically said, Go and completely destroy the Amalekites, and pursue them until they are completely wiped out. **19** Why, then, did you not obey Adonai's command, but rushed to accumulate the spoils and did evil in Adonai's sight?"

20 Saul answered Samuel, "I obeyed Adonai's command, and followed His instructions. I captured Agag the king of Amalek and have completely destroyed the Amalekites. **21** The soldiers took the best of the sheep and oxen, to sacrifice to Adonai in Gilgal."

22 Samuel answered, "Adonai's commands are more important than burnt offerings and sacrifices. Obedience is more important than sacrifices and the fat of rams. **23** Rebellion is like the sin of witchcraft, and obstinacy is like wickedness and idol worship. Since you have rejected Adonai's command, He has also rejected you as king."

24 Saul said to Samuel, "I have sinned; for I transgressed Adonai's commandment and your words, because I feared the people and obeyed their voice. **25** Now therefore, please pardon my sin, and return with me, so that I may worship Adonai."

26 Samuel said to Saul, "I will not return with you. For you have rejected Adonai's word, and Adonai has rejected you as king over Israel."

27 As Samuel turned around to leave, Saul took hold of the corner of his robe, and it tore.

28 Samuel said to him, "Adonai has torn the kingdom of Israel from you today and has given it to a neighbor of yours, who is better than you. **29** And also the Eternal One of Israel will not lie or change His mind, for He is not a man that He should change His mind."

30 Then Saul pleaded, "I admit that I have sinned, but please honor me now, before the leaders of my people, and before Israel, and accompany me to worship Adonai."

31 So Samuel accompanied Saul; and Saul worshipped Adonai. **32** Then Samuel said, "Bring me Agag the Amalek king," and Agag, full of smiles, came to Samuel and said, "The enmity between us is over and my life is saved." **33** But Samuel said, "Just as your sword has killed the children of mothers, now your own mother will lose her son." Then Samuel chopped Agag in pieces before Adonai in the city of Gilgal. **34** Then Samuel went to Ramah; and Saul returned to his palace in Gibeah.

INTRODUCTION TO
HAFTARAH for SHABBAT PARSHAT PARAH
Ezekiel 36:16–38

Book of Ezekiel   See haftarah Vayigash, page 105.

History   In the six weeks before Passover, there occur four special Sabbaths. The third of the four Sabbaths is called Shabbat Parah. On this Sabbath we read about the laws concerning the red heifer (*parah adumah*). All Israelites pilgrimage to the Temple in Jerusalem on Passover in order to offer the Pascal lamb. They had to be in a state of ritual purity to perform this ceremony. Since the ashes of the *parah adumah* were used in the process of purification, this Torah and haftarah reminded those who were not yet in a state of purity to take the necessary steps.

Text   Ezekial says that Adonai has deliberately sent Israel into exile and disaster as a sign of His disapproval of their morality and ritual impurity. However, Israel's captivity made the surrounding nations conclude that Adonai was powerless and could not help them, so His name and reputation were disgraced:

> *Wherever they lived, they disgraced My holy name; people said of them, "These are Adonai's chosen people, yet He forced them to leave His land."* **36:20**

Now Adonai has been forced to redeem His own honor and restore the people of Israel to their own home. Adonai says:

> *I will clear the holiness of My great name, which was contaminated among the nations. . . . gathering you from among the nations and countries and bringing you into your own land.* **36:23–24**

> *I will cleanse you from your stupid idols. I will give you a new heart, and put a new spirit into you; and I will remove the stony heart from you and give you a heart of holiness.* **36:25–26**

And people will say, "This land that was waste has flowered like the Garden of Eden and the wasteland and desolate and ruined cities are now fortified and filled with people." Then the nations that are still around you will really know that I, Adonai, rebuilt the ruined cities. . . . I, Adonai, have promised it, and I will do it. **36:35–36**

Connection   The theme of purification in both the sidrah and the haftarah is the connection to the festival of Passover. This reading several weeks before Passover is a reminder to the communities that they must begin the holiday in a proper spiritual state.

Haftarah for Shabbat Parshat Parah
(Ezekiel 36:16–38)

36 **16** I received a message from Adonai, saying, **17** Ezekiel, son of man, when the Israelites lived in their own land, they made the land unclean by their conduct and their deeds. They behaved toward Me just as a woman's monthly period makes her unclean. **18** So I was angry at them for the murder they had committed, and for their idols with which they worshipped. **19** So I exiled them through the nations and scattered them to many countries; I punished them for the evil way they lived. **20** Wherever they lived, they disgraced My holy name; people said of them, "These are Adonai's chosen people, yet He forced them to leave His land." **21** But I am concerned for the reputation of My holy name, which the Israelites profaned among the foreigners where they settled.

22 Adonai Almighty says, I want you to tell the Israelites, this is what Adonai the Almighty says: O House of Israel, you do not deserve what I am going to do, because you have disgraced My reputation among the nations where you now live. **23** I will clear the holiness of My great name, which was contaminated among the nations. They will know that I am holy when I demonstrate My holiness before their eyes, **24** by gathering you from among the nations and countries, and bringing you into your own land.

25 Then I will sprinkle your homeland with clean water, and you will be cleansed from all your sins, and I will also cleanse you from your stupid idols. **26** I will give you a new heart, and put a new spirit into you and I will remove the stony heart from you and give you a heart of holiness. **27** I will put My spirit into you and make you eager to live by My commands, and observe all My laws.

28 You will once again live in the land which I gave to your ancestors, and you will once again be My people, and I will once again be your Adonai. **29** I will also cleanse you from all your sins. Your grain harvest will overflow, and I will not allow any famine to fall on you. **30** Your trees will be filled with the fruit from the tree, and your crops will overflow your fields, so that you will no longer suffer from the disgrace of famine. **31** Then you will regret your own evil ways, and you will hate yourselves because of your sins and your disgusting behavior. **32** It is not for your sakes that I do this, Adonai the Almighty says. I said I want you to remember. I want you to be ashamed and disgraced for your conduct.

33 This is what Adonai the Almighty says: When I cleanse you from all your sins, I will let you resettle the cities and allow you to rebuild. **34** And the empty fields will once again be farmed, instead of lying desolate. **35** And people will say, "This land that was waste has flowered like the Garden of Eden and the wasteland and desolate and ruined cities are now fortified and filled with people." **36** Then the nations that are still around you will really know that I, Adonai, rebuilt the ruined cities, and planted the fields that were once desolate; I, Adonai, have promised it, and I will do it.

(Sephardim conclude here)

37 This is what Adonai the Almighty says: "Once again, I will do what the house of Israel asks Me to do for them; I will increase them like a flock of sheep.

38 Like the flocks brought for sacrifices, like the flocks of Jerusalem during the festival, so will the desolate cities be crowded with people, and then everyone will know that I am Adonai.

HAFTARAH for SHABBAT HACHODESH
Ezekiel 45:16–46:18

Book of Ezekiel   See haftarah Vayigash, page 105.

History   Ezekiel, who lived during the last days of the first Temple, received inspiration from the prophecies of Jeremiah, who prophesied in Babylon for twenty-two years, having been taken into captivity eleven years before the fall of Jerusalem.

Before the destruction of the Temple, 586 B.C.E., Ezekiel's prophecies were messages of doom: after, they were messages of hope and assurances of restoration.

After the destruction of the Temple, the Judeans were overwhelmed by the devastation. How could it have happened? They had lost everything: country, Temple, freedom, and thousands of lives. Ezekiel lifted their spirits and showed them that Adonai was at work in the devastation. He prophesied that the Judeans would emerge from the catastrophe renewed, reenergized, and full of hope.

The last chapter of the Book of Ezekiel is a description of the rebuilt Jerusalem that would arise after the exile was over. Ezekiel describes the reconstructed Temple, the duties of the priesthood, and the reorganized kingdom when the tribes returned from exile. Ezekiel's vision ends with Adonai returning in glory to a new Temple in the midst of Jerusalem, never to depart.

Text   The haftarah starts with a description of the requirements for contributions to be brought by the entire population. The ruler will be responsible for the supply of sacrifices. From the contributions:

> *All the people of the land shall bring offerings to the ruler in Israel. And it shall be the ruler's responsibility to provide burnt offerings, grain offerings, and drink offerings, on the feasts, the New Moons, and the*

Sabbaths, at all the religious events, in the house of Israel. **45:16–17**

This is followed by a description of the gifts to be distributed by the prince to his heirs.

Now Ezekiel suggests that to ensure the holiness and purity of the rebuilt Temple, Passover and Shabbat are to be preceded by a day of atonement.

Ezekiel also restates some of the laws of the offerings of the feasts of Passover and Sukkot.

The haftarah ends with a statement that guarantees equality under the law:

Moreover, the ruler must never take a person's property by force; he must give his child land from his own property: none of My people shall be forced from their own land. **46:18**

Connection   The connection between the sidrah and haftarah is that Passover sacrifices are to be found in both readings. The haftarah also includes the preparation for Passover.

(*Ashkenazim begin here*)

45

16 All the people of the land shall bring offerings to the prince in Israel.

17 And it shall be the prince's responsibility to provide burnt offerings, grain offerings, and drink offerings, on the feasts, the New Moons, and the Sabbaths, at all the religious events, in the house of Israel. He shall provide the sin offerings, the grain offerings, the burnt offerings, and the peace offerings, to ask forgiveness for the house of Israel.

18 This is what Adonai the Almighty says: On the first day of each new year, you shall take a young, healthy bull, and purify the Temple. **19** The priest shall take some of the blood of this sin offering, and smear it on the doorposts of the Temple, the four corners of the altar, and the doorposts of the gate which leads into the inner court. **20** Do this same ceremony on the seventh day of the month for every one who accidentally sins in error or without being aware; this is how My Temple will retain its holiness.

21 Starting on the fourteenth day of the first month, you shall celebrate the Passover, and for seven days eat only unleavened bread. **22** On that day, the ruler shall offer a bull as a sin offering for his sins and for the sins of the land. **23** During each of the seven days of the festival of Passover he shall sacrifice a burnt offering to Me, seven healthy bulls and seven healthy rams, and each day a goat as a sin offering. **24** For a grain offering he shall prepare a pound of flour for each bull, 20 pounds of flour and a gallon of olive oil for each ram. **25** He shall do the same during the festival of Sukkot in the seventh month (Tishrei) on the fifteenth day of the month, and during the seven days of the festival and provide the same number of animals for the sin offering, the burnt offering, the meal offering, and the oil.

46

This is what Adonai the Almighty says: The east gate of the inner court must be closed during the six working days, but on the Sabbath and on the day of the New Moon the gate shall be opened. **2** The ruler shall enter through the gate and stand by the Temple doorway. The priests shall prepare the burnt and peace offerings, and he shall worship at the doorway of the gate. Then he shall go out, and the gate shall not be shut until evening. **3** Every Sabbath, and on the festivals of the New Moon, the people of Israel shall also worship Adonai at the door of the gate.

4 On the Sabbath, the ruler shall offer to Adonai a burnt offering, which shall be six healthy lambs and a healthy ram. **5** The meal offering shall consist of 20 pounds of flour for each ram, and as much as he can afford for the lambs, and a gallon of olive oil to every 20 pounds of grain. **6** On the day of the New Moon, he shall offer a young, healthy bull, six healthy lambs, and a healthy ram. **7** For the grain offering, he shall prepare 20 pounds of grain for each bullock, and as much as he can afford for each of the lambs, and a gallon of olive oil with every 20 pounds of grain.

8 When the ruler enters the Temple, he shall enter through the gate, and he leaves by the same gate. **9** But when the people of Israel come to worship during the festival, they shall enter through the north gate and leave through the south gate, and everyone who enters through the south gate shall leave by the north gate; the worshippers must leave through the opposite gate from which they came. **10** The ruler shall enter with them, and he shall leave as they go out.

11 During the festival and the holidays, the grain offering shall consist of 20 pounds of grain for each bull, and 20 pounds of grain for a ram, as much as he can afford for each of the lambs, and a gallon of olive oil to every 20 pounds of grain. **12** When the ruler voluntarily offers a burnt or peace offering to Adonai, the priest shall open the gate for him, and he shall offer his burnt and peace sacrifices just as he does every Sabbath; then he shall leave, and after he has left they shall shut the gate.

13 Every morning, you shall prepare a burnt offering of a healthy young lamb, to Adonai. **14** At the same time, you shall provide a meal offering consisting of 3 pounds of grains mixed with one quart of olive oil; this grain offering to Adonai will never change. **15** The lamb, the grain offering and the oil shall be provided every morning without fail.

(Sephardim conclude here)

16 This is what Adonai the Almighty says: If the ruler gives a gift of land to one of his sons, it will be their inheritance, and also belong to his descendants. **17** However, if he gives a gift of his inheritance to one of his servants, then the servant shall own it until the year of jubilee, then it shall return to the ruler; only the ruler's children may keep a gift from their inheritance. **18** Moreover, the ruler must never take a person's property by force; he must give his child land from his own property; none of My people shall be forced from their own land.

HAFTARAH for SHABBAT HAGADOL
Malachi 3:4–24

Book of Malachi   See haftarah Toldot, page 78.

History   The Sabbath before Passover is called Shabbat HaGadol, meaning the Great Sabbath. There are several reasons for the title "great"

Some say that the Sabbaths before each of the holidays were called great because of the importance of the approaching festival.

According to tradition, the tenth of Nisan in the year of the exodus was on a Saturday. It was a great event since on that day the Israelites could select a lamb for sacrifice even though the lambs were worshipped by the Egyptians.

From the general situation as revealed in the text, the Israelites were ruled by a governor who was appointed by the Persian emperor. The Second Temple, built by Zerubbabel in 520–511 B.C.E., was in existence, and sacrifices were being offered. Yet by this time the return from exile was only a trickle and both priests and people were corrupt.

Text   In this message, the prophet enumerates the reasons Adonai has disregarded His people and condemned them to be punished for their sins. Malachi warns the Israelites that judgment will be executed upon those:

who oppress the worker, the widow, the orphans, and those who rob the foreigners, and do not respect Me. **3:5**

He continues:

Those who respected Adonai supported each other; and Adonai listened to them; a scroll of honor was written and recorded the names of those who respected Adonai and followed his commandments. **3:16**

And when that great day arrives:

Soon the day will come, and will burn like a fiery furnace; and all the wicked people will be consumed like straw. Not leaf nor branch will survive. **3:19**

However, if they repent:

Remember the laws of the Torah which I gave to My servant Moses at Mount Horeb (Sinai) to give to Israel. Observe all the laws and commandments. **3:22**

The people ask, "Where is Adonai?" Malachi answers:

I will send Elijah the prophet before the dreadful day of judgment. **3:23**

Connection   Elijah is mentioned in both the sidrah and the haftarah.

The haftarah ends with a pronouncement of the reappearance of Elijah the prophet. Elijah is traditionally regarded as the advance messenger who would arrive at Passover time and announce the arrival of the Messianic era.

3 **4** The offering of Judah and Jerusalem will then be acceptable to Adonai, as in former years. **5** Then I will visit you for the judgment; I will be a ready witness against sorcerers, adulterers, liars, and those who oppress the worker, the widow, the orphan, and those who rob the foreigners, and do not respect Me, says Adonai Tzvaot. **6** For I, Adonai, do not change, and you, children of Jacob, are not yet destroyed.

7 Since the days of your ancestors you have turned away from My laws, and have not observed them. Return to Me, and I will return to you, says Adonai Tzvaot. But you ask, "How are we to return?"

8 Will a human cheat Adonai? Yet you are cheating Me. But you ask, "How have we cheated you?" By tithes and contributions.

9 You are cursed; this whole nation has cheated Me.

10 Adonai Tzvaot says, Bring all the tithes and contributions into the treasury, so that there may be food in My Temple, and put Me to the test, and see if I do not open the floodgates of heaven and pour out an abundant blessing upon you. **11** Adonai Tzvaot says, I will banish the devouring locust, so that it will not destroy the fruits of your soil, nor make the vine in the field fail to ripen.

12 Adonai Tzvaot says, All the nations will call you blessed; for you will be a land of delight, says Adonai Tzvaot. **13** You have said harsh things about Me, says Adonai. Yet you ask, "What have we said against you?"

14 You have said, "It is useless to serve Adonai; what have we gained by observing His commandments and sadly walking around because we are sorry for our sinful behavior? **15** And now we see that the arrogant are happy, and the evildoers and those who defy Adonai escape."

16 Those who respected Adonai supported each other; and Adonai listened to them; a scroll of honor was written and recorded the names of those who respected Adonai and followed His commandments.

17 Adonai Tzvaot promises: On that day of judgment, they will be My treasure; and I will protect them, just as parents protect their own children who obey them.

18 Then you will see how I will judge the righteous and the wicked, and how I judge those who ignore His commandments.

19 Adonai Tzvaot promises: Soon the day will come, and will burn like a fiery furnace; and all the wicked people will be consumed like straw. Not leaf nor branch will survive. **20** But for those of you who honor My name, the sun of righteousness will arise with healing rays. You will arise and grow strong. **21** On that day that is coming, you will trample the wicked, for they will be ashes under the soles of your feet.

22 Remember the laws of the Torah which I gave to My servant Moses on Mount Horeb (Sinai) to give to Israel. Observe all the laws and commandments. **23** I will send Elijah the prophet before the dreadful day of judgment. **24** Elijah will teach the parents and children to love and respect each other; otherwise I will come and destroy the earth with a curse. I will send Elijah the prophet before the dreadful day of judgment.

INTRODUCTION TO
HAFTARAH for the FIRST DAY
OF PASSOVER
Joshua 3:5–7, 5:2–6:1, 27

Book of Joshua   See haftarah Shelach Lecha, page 224.

History   Moses, the great leader, grew old. The time had come to choose someone to take his place after he was gone. Moses' choice fell on Joshua, a man respected by the people and possessing a gift for military strategy. Into Joshua's capable hands Moses placed the task of invading Canaan.

As the Israelites crossed the Jordan, its flow miraculously stopped—just like at the miraculous crossing of the Sea of Reeds. A new base camp was set up in a place called Gilgal between the Jordan River and the first military objective, Jericho. Here in Gilgal (meaning circle), Joshua erected a memorial of a circle with twelve boulders (one for each tribe) from the river bottom.

Text   The slave generation, who doubted Adonai's power, had died in the desert. Now Joshua stopped and all the males were circumcised.

> *So Joshua made flint knives, and circumcised the foreskins of the Israelites at the Gibeath of Araloth.* **5:3**

The circumcision of the new generation marked the renewal of the relationship between the Israelites and Adonai.

In addition the Passover feast was celebrated and the born-free Israelites celebrated the hard-won freedom from slavery in Egypt.

> *The Israelites camped in Gilgal, and on the evening of the fourteenth day of the month, they celebrated Passover in the plains of Jericho.* **5:10**

Now the daily providing of manna and quail stopped, and the Israelites lived on locally grown foods.

As the Israelites moved closer to Jordan, Joshua was confronted by an armed man. Joshua asked him who he was.

He answered, "I am the Commander of the army of Adonai." Then Joshua bowed down and said to him, "What does my master command his servant?" **5:14**

The man then instructed Joshua how to capture Jericho with no loss of life just by using psychology.

Connection The Torah reading on the first day of Passover deals with the first celebration of Passover in the desert.

The haftarah refers to the first Passover celebrated in the soon-to-be-occupied land of Canaan.

Haftarah for
the First Day of Passover
(Joshua 3:5-7, 5:2-6:1, 27)

3 **5** Joshua said to the people, "Sanctify yourselves, for to-morrow Adonai will perform wonders among you.

6 To the priests, Joshua said, "Lift up the Ark of the Covenant, and parade it before the people." So they lifted up the Ark of the Covenant and marched it before the people.

7 Adonai said to Joshua, "Today I will begin to raise your stature in the eyes of all Israel so that they will realize that, just as I supported Moses, I will also support you.

(Sephardim begin here)

5 **2** At this time, Adonai said to Joshua, Make flint knives, and circumcise the Israelites who were not circumcised. **3** So Joshua made flint knives, and circumcised the fore-skins of the Israelites at the Gibeah of Araloth. **4** The reason Joshua had to circumcise them was that all the males who had left Egypt, including all the soldiers who came out of Egypt, died in the wilderness, **5** and Israelites born in the wilderness after they had come out of Egypt had not been circumcised. **6** The Israelites traveled through the wilderness for forty years, until all the men, including the soldiers who had come out of Egypt, died because they disobeyed Adonai, who swore that they would not enter the land, which He had sworn to their ancestors that He would give us, a land flowing with milk and honey. **7** So Joshua, along the road to the promised land, circumcised their children, who had taken their place, for they had not been circumcised during the journey in the desert.

8 When all the males had been circumcised, they remained in their places in the camp, until they were healed. **9** Adonai said to Joshua, Today I have rolled away the shame of your slavery in Egypt. So the name of that place is called Gilgal (meaning to roll away) to this day.

10 The Israelites camped in Gilgal, and on the evening of the fourteenth day of the month, they celebrated Passover in the plains of Jericho. **11** On the very next day after the Passover, they ate food grown in the land, Canaan, unleavened bread and roasted barley.

12 The manna stopped the day after they ate food grown in Canaan. The Israelites no longer had manna; but that year, they ate from the food grown in the land of Canaan.

13 When Joshua was close to Jericho, he looked up and saw a man with a sword drawn in his hand standing near him. Joshua asked him, "Are you our friend or our enemy?"

14 He answered, "No, I am the commander of the army of Adonai." Then Joshua bowed down and said to him, "What does my master command his servant?"

15 The captain of Adonai's army said to Joshua, "Remove the sandals from your feet; for you are standing on holy ground," and Joshua did so.

6 **1** The walls of Jericho were shut tightly because the residents feared Israelites; no one came out and no one came in.

27 So Adonai supported Joshua; and his reputation spread throughout the land of Canaan.

HAFTARAH for the SECOND DAY OF PASSOVER
2 Kings 23:1–9, 21–25

Books of Kings I and II See haftarah Vayera, page 68.

History The Assyrian empire was invaded by the Scythians, a people from the Black Sea region. While the Scythian hordes swept through ancient empires, a new king had come to the throne of Judah. Josiah, the son of Amon, was a very different man from his father. Josiah heeded the words of the prophet Zepheniah, who had criticized the corruption that prevailed in Judah in the days of Amon. Josiah is known as the most righteous of all Judean kings. He implemented religious reforms known as the Reformation of Josiah. His reformation was a crusade against idolatry.

The new king rid the land of idols and corrupt officials and returned to the laws of Israel and the worship of Adonai. Josiah had all the idols destroyed and the Temple thoroughly cleansed. All objects associated with pagan worship were burned. Idol-worshipping priests were rounded up and slain. This occurred in the eighteenth year of Josiah's reign, in 621 B.C.E.

Text During the process of cleansing the Temple, a great discovery was made. A scroll was found which had lain forgotten and lost for generations. When examined, the scroll was found to be the Book of Deuteronomy, the last of the Five Books of Moses. It summarized and explained the Ten Commandments and the laws of Israel. Hilkiah, the high priest, and Huldah, a prophetess, encouraged the king to study this long-lost book and read it aloud to the people of Judah. Standing before a large assembly, Josiah read from the Book of Deuteronomy as the people, young and old, stood listening in awe to the ancient words.

Then the king went up to the Temple of Adonai. All the people of Judah, all the inhabitants of Jerusalem, the priests, the prophets, and all the people, both small and great, went with him; and he read to them all the words of the Book of the Covenant which was discovered in the Temple of Adonai. **23:2**

During the reigns of Joshua's father and grandfather, Passover had been mostly neglected.

Then Josiah instructed all the people, "Observe the Passover to Adonai, just as it is recorded in the Book of the Covenant." **23:21**

An important part of the King Josiah's Reformation was the Passover that was celebrated.

Now, all over Judah priests assembled and read to the people from the book. The people became familiar with their history and traditions. Most important of all, the Book of Deuteronomy taught the people the meaning of their laws. Strengthened by this knowledge, the people of Judah regained faith and dignity.

Such was the state of Judah when Assyria was dealt its final blow. Two prophets, Nahum and Zepheniah, had prophesied that the destruction of Assyria was at hand. Josiah had heard and believed these prophecies.

Assyria was like a wounded animal. Its massive structure was held together by sheer force. Enemies within and without circled the weakened giant and destroyed it.

Connection This section of the Book of Kings was chosen for this date because of the rejuvenated Passover which was celebrated in the eighteenth year of Josiah's reign.

The king ordered all the people to observe the Passover of Adonai as prescribed in this Torah scroll. It was a momentous occasion.

There had never been such a Passover since the days of the judges, or during the reign of the kings of Israel and Judah. During the eighteenth year of the reign of King Josiah, this Passover was celebrated to Adonai in Jerusalem. **23:21–22**

Haftarah for
the Second Day of Passover
(2 Kings 23:1-9, 21-25)

23 The king assembled all the leaders of Judah and Jerusalem. **2** Then the king went up to the Temple of Adonai. All the people of Judah, all the inhabitants of Jerusalem, the priests, the prophets, and all the people, both small and great, went with him; and he read to them all the words of the Book of the Covenant which was discovered in the Temple of Adonai. **3** The king stood on the official platform and renewed the covenant to obey Adonai, to observe His commandments and laws with all his heart and soul, and and to follow all the words of this covenant that were written in this book; and all the people pledged to observe all the laws of the covenant.

(Some start here)

4 The king commanded Chilkiah the High Priest, and the assistant priests, and the guards to remove from Adonai's Temple all the implements used to worship Baal and Asherah, and all the heavenly lights. He burned them outside Jerusalem in the fields of Kidron and removed their ashes to Bethel. **5** He removed the pagan priests, whom the kings of Juudah had appointed to burn incense in the Temples in the cities of Judah and around Jerusalem; and also those who burned incense to Baal, to the sun, to the moon, to the planets, and to all the heavenly bodies. **6** He removed the Asherah idol from Adonai's Temple, outside Jerusalem, and brought it to the brook Kidron; and he burned it, ground it into dust, and threw its dust on the graves of the common people. **7** He destroyed the house of prostitution, near Adonai's Temple, where the women wove decorations for the idols of Asherah.

8 Then Josiah brought back all the priests who were living in the cities of Judah. He destroyed the pagan shrines where the priests burned incense, from Gibeah to Beer-sheeba, and smashed down the altars at the entrance to the gate of Joshua, the governor of Jerusalem. The gate was located at the entrance of the city. **9** The pagan priests were not allowed to officiate at Adonai's altar in Jerusalem, but they were allowed to eat unleavened bread among the other priests.

21 Then Josiah instructed all the people, "Observe the Passover to Adonai, just as it is recorded in the Book of the Covenant." **22** There had never been such a Passover since the days of the judges, or during the reign of the kings of Israel and Judah. **23** During the eighteenth year of the reign of King Josiah, this Passover was celebrated to Adonai in Jerusalem.

24 Josiah removed the magicians and wizards, the statues and the idols, and all the pagan ceremonies that were prevalent in the land of Judah and Jerusalem. He obeyed all the laws which were written in the scroll that Chilkiah the priest found in Adonai's Temple. **25** Never had there been such a king who listened to Adonai with all his heart, all his soul, and all his strength, and obeyed all the laws of Moses; since then, there has never been another sincere ruler like him.

INTRODUCTION TO
HAFTARAH for SHABBAT CHOL HAMOED
(THE INTERMEDIATE SABBATH OF PASSOVER)
Ezekiel 36:37–38, 37:1–16

Book of Ezekiel   See haftarah Vayigash, page 105.

History   During the last days of the First Temple, Nebuchadnezzar destroyed the land, devastated Jerusalem, killed thousands, and deported survivors. The first half of Ezekiel chapter 37 contains the vision of the valley of the dry bones. The vision was a parable of the resurrection and the return of the exiles to Jerusalem.

Text   In his vision, Ezekiel finds himself in a valley of dried bones. The bones represent the kingdom of Israel and Judah. Now Ezekiel says that Adonai spoke:

> Then he said to me,
> Son of man, can these dry bones come to life?
> I answered,
> "Adonai Almighty, only You know the answer." **37:3**

Adonai speaks to Ezekiel once again and tells him to talk to the dry bones and say:

> "Dry bones, listen to the word of Adonai." **37:4**

Adonai continues:

> I will cause breath to enter into you
> and you will become alive. **37:5**

So Ezekiel prophesies as commanded:

> Bone became attached to bone. As I watched, the muscle and flesh formed over the bones and stretched over them, but the bodies were not breathing. **37:7–8**

Then Adonai speaks:

> Son of man,
> prophesize to the wind. **37:9**

413

So Ezekiel follows the instructions:

And breath came into them,
and they came to life and stood up,
and they were as numerous as a very great army. **37:10**

Now Adonai tells Ezekiel to announce to the exiles:

I will open your graves of exile,
raise you up, and bring you back to the land of Israel . . .
you will realize that I am Adonai. **37:12–13**

Adonai promises the exiles the full blessing of future redemption.

Connection The holiday of Passover recalls past deliverances and calls for the prophet Elijah to enter our homes.

There is a tradition that the resurrection of the dry bones will occur during this holiday.

The modern state of Israel is testimony to the resurrection and rebirth of the ancient homeland.

At the end of World War II, the emaciated survivors of the Nazi death camps were given refuge and homes in the soon to be created modern state of Israel. Israel at that time was underdeveloped, like a valley of dried bones. The refugees breathed life, sinew, and skin into the land and Israel became alive. Today the blue and white flag of Israel proudly waves over Mount Zion in Jerusalem and in hundreds of diplomatic embassies all over the world.

Haftarah for Shabbat
Chol Hamoed of Passover
(Ezekiel 36:37-38, 37:1-16)

36 **37** This is what Adonai the Almighty says: I will allow the nation of Israel to grow until they become as many as a flock. **38** Just like the numerous sheep that were brought to Jerusalem during her festival times, crowds of people will fill the once empty cities, and then everyone will realize that I am Adonai.

37 Adonai took me by the hand; Adonai's spirit carried me out and set me down in the midst of a valley full of bones. **2** In the open valley, He showed me the old dry bones, and **3** then he said to me, Son of man, can these dry bones come to life?
I answered, "Adonai Almighty,
only You know the answer."
4 Once again He said to me,
Speak to these dry bones.
Say to them,
"Dry bones, listen to the word of Adonai."
5 This is what Adonai Almighty says to these bones:
Watch, I will cause breath to enter into you,
and you will become alive.
6 I will put muscle and flesh on you,
cover you with skin,
and I will place breath into you,
and you will become alive;
then you will realize that I am Adonai.
7 So I prophesied as I was commanded; and as I prophesied, there was a sound, and then a rattling; the bones moved together. Bone became attached to bone. **8** As I watched, the muscle and flesh formed over the bones and stretched over them, but the bodies were not breathing. **9** Then He said to me,

Son of man,
prophesy to the wind,
prophesy and say:
"This is what Adonai the Almighty says:
O breath, come from the four winds,
and breathe into these dead bodies
and bring them to life."
10 So I prophesied as He commanded me,
and breath came into them,
and they came to life and stood up,
and they were as numerous as a very great army.
11 Then He said to me,
Son of man, these bones represent the entire house
of Israel.
They are saying, "Our bones are all dried,
our hope is all gone."
12 Now prophecy again, and say to them,
"This is what Adonai the Almighty says:
I will open your graves of exile,
raise you up, and bring you back to the land of Israel.
13 When I open your graves, and raise you up,
then you will realize that I am Adonai.
14 You will live because I will put My spirit in you,
and I will return you to your own land;
then you will realize
that I, Adonai, have kept My promise."

(*Some congregations continue*)

15 Once again Adonai's message came to me, saying,
16 Son of man, take a stick, and write on it: For the
kingdom of Judah, and the southern tribes of Israel,
his companions; then take another stick, and write on
it: For Joseph, the stick of Ephraim, and all the northern tribes of Israel, his companions. **17** Now tie the
two sticks together into one stick, and they will look
like one in your hand.

INTRODUCTION TO
HAFTARAH for the SEVENTH DAY
OF PASSOVER
2 Samuel 22:1-51

Books of Samuel I and II   See haftarah Shemini, page 174.

History   David in his meteoric rise to power naturally made many enemies. King Saul, his mentor and father-in-law, was jealous of David's fame. Ishbosheth, Saul's son who assumed the throne after his father died, feared David, who ruled in Hebron, the capital of Judah. The Philistines were eager to prevent the land of Judah from uniting. Power is a magnet and attracts competitors and danger.

Text   In the haftarah reading David thanks Adonai for his many escapes, David says:

> *In my distress, I called upon Adonai.*
> *Yes! I called to Adonai,*
> *from His Sanctuary,*
> *He heard my plea,*
> *and my cry reached His ears.* **22:7**

David called upon Adonai because he trusted Him.

> *He rescued me from powerful enemies*
> *who were stronger than me.*
> *They attacked me when I was weak,*
> *but Adonai defended me.* **22:18–19**

Connection   The Torah reading for the seventh day includes the Song of Triumph, which Moses and the Israelites sang on the seventh day after the miraculous escape from Egypt.

David's song of deliverance from his enemies is similar to the Song of Triumph by Moses.

Haftarah for
the Seventh Day of Passover
(2 Samuel 22:1-51)

22 And David sang this song on the day when
Adonai saved him from his enemies, especially the
hand of Saul;

2 He sang:
Adonai is my Rock,
and my fortress,
and my Deliverer;

3 I find safety within Elohim,
who is my Rock;
He is my Shield,
my Horn of Salvation,
my high Tower,
and my Refuge, my Savior.
You rescued me from violence.

4 I sing,
"Praised is Adonai,"
and I am saved from my enemies.

5 Waves of death crashed over me,
the floods of destruction attacked me.

6 The ropes from the Sheol (grave) were tied around
me
and death traps blocked my way.

7 In my distress, I called upon Adonai.
Yes! I called to Adonai,
from His Sanctuary,
He heard my plea,
and my cry reached His ears.

8 Then the earth shivered and trembled,
the foundations of heaven rocked,
and they shook, because He was angry.

9 Smoke rose from His nostrils,
and the flames leapt from His mouth;

glowing coals flamed forth from Him.
10 He opened the heavens
and came down;
black darkness was under His feet.
11 He rode upon a flying cherub
and flew on the wings of the wind.
12 Darkness surrounded Him;
wild rainstorms of water
and thick clouds surrounded Him.
13 Through brightness before Him,
glowing coals of fire lit the sky.
14 Adonai the Most High
thundered from heaven.
15 He shot arrows
and scattered the enemy;
He sent lightning and confused them.
16 At Adonai's command,
the ocean's floor appeared,
and at the blast of breath from His nostrils,
the foundations of the world appeared.
17 He reached down from heaven;
He took me;
He pulled me out of the waters.
18 He rescued me from powerful enemies
who were stronger than me.
19 They attacked me when I was weak,
but Adonai defended me.
20 He brought me to safety;
He saved me, because He delighted in me.
21 Adonai rewarded me for my righteousness;
He rewarded me because I was innocent.
22 I have observed Adonai's commandments,
and have not strayed from Adonai to do evil.
23 All His laws are always on my mind;
and I did not stray from His commandments.
24 I completely obeyed Him,
and I guarded myself from doing evil.

25 Therefore,
Adonai has rewarded me for my righteousness,
and the purity of my thoughts.
26 You are merciful
with those who are merciful;
with the faithful people,
You are faithful.
27 You show Your purity
with those who are pure;
You show Your hostility
with those who are wicked.
28 You save the troubled people,
but you humble the snobs.
29 Adonai, You are my lamp;
Adonai, you brighten my darkness.
30 You help me defeat armies;
with Your help, I can scale walls.
31 Adonai, Your way is perfect;
Adonai, Your word is true;
Adonai, You are a shield
to all who place their trust in You.
32 There is no other but Adonai;
there is no refuge except Adonai.
33 Adonai is my strong fortress,
and Adonai removes obstacles in my path.
34 He makes My feet swift
like the feet of deer
and helps me climb to great heights.
35 He strengthens my hands for combat,
so that my arms bend a brass bow.
36 You are my saving shield;
and Your help has made me great.
37 You cleared the road before me
and my feet did not stumble.
38 I chased my enemies
and destroyed them;
I did not stop until they were defeated.

39 I fought with my sword
and wounded them,
and they fell at my feet.
40 For You have armed me with strength of war;
You have defeated my enemies who attacked me.
41 You made my enemies run away from me,
so I destroyed those who hated me.
42 They cried for help,
but there was no one to help them;
they even cried to Adonai,
but he refused to answer.
43 I smashed them into the dust of the earth;
I stamped and squashed them down
like mud of the streets.
44 You rescued me from my accusers;
You made me to be the leader of nations;
a people whom I did not know serve me.
45 As soon as they hear of me,
foreigners are frightened of me; they obey.
46 Strangers surrender,
and come crawling out of their hiding places.
47 Adonai lives—
blessed be my Rock;
Adonai is my Rock of salvation.
48 Adonai takes revenge for me
and defeats nations for me.
49 He rescues me from my enemies.
You raised me high
above my enemies;
You save me from the violent enemies.
50 Adonai, for Your sympathy,
I will give thanks to You among the nations,
and sing praises to Your name.
51 Adonai is a tower of strength
to His chosen king,
and shows mercy to David, His anointed,
and to His descendants forever.

INTRODUCTION TO
HAFTARAH for the EIGHTH DAY
OF PASSOVER
Isaiah 10:32–12:6

Book of Isaiah See haftarah Bereshit, page 51.

History Ancient Israel's Golden Era was the tenth century B.C.E., when David and Solomon ruled Israel, and Israel was a power in Western Asia. It was this period the prophets had in mind when they urged the restoration of a united Israel and called for revenge on their enemies around them.

Text It was only among the descendants of David that the prophets assumed the leader would be found who could make the unification of Israel possible and defeat the mighty army of Assyria. Isaiah says:

> *Someone from David's family*
> *will some day come to power.*
> *The spirit of Adonai will rest on him;*
> *the spirit of wisdom and understanding,*
> *the spirit of insight and might,*
> *the spirit of knowledge and respect for Adonai.* **11:1–2**

The new ruler, a descendant of David, will unite the two kingdoms, Ephraim and Judah, and together they will defeat the enemies. Then the exiles will return from Assyria and cross the Euphrates River without wetting their feet, just like the Israelites did as they escaped Egypt through the Sea of Reeds.

The haftarah ends on a joyful and triumphant note.

> *Sing to Adonai;*
> *for He has done miraculous deeds;*
> *make Him known around the world.*
> *People of Jerusalem,*
> *sing and shout;*
> *the great Holy One of Israel lives among you.* **12:5–6**

Connection   There are several points of connection between the Torah reading and the haftarah. Both deal with an exodus to freedom, from Egypt and Babylon through a body of water, the Sea of Reeds and the Euphrates River, respectively.

In both cases, the exodus will be led by charismatic leaders, Moses and a descendant of David, respectively.

Haftarah for
the Eighth Day of Passover
(Isaiah 10:32–12:6)

10 **32** Today the enemy camps at Nob
shake their fist at Mount of Zion in Jerusalem.
33 But Adonai Almighty with strength
will chop down the mighty tree;
the tall in height will be chopped down,
and the mighty army of Assyria
will be defeated.
34 He will chop down the enemy
and they will fall
like the trees of Lebanon.

11 Someone from David's family
will some day come to power.
2 The spirit of Adonai will rest on him;
the spirit of wisdom and understanding,
the spirit of insight and might,
the spirit of knowledge and respect for Adonai.
3 He will be filled
with a spirit of the fear of Adonai;
he will not make decisions
by what his eyes see,
or decide by what his ears hear.
4 But he will judge the poor
with righteousness
and make fair decisions
for the needy of the land;
he will rule against the wicked
with the rod of his mouth,
and slay the wicked
with the decision from his lips.
5 And righteousness will be a belt around his waist,
and faithfulness the sash around his loins.

6 The wolf will live with the lamb;
the leopard will lie down with the goat;
the calf and the young lion with
the yearling;
and a little child will lead them.
7 The cow will eat along with the bear;
their offspring will lie down together;
the lion will eat straw like the ox.
8 Babies will play with deadly snakes,
and the small children
will safely place their hands in the snake's nest.
9 They will not hurt or destroy
in all My holy mountain.
Just as waters fill the sea,
so will the earth be full of knowledge of Adonai.
10 On that day,
a descendant of David will become a banner of
hope; nations will follow him;
and his kingdom will be famous.
11 On that day,
Adonai, for a second time,
will stretch out His hand,
and bring back the refugees from Assyria,
from Egypt, from Pathros, from Cush, from Elam,
from Shinar, from Hamath,
and from the islands of the sea.
12 He will raise a banner among the nations,
and assemble the exiles of Israel,
and assemble the refugees from Judah
from the four corners of the earth.
13 Ephraim's jealousy will disappear
and Judah's enemies will be cut off.
Ephraim will not be jealous of Judah,
and Judah will not fight Ephraim anymore.
14 Instead they will become allies
against the Philistines in the west;
together they will defeat the enemies in the east.

Together they will battle
against Edom and Moab and the Ammonites.
15 Adonai will utterly dry up the water of Egypt;
He will send a hurricane over the Euphrates River
and divide it into seven tiny streams,
so that people cross without wetting their feet.
16 There will be a clear pathway for His people,
from Assyria;
just as there was a road for Israelites
when they escaped from the land of Egypt.

12

On that day, you will sing,
"Adonai, I praise you;
You were angry with me.
Now Your anger has ceased;
You comfort me.
2 Yes, Adonai,
You are my lifeline;
I trust you;
I will not be afraid.
Adonai the Almighty is my power
and my joy;
 He is my lifeline.
3 Joyfully you will drink water
from the fountain of victory.
4 On that miraculous day you will sing:
Thank Adonai,
praise His name;
tell the world of His deeds.
Praise be His holy name.
5 Sing to Adonai;
for He has done miraculous deeds;
make Him known around the world.
6 People of Jerusalem,
sing and shout;
the great Holy One of Israel lives among you.

HAFTARAH for the FIRST DAY
OF SHAVUOT
Ezekiel 1:1–28, 3:12

Book of Ezekiel   See haftarah Vayigash, page 105.

History   The date of Ezekiel's prophecy is fixed in his opening statement:

> *In the thirtieth year, in the fourth month.*
> *On the fifth day of the month.* **1:1–2**

The date would be 593 B.C.E. Ezekiel was one of the leaders of Judah who Nebuchadnezzar, king of Babylon, carried away after his first conquest of Judah, in 599 B.C.E.

He was a man who saw beyond the immediate evidence of his eyes and understood the implication "behind" the events.

Text   Divinely inspired dreams and visions are a feature of the *Tanak* starting from the period of the Patriarchs. Dreams and visions were closely associated with prophecy and revelations from Adonai. The three major classical prophets—Isaiah, Jeremiah, and Ezekiel—relate how Adonai's call first came to them as an overpowering experience in a dream or vision.

Ezekiel, one of the Jewish exiles in Babylon, was standing beside the river Chebar, when

> *the heavens were opened*
> *and I saw visions of Adonai.* **1:1**

Ezekiel then describes in detail his vision of the glory of Adonai. He sees four living lifelike creatures who glow like burning coals and roll around in carts on jeweled wheels.

Then Ezekiel describes a glowing figure on a throne.

> *I saw the vision of the glory of Adonai,*
> *and when I saw it I bowed down.*

Then I heard a voice speak.
Then the spirit lifted me up,
and behind me,
I heard a great roaring sound saying,
"Blessed is the presence of Adonai in this place." **2:28, 3:12**

Connection   In this haftarah the language in several cases recalls the revelation at Mount Sinai.

I looked and saw a stormy wind
blowing from the north.
It brought a great cloud
surrounded by flashes of lightning. **1:4**

I heard a great roaring sound saying,
"Blessed is the presence of Adonai in this place." **3:12**

Haftarah for
the First Day of Shavuot
(Ezekiel 1:1–28, 3:12)

1 The heavens were opened
and I saw visions of Adonai
while I was among the captives
on the river Chebar,
in the thirtieth year, in the fourth month.
2 On the fifth day of the month
(it was the fifth year of the captivity of King Jehoiachin),
3 Adonai's word came to Ezekiel ben Buzi the priest;
in the land of the Chaldeans
on the river Chebar,
and Adonai placed His hand upon him.
4 I looked and saw a stormy wind (*ruach*)
blowing from the north.
It brought a great cloud
surrounded by flashes of lightning;
in the midst of the fire,
there was a bright, shiny metal object.
5 Within the fire
I saw the form of four Living Creatures—
they looked like humans.
6 Each one had four faces and each one had four wings.
7 Their legs were straight, and their feet looked like those of a calf,
and they sparkled like polished copper.
8 There were human hands
on all four sides
under their wings,
and all four had faces and wings.
9 Their wings touched each other,
and when they moved they did not turn their bodies.
Each one moved straight ahead as they went.
10 Their faces in the front looked like this:

in front, the face of a human,
with the face of a lion to the right side,
the face of an ox to the left,
and the face of an eagle in the back.
11 Their wings were separated on tip.
Each spirit had two wings
touching each other,
and two wings covered their bodies.
12 Each individual moved straight ahead
in the direction of his face.
They went to where the spirit went.
They went straight ahead.
13 The living creatures
looked like burning coals of fire.
Moving between the creatures
were flaming torches,
and a glow (*nogah*)
and from the fire sparked living bolts of lightning.
14 The creatures moved
like a flash of lightning.
15 As I watched the creatures,
I saw a single one (wheel)
of the four-faced creatures on the ground.
16 The wheels sparkled like jewels
and all four wheels looked the same;
the wheels looked like a wheel inside a wheel.
17 As they moved straight ahead
in each of the four directions,
they did not turn as they went.
18 Their wheels had large rims
and all four rims were filled with eyes.
19 When the creatures moved,
the wheels moved in the same direction.
When the creatures stood,
the wheels also rose.
20 The spirit of the four living things told them to move,
and the wheels also rolled along

21 When the creatures moved,
the wheels moved,
when the creature stopped,
the wheels did not move.
When the creature rose up,
the wheels also raised up,
because the spirit of the creatures
was also in the wheels.
22 Spread above the heads of the creatures
was a large slab of sparking crystal.
23 The wings of the creature
were straight out,
one toward another.
For each creature spread its wings
and each creature
had two wings which covered its body.
24 Then I heard the sound of their wings;
it was like the sound of roaring waters.
It was just like the voice of the Almighty
when they moved.
Their movement
sounded like the noise of an army on the march;
when the creatures stood
still, they lowered their wings.
25 When there was a sound
from the crystal which was above their heads;
the creatures stood still,
and they lowered their wings.
26 Over the heads of the creatures
was a dome.
I saw a throne
that looked as bright as a sapphire,
and sitting on the throne
there was a figure that looked like a human.
27 From the waist up
it seemed like the figure
glowed like white hot metal,

and from the waist down
it looked like a blazing fire around it.
28 It was as bright as a rainbow
after a storm.
I saw the vision of the glory of Adonai,
and when I saw it I bowed down.
Then I heard a voice speak.

3 **12** Then the spirit lifted me up,
and behind me
I heard a great roaring sound saying,
"Blessed is the presence of Adonai in this place."

HAFTARAH for the SECOND DAY OF SHAVUOT
Habbakuk 2:20–3:19

Book of Habbakuk   The Book of Habbakuk is the eighth volume of the *Trey Asar*, the twelve minor prophets. Very little is known of his life and background. It has been assumed that he was a Levite, on the strength of a phrase in chapter 3 regarding stringed instruments. Only Levites were authorized to use such instruments.

History   The Babylonians defeated the Egyptians in 606 B.C.E. and became the new masters of the Middle East. Eight years later, in 598 B.C.E., they invaded Judah and occupied Jerusalem. It is believed that Habbakuk, a sensitive individual, was troubled by Adonai's silence in the face of evil, violence, and repression.

Text   In this chapter the prophet begs Adonai to intervene on behalf of the Israelites.

Habbakuk's vision starts with a plea:

> *Adonai, I heard your reputation*
> *and I was overwhelmed with all.*
> *Adonai, please renew Your deeds in our time.*
> *Help us, as You did in times of need.* **3:2**

Then in the body of the vision is the appearance of a vengeful Adonai spreading havoc for the foreigners who have terrorized the Israelites.

> *He makes the nations shake in fear.*
> *Eternal mountains fall to pieces*
> *and ancient hills collapse.* **3:6**

In the vision good triumphs over evil.

> *You came to rescue Your people*
> *to save Your anointed one.*

You crushed the rulers of the wicked nations
and destroyed them totally. **3:13**

At the end of the vision, despite all the calamities that have befallen the Israelites, Habbakuk still has a firm belief in Adonai. He says:

I will rejoice because Adonai is my salvation.
Adonai the Almighty is my strength.
He makes my feet as speedy as a deer
and helps me climb high places. **3:18–19**

Connection   The Torah reading for the second day of Shavuot contains references to the three Pilgrimage Festivals: Passover, Shavuot, and Sukkot. The haftarah also contains language that recalls the revelation at Mount Sinai.

Adonai is coming from Teman.
The Holy One from Mount Paran.
Selah.
His glory illuminates the heavens
and your praises echo throughout the earth. **3:3**

Haftarah for
the Second Day of Shavuot
(Habbakuk 2:20–3:19)

2 **20** Let all the world be silent; now Adonai is in His holy Temple.

(Some Ashkenazim begin here)

3 This prayer by the prophet Habbakuk was accompanied by a musical instrument called the Shegionoth.
2 Adonai, I heard Your reputation
and I was overwhelmed with all.
Adonai, please renew Your deeds in our time.
Help us, as you did in times of need.
Turn from anger to mercy.
3 Adonai is coming from Teman,
the Holy One from Mount Paran.
Selah.
His glory illuminates the heavens
and your praises echo through the earth.
4 A brilliant light
flashes from His powerful hand,
where His power was hidden.
5 Plagues spread before Him;
pestilence follows at His approach.
6 When He stands, the earth trembles;
when He looks,
He makes the nations shake in fear.
Eternal mountains fall to pieces
and ancient hills collapse.
His paths are eternal.
7 In distress
I see the tents of Cushan;
the dwellings of Midran tremble.
8 Adonai, were You angry with the rivers?

Were You angry at the river,
or at the sea, when You attacked
with Your horses and chariots
and defeated them?
9 You readied Your bow
and at His command shot Your arrows.
Selah.
You split the earth with roaring rivers.
10 The mountains saw You
and trembled;
the waters overflowed;
the depths roared,
and the waves rose high.
11 The sun and the moon stood motionless;
at the light of Your arrows
and Your speeding spear.
12 In anger,
You marched through the world in fury;
and You trampled nations in anger.
13 You came to rescue Your people
to save Your anointed one.
You crushed the rulers of the wicked nations
and destroyed them totally.
14 With their own clubs You smashed their heads
when they attacked Israel like a whirlwind
hoping to defeat the poorly armed nation.
15 Through the foaming of mighty waters,
You trampled the sea
with Your horses.
16 I heard and my body trembled;
my lips quivered in fear;
terror melted my bones,
and I trembled.
Now I stand back,
and I quietly wait for the day of disaster,
which will strike the people
whom he will invade with his troops.

17 Fig trees will not blossom,
there will be no grapes
in the vines.
The olive trees will not produce fruit,
and the farms will have no crops.
There will be no sheep in the flock,
and there will be no animals in the barns.
18 But I will rejoice;
I will rejoice because Adonai is my salvation.
19 Adonai the Almighty is my strength.
He makes my feet as speedy as a deer
and helps me climb high places.

(For the musical director. This prayer was to be accompanied with stringed instruments.)

INTRODUCTION TO
HAFTARAH for TISHA B'AV
(THE MORNING OF THE FAST)
Jeremiah 8:13–9:23

Book of Jeremiah   See haftarah Bo, page 122.

History   The holiday of Tisha B'av is the saddest day of the Jewish year. On this day, many Jewish tragedies took place. On the ninth of Av in 586 B.C.E., Solomon's Temple was destroyed; six centuries later in 70 C.E., on the same day, the Second Temple was destroyed; and in 1492 C.E., again on the same day, the Jews were driven out of Spain.

In addition to these, many other tragic events occurred on Tisha B'av. On that date in 1290, King Edward signed an edict expelling the Jews from England. Tisha B'av also marked the beginning of World War I and a long period of suffering for the Jewish people. This period was filled with pogroms and massacres of Jews in Eastern Europe. Tisha B'av also marked the beginning of World War II and the Holocaust, in which six million Jews were slaughtered.

Text   The text covers 597–581 B.C.E., the reigns of Kings Josiah and Jehoiakim.

Jeremiah was not a happy prophet. He was continually rejected by the Israelites because of his message of doom. Jeremiah predicted harsh consequences if society did not reform itself. These messages were continually in opposition to the ruling political and religious authorities. He was harassed, arrested, and imprisoned. The ruling class feared his message and saw Jeremiah as the enemy.

The text is filled with doom and predicts the destruction of Judah and Jerusalem if the people do not repent. Jeremiah predicts invasion, defeat, destruction, exile, and death because they had abandoned Adonai's principles of justice and morality. The anguished people ask:

Is Adonai no longer in Zion?
Is Adonai no longer her King? **8:19**

Then Adonai accuses the people:

> *They are all adulterers,*
> *A band of unfaithful people.*
> *Lies fly from their mouths.* **9:1–2**

Now Adonai tells the people why they have been doomed:

> *It is because they have abandoned My Torah*
> *which I gave them;*
> *they did not listen to My commandments,*
> *and they did not follow My laws.* **9:12**

The selection ends with a warning and advice to the people:

> *Do not allow the wise man*
> *To boast of his wisdom,*
> *And do not allow the strong man*
> *to boast of his strength.* **9:22**

Connection   This is an ideal haftarah for Tisha B'av since it contains some of Jeremiah's saddest prophecies of doom and anguish. The themes of siege, doom, and defeat reflect the mood of Tisha B'av.

Haftarah for Tisha B'av

8 **13** Adonai says,
I will wipe them out.
There are no grapes on the vine
and no figs on the fig tree,
and what I have given them
will be taken from them.
14 Why do we sit still?
Let's assemble
and escape into the walled cities,
and let us die there,
for Adonai has sentenced us
to drink poisoned water,
because we have sinned against Adonai.
15 We looked for peace,
but nothing happened;
and for a time of healing
and found only confusion.
16 The snorting of the horses is heard in Dan (in the north);
the noises from the stallions quake the whole land
—the enemy is here devouring the land
and everything in it;
the city and its people.
17 Now I am sending poisoned serpents;
vipers, such as none can stop their bites,
says Adonai.
18 I am burdened with sorrow;
my heart is sick.
19 I hear the anguish of my people
from a faraway land:
"Is Adonai no longer in Zion?
Is Adonai no longer her King?"

Why have they angered Me
with their graven images
and with foreign idols?
20 The harvest is past,
summer is ended,
and we are not saved.
21 I am shattered
over the pain of my people,
I am clothed in black,
and horror has overcome Me.
22 Is there no cure in Gilead?
Are there no doctors there?
Why then has the health of My people
not been restored?
23 Oh, that my head were spring water
and my eye a fountain of tears,
so that I might cry day and night
for my people who were slain.

9 Adonai says,
Oh, I wish I could find a shelter
in the desert for travelers,
so that I might leave My people,
for they are all adulterers,
a band of unfaithful people.
2 Lies fly from their mouths
like a bow, shooting lies,
and it was not by the truth
that they seized power in the land.
Adonai says,
They move from evil to evil
and they do not know Me.
3 Beware of your neighbors
and do not trust your brothers,
for brothers are deceivers,
and neighbors tell lies.
4 People cheat their neighbor

and they do not speak truthfully;
their tongues are trained to tell lies.
They tire themselves out committing sins.
5 You exist in the midst of dishonesty,
and because of their falseness
they refuse to acknowledge Me,
says Adonai.
6 Therefore, says Adonai Tzvaot,
I will refine them and purify them.
How else could I act
toward the daughter of My people?
7 Their tongue can speak deceit like deadly arrows.
His friendly mouth speaks to his neighbor,
but he secretly sets a trap for him.
8 Adonai says,
Shouldn't I punish them for these sins?
Shouldn't I revenge Myself upon such a nation?
9 I weep for the mountains,
and I mourn for the pastures of the wilderness,
because they are burnt out
and are without travelers,
and they no longer echo the sound of cattle;
the birds in the sky
and the animals have fled.
10 I will make Jerusalem
into a heap (of ruins),
a place for jackals;
and I will desolate the cities of Judah,
so no one can live there.
11 I said to Adonai,
"Who is wise enough to understand this,
and where is the person to whom Adonai has spoken
that can explain?
Why is the land ruined,
dry like a desert
so that no person crosses it?"
12 So Adonai said,

It is because they have abandoned My Torah
which I gave them;
they did not listen to My commandments,
and they did not follow My laws.
13 Instead, they followed the stubbornness of their hearts;
they follow the Baal idols
just as their ancestors had taught them.
14 Therefore, Adonai Tzvaot,
the Savior of Israel, says,
I will feed this people
with bitter food
and will make them drink contaminated water.
15 I will scatter them among the nations
their ancestors never knew,
and I will chase them with the sword
until I have destroyed them.
16 So says God Tzvaot,
Call the wailing women
and send for most skilled women
so that they may come.
17 Let these come quickly
and raise a wail
for us till our eyes overflow with tears
and our eyelids stream with water.
18 The cries of wailing are heard in Zion:
"We become ruined!
We are shamed
because we have deserted our land;
because our enemies
have demolished habitations."
19 Ladies,
listen closely to the words of Adonai,
teach your daughters how to mourn
and teach every one a funeral song.
20 Death has climbed through our windows,
it has entered our palaces,

it has carried away children at play
and young men from the public square.
21 Adonai has said,
Dead bodies of men
will cover the ground
like the bundles of grain behind the reaper
which no one will gather.
22 Adonai says,
Do not allow the wise man
to boast of his wisdom,
and do not allow the strong man
to boast of his strength,
and do not allow the rich man
to boast of his wealth.
23 Adonai says,
But if one needs to boast,
let him boast that he understands
and knows Me, that I am Adonai.
I provide kindness,
justice, and righteousness
on earth.
It is in these gifts that I take delight.

INTRODUCTION TO
HAFTARAH for MINCHA OF TISHA B'AV
Isaiah 55:6–56:8

Book of Isaiah   See haftarah Bereshit, page 51.

History   This haftarah seems to have been written about 539 B.C.E., after Cyrus the Mede had defeated Babylonia. Cyrus was an enlightened ruler and encouraged the conquered people to continue to practice their own religions and customs. In 538, after the conquest of Babylonia, he issued a royal proclamation which led to the Return. In the Book of Ezra, Cyrus says, "God has given me all the kingdoms of the earth and has charged me to build Him a house in Jerusalem, which is in Judah. Whoever among His people may go up to Jerusalem, which is in Judah, and rebuild the House of Adonai."

Many scholars are of the opinion that chapters 40–66 were written by Second Isaiah.

Text   The afternoon Yom Kippur reading is from the Book of Isaiah, the prophet of hope and restoration

The reading opens with a call for repentance.

> *Let the wicked repent his wicked deeds*
> *and the corrupt person his thoughts.* **55:7**

The prophecy then calls for repentance with a promise of salvation and reward.

> *This is Adonai's message:*
> *Practice justice and do what is right.*
> *Deliverance is near at hand*
> *and My righteousness will be revealed.* **56:1**

At the end of the haftarah, Isaiah's prophecy broadens. He says that there is a place for all believers who are willing to observe the laws of the covenant and obey the rules and regulations of Torah.

The haftarah ends with a promise of salvation for all people.

These will I bring to My holy mountain and they will celebrate in My Temple, where people pray to Me.

Their offerings and their sacrifices will be joyfully accepted on My altar, for My Temple shall be known as a house of prayer for all people. **56:7**

Connection   In the Torah reading, Moses asks Adonai:

"Forgive our iniquities and our sin and choose us for Your inheritance as Your people."

In the haftarah the prophet calls on the Israelites to repent of their evil ways:

Blessed is the mortal person who observes the Sabbath without desecrating it, and blessed is the person who does no wrongdoing. **56:2**

Haftarah for
*Mincha of Tisha B'av
(Isaiah 55:6–56:8)

55 **6** Turn to Adonai
while He can easily be found;
call Him while He is close at hand.
7 Let the wicked repent his wicked deeds
and the corrupt person his thoughts.
Let him turn to Adonai
and He will have mercy on him,
and He will surely
forgive him.
8 Adonai says,
My way of thinking
is not like your way of thinking,
and your ways are not as My ways.
9 As the heavens are far above the earth,
so are My ways of thinking
higher than your ways
and My thoughts superior to your thoughts;
10 just like the rain that falls from the sky
and never returns
until it waters the earth,
making it blossom,
producing seeds for the farmer
and food for the hungry;
11 it is the same with the words
that come from My mouth.
They do not return to Me
without accomplishing everything I desire
and succeeding in the purpose
on which I sent it.
12 So you will leave joyously
and return in song
and all the trees of the forest

* Also mincha for fast days.

447

will clap with happiness.

13 Fir trees will grow thorns instead,
and instead of briars and thorns,
myrtles will spring up,
this miracle
will bring everlasting honor
to Adonai,
which can never be destroyed.

56

This is Adonai's message:
Practice justice and do what is right.
Deliverance is near at hand
and My righteousness will be revealed.
2 Blessed is the mortal person
who observes the Sabbath
without desecrating it,
and blessed is the person
who does no wrongdoing.
3 Let no foreigner
who has decided to worship Me say,
"Adonai will segregate me from His people."
Do not allow the physically challenged
person complain,
"I do not belong with these people."
4 God assures the physically challenged person who observes my Sabbaths and follows my commandments and who observes My covenant. **5** To them, within My Temple and within its walls I will honor them even more than sons and daughters—I will provide them with special honor which will always remain and never perish. **6** And as for the foreigners who have committed themselves to Adonai, who serve and love and worship Him; all who observe the Sabbath and do not violate it—and observe My covenant.

7 These will I bring to My holy mountain and they will celebrate in My Temple, where people pray to Me.

Their offerings and their sacrifices will be joyfully accepted on My altar, for My Temple shall be known as a house of prayer for all people.

8 Adonai, who gathers the exiles of Israel, says, I will bring still more to those who have already been gathered.

Index